An indian officer

Russia's march towards India

Vol. I

An indian officer

Russia's march towards India
Vol. I

ISBN/EAN: 9783743338760

Manufactured in Europe, USA, Canada, Australia, Japa

Cover: Foto ©ninafisch / pixelio.de

Manufactured and distributed by brebook publishing software (www.brebook.com)

An indian officer

Russia's march towards India

RUSSIA'S MARCH TOWARDS INDIA

VOL. I

PRINTED BY
SPOTTISWOODE AND CO., NEW-STREET SQUARE
LONDON

RUSSIA'S MARCH

TOWARDS

INDIA

BY 'AN INDIAN OFFICER'

VOLUME I.

WITH A MAP

LONDON
SAMPSON LOW, MARSTON & COMPANY
(LIMITED)
St. Dunstan's House
FETTER LANE, FLEET STREET, E.C.
1894

PREFACE

The following pages contain an account of Russia's advance towards India from the earliest times up to the present day. During the past thirty years a very large number of books has been written on this subject; but while each of the various episodes of this great movement have been separately described, and although the political and strategical aspects of the question have been frequently discussed, no recent work has, to my knowledge, been published which gives a clear historical account of Russia's March through Central Asia in all its stages.

This want I have endeavoured to supply; but it is with many misgivings that I place before my countrymen the result of several years' close study of a question which is of the greatest importance to all who are concerned in the safety and welfare of our great Eastern dependency.

In former years it used frequently to be said that a Russian attack on India was, if not impossible, at all events, highly improbable, and some politicians even went so far as to scoff at the danger and declare that it was nothing but the phantasy of a disordered mind. I know not if any Englishmen still adhere to these optimistic opinions; but, if there be any, I trust that the following unvarnished statement of Russian aggression will go far to convince them that a real danger does exist, and that the time has come when England can no longer place any reliance on Muscovite assurances, but must be prepared to resolutely oppose any further encroachments on the part of Russia.

I have no desire to pose as an alarmist, for I confidently believe that Russia will never successfully invade India if the English people make up their minds to keep the Cossacks behind the limitary line agreed upon in 1873. But if they fail to do this, and permit the Russians to consolidate themselves at Herat or in Afghan-Turkestan, then England's real troubles will commence. I believe that a war fought under existing conditions would undoubtedly result in a triumph for Great Britain; but if the Muscovites be allowed to establish themselves on the frontiers of India, our political and financial difficulties would be increased a hundredfold, and the result would be by no means so well assured.

The existing military situation has not been dealt with, and all questions of strategy have been carefully avoided, for I consider it to be highly injudicious—even for irresponsible writers—to discuss these matters. The War Office and Army Headquarters at Simla are fully competent to determine what action should be taken in certain eventualities, and the discussion of the strategical situation can only tend to draw attention to the weak points which may exist in our armour without affording any assistance to those who are responsible for the defence of India. But one thing I will say, and that is, that, in spite of the recent attempts which have been made to revive the antiquated theory that the Indus is the true first line of defence for India, I believe that it would be nothing less than an act of political suicide to permit the tide of invasion to reach the Indus Valley without employing all the resources of the Empire to avert such a catastrophe, and that no British commander will ever be found who would be willing to stake all on the result of a great battle fought on Indian soil.

The most important publications which have been consulted by me in the preparation of this work are given in the following list of references.

THE AUTHOR.

LONDON: *October* 1, 1893.

LIST OF REFERENCES

The History of Russia from the Earliest Times to 1882. By Alfred Rambaud. Translated by L. B. Lang, and edited and enlarged by N. H. Dole.
Russia. By Sir D. M. Wallace.
The History of Russia. By H. Tyrrell and Henry A. Haukeil.
The Eastern Question, from the Treaty of Paris, 1856, *to the Treaty of Berlin,* 1878, *and to the Second Afghan War.* By the Duke of Argyll.
History of Bokhara. By A. Vambéry.
Collection of Treaties, Engagements, and Sunnuds relating to India and the Neighbouring Countries. By Sir C. U. Aitchison.
History of Afghanistan, from the Earliest Period to the Outbreak of the War of 1878. By Colonel G. B. Malleson.
History of the War in Afghanistan. By Sir J. W. Kaye.
The Afghan War of 1879-80. By H. Hensman.
The Afghan Campaigns of 1878-80. By S. H. Shadbolt.
Kandahar in 1879. By Major A. Le Messurier.
Herat, the Granary and Garden of Central Asia. By Colonel G. B. Malleson.
The History of Persia. By Sir J. Malcolm.
A History of Persia, from the beginning of the 19*th Century to the Year* 1858. By R. G. Watson.
The Annual Register (1758 to 1892).
The Russians in Central Asia. By M. Veniukoff and Captain Valikhanoff. Translated by J. and R. Michell.
Various other translations from the Russian by J. and R. Michell.
Narrative of a Mission to Bokhara. By Joseph Wolff.
Journey from Herant to Khiva, Moscow, and St. Petersburgh. By Colonel James Abbott.
Progress and Present Position of Russia in the East. By Sir J. McNeill.

England and Russia in the East. By Sir H. C. Rawlinson.
England and Russia in Central Asia. By M. F. Martens.
Travels into Bokhara. By Sir A. Burnes.
The Life of Peter the Great. By Eugène Schuyler.
Turkistan. By Eugène Schuyler.
The Russians in Central Asia. By F. von Hellwald.
Mémoires du Chevalier d'Eon. Par Frédéric Gaillardet.
Des Progrès de la Puissance Russe. Par M. L . . . . (Lesur).
Journey to the Source of the River Oxus. By J. Wood. With an Essay on the Geography of the Valley of the Oxus by Colonel Henry Yule.
Cathay and the Way thither. By Colonel Henry Yule.
The Travels of Marco Polo. Translated and edited, with notes, by Colonel Henry Yule.
Report of a Mission to Yarkand in 1873, under command of Sir T. D. Forsyth.
The Roof of the World. By Lieutenant-Colonel T. E. Gordon.
The Shores of Lake Aral. By Major Herbert Wood.
Russian Projects against India. By H. S. Edwards.
Caravan Journeys and Wanderings in Persia, Afghanistan, Turkestan, and Beluchistan; with Historical Notices of the Countries lying between Russia and India. By J. P. Ferrier.
Russia and England in the Struggle for Markets in Central Asia. By Captain M. A. Terentieff. (English translation.)
From Kulja, across the Thian-Shan, to Lob-Nor. By N. M. Prjevalsky. Translated by E. D. Morgan. With Notices of the Lakes of Central Asia.
Russia's Advance Eastward. By C. E. H. Vincent.
Russia in Central Asia. By H. Stumm.
A Ride to Khiva. By Colonel F. Burnaby.
Campaigning on the Oxus. By J. A. MacGahan.
The Merv Oasis. By E. O'Donovan.
Narrative of a Journey through the Province of Khorassan, and on the North-west Frontier of Afghanistan. By Sir C. M. MacGregor.
Wanderings in Baloochistan. By Sir C. M. MacGregor.
Travels in Central Asia. By A. Vambéry.
Clouds in the East. By Colonel Valentine Baker.
A Short History of China. By D. C. Boulger.
Central Asian Questions. By D. C. Boulger.
England and Russia in Central Asia. By D. C. Boulger.
Central Asian Portraits. By D. C. Boulger.
Life of Yakoob Beg. By D. C. Boulger.
Russian Central Asia. By Rev. H. Lansdell, D.D.

LIST OF REFERENCES

The Eye-witnesses' Account of the disastrous Russian Campaign against the Akhal Tekké Turkomans. By C. Marvin.
Merv, the Queen of the World. By C. Marvin.
The Russians at Merv and Herat. By C. Marvin.
The Russian Advance towards India. By C. Marvin.
Grodekoff's Ride from Samarkand to Herat. By C. Marvin.
The Russian Railway to Herat. By C. Marvin.
The Russian Annexation of Merv. By C. Marvin.
Reconnoitring Central Asia. By C. Marvin.
The Russians at the Gates of Herat. By C. Marvin.
Russia's Power of attacking India. By C. Marvin.
England and Russia face to face in Asia; Travels with the Afghan Boundary Commission. By Lieutenant A. C. Yate.
Northern Afghanistan, or Letters from the Afghan Boundary Commission. By Major C. E. Yate.
'La Campagne des Russes dans le Khanat de Khokand (1875-76).' Published in *Le Journal des Sciences Militaires.*
Official Report on the Siege and Assault of Denghil Tepé. By General Skobeleff. (English translation.)
Through the Heart of Asia: Over the Pamirs to India. By G. Bonvalot.
Russia in Central Asia. By Hon. G. N. Curzon.
Persia, and the Persian Question. By Hon. G. N. Curzon.
Hansard's Parliamentary Debates.
Haydn's Dictionary of Dates.
Markham's Geographical Magazine.
Proceedings and *Journals of the Royal Geographical Society.*
Parliamentary Reports regarding Central Asia, Afghanistan, Persia, and Beluchistan.

CONTENTS

OF

THE FIRST VOLUME

CHAPTER I

1220–1689

EARLY HISTORY OF RUSSIA

PAGE

Mongol devastations in Asia and Europe—Russia freed from the Mongols by Ivan III.—Russia's first advance into Asia—Conquests of Ivan the Terrible—The British-Muscovy Company—First Russian Embassy to England—Reign of Michael Feodorovitch, the first of the Romanoffs—Russia's Siberian conquests—Cossack invasions of Khiva—English intervention between Sweden and Russia—England seeks a Siberian route to Hindustan—Russian mission to the Khan of Bokhara—Advance of Russia towards the Pacific checked by the Chinese—Persia refuses Russia's commercial proposals—Expeditions to the Crimea . . . 1

CHAPTER II

1689–1800

'THE KEY AND GATE'

Peter the Great conquers Azof—Pultawa—Peter's loss of Azof and his desire to open a trade with the East—Stories of the wealth of Asia—Submission of the Khan of Khiva to Peter

—Gold-mines of Irket—Omsk and Semipalatinsk—'New Siberian Line'—Failure of Peter's expeditions to Little Bokhara and Khiva—Russian conquests in Persia—Proposed route to India *via* Astrabad—Peter's 'will'—Persia regains her lost provinces—Submission of the Kirghiz-Kazaks to Russia—The 'key and gate to all the countries in Central Asia'—Orenburg—The Persians defeat the Khan of Khiva—Empress Anne and British trade with Persia—The blind Governor of Khiva—Russia again obtains Azof—Russian acquisition of the Crimea—Russian designs on Turkey, and Treaty of Jassy—Russians in Georgia, and their failure in Persia—The struggle for the Caucasian provinces 25

CHAPTER III

1800–1828

COLLAPSE OF PROJECTED INVASIONS OF INDIA

Scheme for a French and Russian invasion of India—The Emperor Paul's manifesto—The Sovereignty of Georgia—Russian advance against Persia—French alliance with Persia—India threatened by an Afghan invasion—Treaty of Tilsit—Revival of project for a Franco-Russian invasion of India—Mission of Sir Harford Jones to Persia—Russo-Turkish War—Franco-Russian War—Persian reverses and Treaty of Gulistan—Submission of Turkoman tribes to Russia—The Gokcheh difficulty and renewal of hostilities between Russia and Persia—Treaty of Turkomanchai—M. Griboiedoff's Mission 50

CHAPTER IV

1829–1840

ATTACKS ON HERAT AND KHIVA

Growth of Russian influence in Persia—Russo-Turkish War, and Treaty of Adrianople—Russia incites Persia to attack Herat—Russian intrigue in Afghanistan—Mission of Burnes to Kabul—Persia's withdrawal from Herat—Lord Auckland's expedition to Afghanistan, the Simla Manifesto, and the restoration of Shuja-ul-Mulk—Russian expedition for conquering Khiva—Russia and the Kirghiz—Failure of Russian advance upon Khiva 89

CHAPTER V
1840–1845
TROUBLES IN AFGHANISTAN

PAGE

Dost Mahommed's attempt to regain his throne—Outbreak in Kabul, and murder of Sir Alexander Burnes and Sir William Macnaghten—Fate of General Elphinstone's army The only survivor of the army—Disaster to Colonel Palmer and his troops—Critical situation in Afghanistan Stoddart's and Conolly's missions to Khiva and Bokhara Failure of Russian mission to Khiva—Russian mission to Bokhara—Russian occupation of Ashurada . . . 126

CHAPTER VI
1846–1858
RUSSIAN ADVANCE ACROSS THE KIRGHIZ STEPPES

Russian frontier-line at the beginning of the nineteenth century—Operations in the Sea of Aral and construction of Fort Raim—Subjection of the Southern Kirghiz to Russia—Founding of Kopal—Collisions between Russians and Khivans—The Aral Sea flotilla—Khokandian attacks on the Russians—Siege of Ak-Mechet and its capture by the Russians—Khokandian expeditions for retaking Ak-Mechet—Further Russian aggression across the Ili—The Crimean War—Two Russian plans for the invasion of India—Herat again besieged by Persia—British force despatched against the Shah—Intrigues and insurrection of Izzet Kutebar—Ignatieff's Missions to Khiva and Bokhara —Further Russian explorations of Central Asia—Khanikoff's Mission 144

CHAPTER VII
1859–1868
ATTACKS ON KHOKAND AND BOKHARA

Civil war in Khokand—Russian forward movement in Khokand Capture of Aulie-ata and Hazret-i-Turkestan—Tchernaieff captures Chimkent British policy of 'masterly inactivity' in India—Prince Gortchakoff's circular—Fall of Tashkent—Russian declarations regarding Tashkent—Russian invasion of Bokharan territory—Capture of Khojent—Capture of Ura-Tepé, and occupation of Jizakh—The 'Steppe Commission' Formation of the Province of

Turkestan—Occupation of Samarkand—Treaty of Peace with Bokhara 183

CHAPTER VIII

THE ANGLO-RUSSIAN AGREEMENT OF 1873

Conferences between Lord Clarendon and Baron Brunnow on Russia's advance towards Afghanistan and India—Prince Gortchakoff's map—Gortchakoff' assurances—Controversy on the limitary line—Russia takes time to consider the Indian Government's proposals—Final settlement of the northern frontier of Afghanistan, and Prince Gortchakoff's letter—Russian pledges to respect the integrity of Afghanistan—An incomplete settlement—Present condition of the boundary question 221

CHAPTER IX

1868-1883

KULJA AND KASHGAR

'Bokharan independence'—Petty native disturbances in Bokhara—The Iskander Kul Expedition—Kulja and its history—Affairs of Kashgar, and the rule of Yakoob Beg—Russian occupation and annexation of Kulja 'in perpetuity'—Yakoob Beg defies Russia—British relations with Kashgar—Russian proposals to Yakoob Beg—Kashgar and the Porte—Treaty of commerce between the Indian Government and Kashgar—Projected Russian invasion of Kashgar—Subjugation of Kashgar by the Chinese—Rendition of Kulja to China 235

CHAPTER X

1869-1873

CONQUEST OF KHIVA

Occupation of Krasnovodsk and its object—Gortchakoff's explanations to Great Britain—Protestations from the Khan of Khiva and the Persian Government—Kirghiz insurrection—Skokeleff and Markozoff's reconnaissances—Council at St. Petersburg—Advance to Khiva and march of the Russian columns—Disasters of Markozoff's column—Bombardment of Khiva—Surrender of Khiva and Kaufmann's triumphal entry—Treaty of peace—Reaction in England against Russia 279

RUSSIA'S MARCH TOWARDS INDIA

CHAPTER I

1220 1689

EARLY HISTORY OF RUSSIA

Mongol devastations in Asia and Europe—Russia freed from the Mongols by Ivan III.—Russia's first advance into Asia—Conquests of Ivan the Terrible—The British-Muscovy Company—First Russian Embassy to England—Reign of Michael Feodorovitch, the first of the Romanoffs—Russia's Siberian conquests—Cossack invasions of Khiva—English intervention between Sweden and Russia—England seeks a Siberian route to Hindustan—Russian mission to the Khan of Bokhara—Advance of Russia towards the Pacific checked by the Chinese—Persia refuses Russia's commercial proposals—Expeditions to the Crimea.

In the early years of the thirteenth century, at the time when Henry III. was king of England, the wild inhabitants of the regions on the extreme eastern borders of Europe were startled by disquieting rumours of the movements of vast hordes of barbarians who were at that time devastating the unknown countries in the heart of Asia. Nor was it long before these reports assumed a more definite shape, for it soon became known that a mighty chieftain had made himself master of the north-eastern portion of Asia, and was then marching with his armies against the kingdoms of Turan and Iran.

This great conqueror was Genghiz Khan, the son of Yissugei, the 'Emperor of the Great Mongols.' In the course of one campaign he had conquered the whole of the vast region which stretches from the Sea of Japan to the inhospitable Pamir Plateau; shortly afterwards Khiva, Samarkand, Balkh, and Bokhara were captured by his warriors; and by the year 1220 the frontiers of his mighty empire had been extended to the southern slopes of the Caucasus and to the eastern shores of the Caspian Sea.

In the following year a considerable Mongol army marched into Europe; but after ravaging the rich valley of the Ural it quickly retired, leaving the startled Russians astonished at the seemingly supernatural visitation. Again, in 1223, one of Genghiz Khan's generals crossed the Caucasus, and, carrying everything before him, speedily subjugated the whole country between the mouths of the Rivers Volga and Dnieper.

At this period the country which is now known by the name of 'Russia' was in a condition of complete anarchy, and was split up into a number of petty principalities. The rulers of these states were perpetually at war with each other, their subjects were devoid of the elements of civilisation, and throughout the country there was no state, or group of states, which was in a position to offer any effective resistance to the onward march of the barbarian invaders. At this time the most powerful of the Russian princes was Mitislaf of Gallicia, and he speedily gathered round him some of the minor chiefs and proclaimed a holy war against the savage unbelievers who appeared to be bent on the extermination of all who attempted to oppose their career of war and bloodshed. But the Russian armies were defeated with great slaughter on the banks of the River Kalka, and after the barbarians had again indulged their appetite for destruction and massacre, they once more retired, leaving behind them a desert to mark their path.

Thirteen years elapsed before these scourges of humanity again appeared in Europe. In the meanwhile Genghiz Khan had died, and was succeeded by his son Ogatai, who, during the first years of his reign, was occupied with the continuation of the war against the Kin emperors of China, which his father had commenced with such remarkable success. In May 1234 the last of the Kin emperors was overthrown, and while Ogatai was employed in a great struggle with the Sung rulers of the southern provinces of China, he sent an army under his nephew Batu Khan to re-establish Mongol supremacy in Eastern Europe.

It is needless here to describe the various campaigns which followed; it is sufficient merely to state that by the year 1241 Batu Khan had completely overthrown the armies of the Russian princes, their chief cities had been captured, and the irresistible hordes of Asiatic barbarians had

B 2

conquered Poland and Hungary, and had gained complete possession of the whole of Eastern Europe. But at this juncture, when Batu was on the point of commencing a new campaign against Austria and the Teutonic knights, he received news of the death of his sovereign Ogatai, and at once made preparations for a retreat. Europe was thus delivered from any further 'carnivals of death,' and the terrible Mongol invasions came to an end.

On his return from Poland and Hungary, Batu settled on the banks of the River Volga, built the city of Sarai, and there established the kingdom of the Khans of the Golden Horde—a name which is said to have been derived from the gorgeous tapestry and sumptuous appointments of the tent of the Mongol prince. For more than two centuries after this the princes of the petty Russian principalities were forced to pay homage to the Khans of the Golden Horde. They were obliged to attend at Sarai to obtain the Khan's decision regarding their various disputes, and could not ascend their thrones without first receiving the 'Iarlikh,' or letters-patent, from the Khan, and they were speedily punished if they made any attempt to throw off the Mongol yoke.

But towards the close of this period the Mongol empire itself had, for many reasons, begun to show signs of decay; and the victory which the Grand Prince of Moscow—Dimitri Donskoi—gained over the Mongol army of Mamai at Koulikovo in 1380 was a sure presage of the approaching overthrow of the supremacy of the Golden Horde. Moscow, at that time, was gradually assuming a leading position among the Russian principalities, and when Ivan III., surnamed the Great, succeeded his father Vassili the Blind in 1463, as Grand Prince of Moscow, the Russians obtained in him a leader who was able to free them from the oppression of the Mongols, and one who laid the foundation of that unity of the Russian people which enabled them to take their place among the nations of Europe.

It would be out of place here to refer to Ivan's actions except in so far as they affect the question of Russian conquests towards the East, and these therefore only will be considered. After subduing Novgorod the Great, which had been hesitating between the rival Grand Princes of Moscow and Lithuania, Ivan conquered the whole of Northern Russia as far as Finland, the White Sea, and the Ural Mountains, and then turned his attention to the Khanates or Czarates of Sarai and Kazan—two of the states which had grown out of the gradual decay of the Golden Horde. He, in 1478, refused to pay tribute to Achmet Khan of Sarai, trampled on the Khan's image, and put all the Khan's envoys to death, excepting one who escaped and conveyed the news to the Horde. Achmet, of course, took the field for the purpose of punishing his rebellious vassal, and, on marching towards Moscow, found that Ivan, with a numerous and well-equipped army, had taken up a strong position on the banks of the River Oka. The Khan seems to have been disinclined to risk everything on a battle, and did not attack; while the Grand Prince, who, in spite of his repeated successes, does not appear to have been possessed of much valour, neglected the advice of his *boyars*, and declined to cross the river to attack the Mongols. The two armies remained thus confronting each other for many weeks, confining themselves to an occasional discharge of arrows and abuse; and it was not until the river became frozen that this extraordinary situation was brought to a close. Then, however, when a bloody battle appeared imminent, an inexplicable panic seized both armies, and they fled in confusion. Such was the final encounter between the Russians and their former oppressors of Sarai—a disgraceful flight of both forces. But the power of the Golden Horde was broken. Achmet on reaching his country was put to death by one of his followers, and the Horde, attacked by Ivan's firm ally, the Khan of the Crimea,[1] only existed as a separate nation for a short time longer.[2]

Ivan then marched against Kazan, captured the city in 1487, and carried the Khan Alegam as a prisoner to Moscow. The people were forced to swear allegiance to the Grand Princes of Moscow; but, as the city was not yet ripe for annexation, it

---

[1] The Khanate of the Crimea was one of the three chief Tartar States which rose out of the ruins of the Golden Horde. Kazan and Sarai were the headquarters of the other two.

[2] Sarai, the great capital of the Golden Horde, where Russian prisoners had grovelled before the Khans, was destroyed in 1502, when the power of the Horde was completely broken.

was placed under the sovereignty of a nephew of Ivan's ally, the Khan of the Crimea.

Two years later Viatka, which had for a short time fallen into the hands of the Khan of Kazan, was reconquered; and in 1499 the governors of Oustiougue, of the Dwina, and of Viatka, advanced as far as the River Petchora, and built a fort on its banks. Then, crossing the Ural Mountains in sledges drawn by dogs, in the depth of winter, they slew fifty Samoyedes and captured 200 reindeer. They then invaded the country of the Vogouls and Ougrians, took forty palisaded enclosures, and finally returned to Moscow with fifty captive chiefs.

This raid had no permanent results, and is only interesting from the fact of its having been the first Russian advance into Asia. This advance across the Urals was made at a time when England was just recovering from the effects of the Wars of the Roses, when India was only known to Europe through vague travellers' tales, and a hundred years before the formation of the first East India Company.

It will be seen that this first advance into Asia was merely a sudden and irregular foray across the border. It had been made without orders from the central Government, and without any idea of permanent advantages being derived from it. It was a natural result of the disordered state of the country, and was merely an episode in the general expansion of a people who had been downtrodden for centuries by a race of barbarous nomads, but who, taking advantage of the gradual decay of their oppressors, and feeling the growth of their own forces, began, under Ivan the Great, that expansion and course of territorial acquisition which has steadily continued ever since, and has brought Russia to the position she now occupies, as one of the most powerful nations in the world, with an empire extending from the Pacific Ocean to the very heart of Europe.

Ivan's conquests towards the east have only been here referred to; but he succeeded also in greatly extending and consolidating Russian power towards the west and north; and Russia day by day took a more important share in European concerns, while eastern potentates also sought the Grand Prince's friendship. Among these was Baber the Great, Mogul Emperor of Dehli, who entered into negotiations with Ivan's son and successor, Vassili Ivanovitch.

Vassili's rule, however, was merely a preparation for the more important reign of his son, Ivan IV., who, on account of his violent acts, earned the surname of 'The Terrible.' Vassili lost the friendship of the Khan of the Crimea, and found that Kazan had fallen away from its allegiance to Moscow. He twice sent expeditions against the city, but both were complete failures; and he therefore devised other means for ruining his enemies. He established a fair at Makarief,[1]

---

[1] The fair of Makarief was afterwards transferred to Nijni Novgorod, where it still flourishes and attracts hundreds of thousands of merchants from all parts of Europe and Asia.

on the Volga, by means of which the trade of Kazan was much injured.

But the final subjugation of Kazan, and the annexation of the Khanates of Kazan and Sarai (or Astrakhan) was not accomplished till some years later by the terrible Ivan IV.

Throughout the first years of the reign of Ivan IV. the Czar[1] found that Kazan was still greatly under the influence of the Khan of the Crimea, and although the Muscovite party at one time obtained the ascendency, a revolution shortly afterwards broke out, when the city gates were shut on the Muscovites, and the people proclaimed a Tartar Khan. Ivan then determined to subdue the Mussulman city once and for ever, and he therefore marched against it with a large army in 1552, and, after a desperate hand-to-hand struggle, gained complete possession of the town, and then massacred the inhabitants. The fall of Kazan was soon followed by the annexation of Astrakhan. The Nogais, who wandered in the adjoining steppes, then submitted to the Czar of Moscow, and their example was followed by the Cossacks of the Don, while the Bashkirs and other tribes on the Volga and Kama, who formerly had been subject to the Khan of Kazan, after a short time paid homage to Ivan the Terrible.

Russia—or, more correctly speaking, Moscow—thus obtained possession of the entire course of the Volga from its source to the Caspian Sea, and

---

[1] Ivan the Terrible was the first Grand Prince of Moscow who assumed the title of 'Czar.'

thus secured one of the main trade routes with the far East. By gaining a footing on the shores of the Caspian, she was able to exert some slight influence over Persia, and her fame began to penetrate far into the unknown lands in the heart of Asia. In 1557, ambassadors from the Khan of Khiva arrived at the court of the Czar to seek permission to trade with Russia; and similar missions visited Moscow in 1563, 1566, and 1583.

Nor were these the only successes towards the East which Ivan the Terrible could boast of. In 1558 he granted to one, Gregory Strogonoff, a strip of land on the banks of the River Kama, where the Strogonoffs settled, and from whence they started on explorations of the mineral resources of the Urals. These colonists, in their raids across the mountains, came into contact with the Siberian hordes of the Irtish, Tobol, and Baratinski Tartars, who were ruled by Kuchum Khan, a lineal descendant of the great Genghiz Khan. The Strogonoffs applied to Ivan for permission and assistance to fight the Tartars. Ivan was at the time fully occupied elsewhere, but he saw a way of furthering the schemes of the Strogonoffs. At that time a band of brigands named 'The Good Companions of the Don' maintained a regular system of blackmail and pillage on the Volga, and had on more than one occasion roused the ire of the Czar. These men he now proposed to utilise, and pardoning one of their chiefs, named Irmak (or Yermak) Timoféevitch, permitted him to take service with the Strogonoffs, with several hundred of his followers—outcasts of every nationality and description. Irmak, with this motley army, crossed the Ural Mountains in 1579, traversed the vast untrodden forests of Tobol, defeated Kuchum in a series of battles in 1581, captured his capital, Sibir, and made the Khan's cousin, Mahmet Kul, a prisoner. Many of the neighbouring chiefs submitted, and the Russians then sailed down the River Irtish, capturing several forts on their way. Thus, before Ivan's death, which occurred in 1584, the Czar received news that a vast tract of hitherto unknown country had been conquered for him by the wild brigand chief and his adventurous followers.

Leaving Irmak's exploits for the present, it is necessary now to refer to the doings of the English in Russia at that time, in order that it may be clearly understood what were then the relative positions and commercial aspirations of the two nations which now are rivals for empire in Asia.

In the reign of King Edward VI. a company of merchants was formed for the discovery of 'kingdoms, islands, and places unknown and unvisited by the highway of the sea.' The great navigator, Sebastian Cabot, was nominated governor for life; and shortly afterwards three vessels, under Sir Hugh Willoughby and Chancellor, were sent towards the North to explore the unknown sea which was believed by some to offer a road to China and the far East. These three ships encountered a violent storm off the Scandinavian coast, and became separated from each other.

Willoughby, with the 'Buona Speranza' and
'Buona Confidenza,' was lost; but Chancellor, in
the 'Edward Bonaventura,' succeeded in rounding
the North Cape, and found himself first in a
strange sea, and then at the mouth of a river, near
to which stood two monasteries.[1] Here he landed,
and found that he was on the territory of the Czar
of Moscow, although, at that time, no Czar had
visited this portion of his dominions.[2] He had
unwittingly reached the White Sea and mouth of
the River Dwina, close to where the town of
Archangel now stands. Chancellor went to Moscow and delivered to Ivan the letters which he
had received from King Edward VI. This happened in 1553.

On the accession of Queen Mary, she confirmed
the privileges of the company, and in 1556
Chancellor again sailed for the Dwina, and after
revisiting Moscow, was accompanied to England
by the first Russian ambassador, Osip Nepei.
Nepei, on his return to Russia, was accompanied
by Anthony Jenkinson, who, by his straightforward
behaviour and wide knowledge, succeeded in
gaining Ivan's favour, and obtained from the Czar
a letter of recommendation to the neighbouring
Asiatic princes. Jenkinson, thus armed, descended
the Volga, and flew the first British flag on the
Caspian Sea. Crossing from Astrakhan to the

---

[1] These were the monasteries of Saint Nicholas and Saint
Michael, near to the latter of which the town of St. Michael the
Archangel—or, shortly, Archangel—was afterwards built.

[2] Peter the Great was the first Czar who visited Archangel and
the White Sea.

Mangishlak peninsula, he thence made his way to Bokhara. There he was obliged to sell his wares at a price which brought him little or no profit, and he thus returned to Russia, having gained but small remuneration for his difficult and dangerous undertaking. In another journey which Jenkinson made in 1562, he again sailed down the Caspian Sea from Astrakhan to Derbent, and from thence proceeded to Kasvin, which was at that time the capital of Persia. He, however, received but scant courtesy from the Shah, and returned to Russia, taking with him the princes of Georgia and Shirwan, and other chiefs who wished to gain the friendship of the Czar of Moscow.

These ventures of Jenkinson's were repeated by other factors of the British-Muscovy Company during the next nineteen years; but none of them had any tangible result, and they merely demonstrated that the time had not yet arrived when a profitable trade could be carried on with the countries of Central Asia, and the English were therefore obliged to content themselves with trading in the territories of the Czar. Ivan, however, in acknowledgment of Jenkinson's services, had authorised the English Merchant Company to trade on all rivers in the north of Russia, from the Dwina to the Obi, and permitted them to establish themselves in the principal Russian towns.

Thus it will be seen that while Russia was engaged in forming an united empire out of the various elements which had been scattered and suppressed by the Mongol invasions, and one which could take its place among the nations of Europe, England and other Western nations (which had escaped from the disastrous results of the barbarian invasion, and were in a more advanced state of civilisation), began to turn their attention to commercial enterprises, and became desirous of obtaining some share in the riches of the East. But none knew how these riches were to be acquired, or by what road the countries which possessed such fabulous wealth could be reached. It was only known that those states through which the commerce of India and the East passed invariably became in their turn wealthy; and this knowledge merely increased the desire to obtain some share in the traffic. Since Vasco de Gama had discovered the Cape route in 1497, Portugal had obtained complete command over the Eastern seas, and had monopolised the Eastern trade. None of the other nations in Europe for many years attempted to contest the naval supremacy of the Portuguese in the East, and they were therefore obliged to seek some other route in their endeavours to obtain a share in the trade. Thus England, through a want of geographical knowledge, first endeavoured to obtain a trade route to India and Central Asia through Russia—a fact which it is strange to contemplate, when Great Britain, through her maritime supremacy and the hardihood of her sons, has succeeded in building up for herself a great empire in the East to find herself there confronted and even threatened by the State which first was believed to offer the best means of communication with India, but which now appears as a dangerous and powerful rival.

It is impossible here to review the effects which 'the times of troubles' had on Russian expansion; and it is sufficient merely to state that when Ivan the Terrible, in a fit of uncontrolled rage, slew his favourite son, Ivan, in 1581, he committed an act which had the most disastrous results for Russia, and threatened to overthrow the empire which he and his immediate predecessors had built up. The country became the theatre of war for two rival Powers who determined to profit by the internal disorder and weakness of the Russian State. Russia, which had just become united, and which was just appearing before Europe as a powerful nation, appeared doomed to destruction, when help came from an unexpected quarter. Tartar Kazan, which had been for so long a thorn in the side of Russia, had gradually been transformed, and now stepped forward as the champion of the empire of Moscow. Joining in, if not actually leading, the national rising for the deliverance of Russia, the citizens of Kazan stepped into the breach, and brilliantly assisted in the popular movement for the salvation of the Muscovite empire, and in defence of the orthodox religion. The foreign invaders were repulsed, and Michael Feodorovitch, the first of the Romanoff dynasty, was proclaimed Czar.

But although, after the death of Ivan the Terrible, Russia lost in Europe much of the power which she had previously gained, she was carving out for herself a new and extensive empire in Asia. Irmak's exploits have already been referred to, and the story of Russian conquests in Siberia must now be resumed.

In the spring of 1584 (the year in which Ivan IV. died), Irmak and his followers were besieged in Sibir by the Tartars; but the Russian leader soon defeated his enemies and then sailed up the Irtish, conquering many strong places during his advance. His brilliant career, however, was fast drawing to a close, for it was destined that he should not long survive the master whom he had latterly served so well. Hearing that a caravan from Bokhara was crossing the Ishim steppe on its way to Kuchum Khan, he halted near the River Bagatai with the intention of surprising the traders. There the Russians lay down to rest, unconscious that their enemy was near. The sleepers were suddenly attacked by Kuchum's followers, and the gallant Irmak was drowned, after having bravely cut his way to the river bank. His followers then recrossed the Urals, and left Kuchum, for a time, master of the situation. But not for long; for news of Irmak's brilliant successes had reached Moscow, and a second expedition was fitted out and despatched to Siberia in 1586. The territory which Irmak had conquered for Ivan was gradually won back for Russia, and by the end of the sixteenth century the Russians had regained possession of Siberia from the Ural Mountains to the River Irtish. The town of Tiumen was built on the site of one of

Irmak's first conquests, and was thus the first permanent Russian settlement east of the Ural Mountains. Tobolsk was also founded, and became the residence of the first Russian governor of Siberia. And Kuchum Khan, bereft of his wives and children, was driven into the wild steppes of Ishim, where he died, or was put to death by the Nogai Tartars.

But, though Russia gained vast additions to her dominions in Siberia, she was less fortunate in her dealings at this time in the Caucasus. A force which was sent by Boris Goudonoff to occupy Daghestan was annihilated; while Alexander, Prince of Kachetia, who had acknowledged himself to be a vassal of Goudonoff, had been assassinated, and was succeeded by his son, who was a staunch defender of Islam, and ally of Shah Abbass of Persia.

During this period Russia had but few dealings with the states of Central Asia; but, nevertheless, the fame of her conquests in Siberia caused the great Abdulla, the Khan of Bokhara, to send an embassy to Moscow in 1589 with the object of obtaining the friendship of the Czar Feodor Ivanovitch. The Khan, however, omitted to address the Czar with his full titles, and his letter was therefore not received. The Boyar, Boris Goudonoff (who subsequently was proclaimed Czar), informed the Khan that 'all sovereigns write to his Czarish Majesty with due respect, and to him, the Boyar, with love and compliments,' and said that it was only due to his intercession that the ambassador had not been refused an audience.

The commencement of the seventeenth century was marked by a series of Cossack invasions of Khiva. In 1602 the Ural Cossacks heard of the riches of Khiva from some Persian merchants whom they had captured in one of their forays. They accordingly resolved to make a raid on the Khanate, and, crossing the Kirghiz Steppes, actually captured the town of Urgenj during the temporary absence of the Khan. They then started to return with large quantities of spoil and about a thousand women, but were overtaken and surrounded by the Khivans. Cut off from water, they still fought for several days, quenching their thirst with the blood of the slain; but finally, after being compelled to abandon their booty, they were almost all massacred.

A second expedition shared the same fate, while a third fared still worse. Caught in severe snowstorms, the invading Cossacks lost their way, and, instead of reaching Khiva, found themselves on the shores of the Sea of Aral. Their provisions became exhausted, and, driven to madness by the pangs of hunger, they killed and ate each other, while the survivors were captured and carried into slavery by the Khivans.

Michael Feodorovitch had no easy task before him when in 1613 he found himself raised to the throne of the Czars of Moscow. His dominions were threatened by Sweden in the north, while the Poles still ravaged the country to the south-west;

and the traces of 'the troublous times' were everywhere apparent. Foreign help was necessary; and after Holland had been first fruitlessly asked for assistance, Michael sent an ambassador to England to entreat for money with which to continue the struggle. In the following year (1614) John Merrick, who had for some years previously traded in Moscow, appeared before the Czar as an ambassador from the English king, James I. Merrick demanded that the English merchants should be permitted to trade with India by the River Obi, and with Persia through Astrakhan and the Caspian Sea. He also applied for concessions of iron and jet mines on the Soukhona, and grants of land near Vologda. These were the English terms for mediation between Gustavus Adolphus of Sweden and the Czar, and are curious in that they show that, fourteen years after the formation of the first East India Company, England was still desirous of obtaining a trade route with Hindustan through Siberia. But the difficulties and dangers of the route were pointed out to the English envoy, and he finally consented to negotiate with the Swedes; and through his good offices the Peace of Stolbovo was concluded between Gustavus Adolphus and the Romanoff Czar. As a reward for his successful mediation, Merrick again urged that the English demands should be conceded; but the merchants of Moscow so unanimously represented to the Czar that such a concession would mean their ruin, that the negotiations fell through.

In 1620 the Czar Michael made a fresh attempt to open up a trade route with Central Asia, and sent an embassy, under Ivan Khokhloff, to the Khan of Bokhara. This mission, however, failed to obtain any concessions from the Khan, and is chiefly remarkable on account of the instructions which were issued to the Russian ambassador in order that the dignity of the Czar might be fully maintained. Khokhloff was ordered to give no presents if such should be demanded in order to admit him to the Khan's presence; and, if he were to be invited to dine with the Khan, he was not to accept the invitation unless it was stipulated that he should be given a higher place than any other foreign envoys who might be present. This ambassador reached Samarkand in safety, and obtained an audience of the Khan; but, on presenting the Czar's compliments, he noticed that the Bokharan ruler did not stand up when the Czar's name was mentioned, and he therefore remarked that all foreign potentates were in the habit of rising on such occasions as a mark of respect towards the Czar. The Khan immediately stood up, and apologised for the unintentional slight which had been offered. This incident, and the earlier treatment of Abdulla Khan's ambassador, show that, although the Russians were unable to obtain a footing in Central Asia at that time, yet they had no intention of permitting their nation to be in any way despised or treated with disrespect—an excellent principle in dealing with Asiatics, and one which has been of much use to Russia in her advances into the heart of Asia.

Two years after the despatch of this embassy to Bokhara diplomatic relations were also entered into with Afghan, the Khan of Khiva, who, having been driven from his kingdom, sought the protection of the Czar, and even offered, if restored to his throne, to become the vassal of Russia.

At the beginning of the seventeenth century the Russians did little more than hold their own in Siberia, and many attacks were made by the native tribes on their posts and settlements. But, profiting by the quarrels of opposing factions, and by opening up trade with the Central Asian khanates, the Russian power in Siberia gradually became consolidated, and communications were entered into with the Chinese and with the Dzungarian Kalmuks which have resulted in the gradual extension of Russian influence, first to Lake Baikal, and then still further eastwards to the shores of the Pacific Ocean.

Their advance through Eastern Siberia, however, was by no means unopposed. The Chinese were naturally alarmed at their movements, and when the first Russian embassy visited Pekin, in 1656, it met with a very cold reception. Some years afterwards the Chinese Emperor Kanghi sent a force to subdue Galdan, the Dzungarian prince, whose pretensions were beginning to imperil the very existence of the Manchu dynasty; and while he was so engaged the Russians, taking advantage of the dispute between the Chinese and Dzungarians, built some forts on the upper waters of the River Amour, the chief of which were Albazin and Astrog, and thus brought about the first conflict between Russian and Chinese troops. The Emperor Kanghi viewed the existence of these forts as a standing menace and insult to his authority; and as soon, therefore, as Galdan had been defeated, he ordered his troops to attack and demolish the objectionable Russian outposts. Albazin was captured and destroyed, the other forts in the neighbourhood shared the same fate, and thus all traces of the first Muscovite settlements on the Amour were completely obliterated.

But a fresh war soon broke out between Galdan and the Chinese, and the Russians were thus for a while left undisturbed in their efforts to retrieve their shattered fortunes in Eastern Siberia. Albazin was rebuilt, and rose from its ruins stronger and more capable of resisting a siege. As soon as the Chinese had once again settled their differences with the Dzungarians, an army marched against the Russians. The first attack was repulsed; but Kanghi sent large reinforcements, when the Russians, finding themselves to be completely overmatched, signed the Treaty of Nipchu in 1689, whereby the fertile regions of the Amour were restored to the Chinese; and thus the Russians were seriously checked in their advance towards the Pacific, and for the next century and a half they were shut out from all communication with the eastern shores of Asia.

Nor was it only in Eastern Siberia that the Russians failed in their endeavours to extend their territories at the expense of their Asiatic neighbours. In 1664 the Czar Alexis Mikhailovitch sent an embassy to the court of Shah Abbass II. of Persia. The filthy habits of the Muscovites, however, utterly disgusted the Persian monarch, who called them the 'Usbegs of the Franks'; and when it was discovered that the object of the mission was solely for the purpose of trade, and that the Russians had adopted the guise of ambassadors to evade the payment of dues, the Shah became incensed, and summarily expelled them from the country. In revenge for this affront the Czar incited the Cossacks of South Russia to attack the Persian province of Mazanderan. The Cossacks promptly took the hint, overran the province, sacked the city of Ferabad, and finally entrenched themselves on the Miankaleh peninsula, north of the Gulf of Astrabad, where they intended to remain for the winter. Here, however, they were attacked by the Persians, and, being defeated, took refuge on the island of Ashurada, where they remained for some time.[1]

Two expeditions were also sent against the Crimea, in 1687 and 1689, but both proved

---

[1] This account of the first Russian occupation of the Island of Ashurada has been taken from the recent excellent work on Persia by the Hon. G. N. Curzon, where the fact is noticed for the first time by an English writer on Central Asian affairs. It is interesting in that it shows that this island was occupied by the Russians 170 years before they permanently settled down there.

complete failures; and thus, when Peter the Great freed himself from the regency of his sister Sophia, and assumed entire control over the affairs of the state, he found that Russia's dealings with her barbarian neighbours were marked by failure and retreat.

CHAPTER II

1689-1800

'THE KEY AND GATE'

Peter the Great conquers Azof—Pultawa—Peter's loss of Azof and his desire to open a trade with the East—Stories of the wealth of Asia—Submission of the Khan of Khiva to Peter—Goldmines of Irket—Omsk and Semipalatinsk—'New Siberian Line'—Failure of Peter's expeditions to Little Bokhara and Khiva—Russian conquests in Persia—Proposed route to India *via* Astrabad—Peter's 'will'—Persia regains her lost provinces—Submission of the Kirghiz-Kazaks to Russia—The 'key and gate to all the countries in Central Asia'—Orenburg—The Persians defeat the Khan of Khiva—Empress Anne and British trade with Persia—The blind Governor of Khiva—Russia again obtains Azof—Russian acquisition of the Crimea—Russian designs on Turkey, and Treaty of Jassy—Russians in Georgia, and their failure in Persia—The struggle for the Caucasian provinces.

PETER THE GREAT had much to occupy his attention in Europe before he was able to turn his thoughts to Asiatic affairs. He discerned that, as air and freedom are essential for the growth and development of mankind, so, for the expansion and progress of a nation, it is equally necessary that external trade and international intercourse should be fostered and extended. Russia had effected her unity, but was still surrounded by a cordon of states which checked her further development and cut her off from commercial intercourse with the Western nations of Europe. Peter saw that before Russia could cease to be merely an Oriental state, and before she could take a befitting place among the European powers, it was necessary that she should obtain a footing on the sea coast, in order that she might be able to trade freely and directly with Western Europe. This was one of the first tasks to which he applied his great powers, and how well he succeeded in his endeavours is generally known.

Shortly after he had assumed supreme authority, he succeeded in conquering Azof, whereby he gained a footing on the sea at the mouth of the River Don, and at the same time took up a position from which he could keep the Tartars of the Crimea in check. But the results of this conquest did not fulfil his expectations. Before his vessels could freely navigate the Black Sea and pass from thence into the Mediterranean, it was necessary that the Sultan of Turkey should give his assent; and as this was not forthcoming, and Peter was not strong enough to cope with the Turks, he had to turn his attention elsewhere to obtain that 'window towards the West' upon which he had set his heart. How he at first met with reverses, but eventually triumphed over his enemies, and effaced the memories of Narva by the great victory at Pultawa, are matters of European history, and require no notice here, except for the purpose of showing that Peter had many matters of vital importance to settle in Europe, which fully occupied all his attention until the commencement of the eighteenth century, and prevented him from interfering to any great extent in Asiatic concerns.

Even after Pultawa had been fought and won in 1709, the Czar found himself confronted by a new enemy who gave him ample occupation. This new foe was the Sultan of Turkey, who, at the instigation of France and Sweden, declared war against Russia, and succeeded in regaining possession of Azof. Peter thus found himself again completely cut off from the Black Sea, and was not in a position to attempt any further struggle with the Turks; and it was after this disaster that he chiefly devoted his energies to the maintenance and extension of his acquisitions on the Baltic, and to the development of commercial dealings with the East. He had gained a firm footing on the Neva, but had lost Azof; and he now desired to obtain some equivalent for the latter by exploiting Asia, and making Russia the great centre of trade between Asia and Europe.

Some time previously, in 1694, he had sent a merchant named Simon Malinki to India provided with government stores and money for the purpose of opening up a trade with the Great Mogul. But his mission appears to have borne no fruit, for no records of his doings have been kept.

In 1713, however, marvellous stories of the mineral wealth of Asia began to reach Peter's ears. The Governor of Siberia reported that gold sand was to be found in abundance near the town of Irket, i.e. Yarkand; and at the same time a

Turkoman chief named Hodja Nefes arrived in Astrakhan, where he related many stories of the gold which was said to be found on the banks of the Amu Daria—River Oxus. This Turkoman also stated that the Oxus used formerly to flow into the Caspian Sea, and professed to explain how its course had been diverted towards the Sea of Aral by the Usbegs, who had constructed dams across its former channel. From Astrakhan he went to Moscow, to propose to the Czar that he should take possession of the countries bordering on the Oxus, and restore the river to its ancient bed.

Some years previously—in 1700—the Khan of Khiva had tendered his submission to the Czar; and Peter had accepted the proffered allegiance. When Hodja Nefes arrived in Moscow, his wonderful reports were confirmed by a Khivan envoy who was there at the Russian Court, and Peter at once decided to despatch a military expedition to take possession of Khiva, and to establish his authority over the districts on the banks of the Oxus which were said to contain such fabulous stores of wealth.

He also issued orders for the despatch of an expedition to Little Bokhara, for the purpose of obtaining possession of the gold-mines of Irket. This undertaking was entrusted to Colonel Buchholtz, who was directed to proceed thither, building forts along the line by which he advanced. But the expedition was a disastrous failure, and its only permanent result was the erection of a fort on the site of the present city of Omsk.

Two years later another fortified post was built at Semipalatinsk; and in 1720 General Likhareff was sent to establish a fort on Lake Zaisan, and to explore the country lying between that point and Irket. Likhareff reached Zaisan Nor, and was continuing his advance up the Irtish when he unexpectedly came across Galdan Tchirin, the Khan of Dzungaria, who, with a large army, was watching his frontier against the Chinese. He managed, however, to deceive the Khan as to the object of his mission and retreated, building a fort at Ust-Kamenogorsk on his way back.

Thus Peter's search for gold in Little Bokhara resulted in complete failure. But although he did not succeed in the immediate object which he had in view, the movements of Russian troops towards the head waters of the River Irtish had a very important influence on the Russian position in Siberia, for in this way the line of forts on the Irtish was commenced, which line, by 1752, was connected with the Orenburg posts by a continuous series of forts which extended across the Ishim Steppe and became known as the 'New Siberian Line.'[1]

Nor did Peter's expedition to Khiva meet with any greater measure of success. The Czar entrusted the command to a Circassian prince named Bekovitch Tcherkasski, who spent three years in surveying the eastern shores of the Caspian, and established forts at Cape Karagan (on the Mangishlak peninsula) and on the Krasnovodsk spit.

[1] No further mention will be made of Russian advances in Siberia except those towards Khokand, *viâ* Vernoye.

He was ordered to approach the Khan in the character of a friendly envoy, and, before resorting to force, to congratulate him on his accession to power, and to explain that the strength of his escort was merely due to a polite desire on the part of the Czar to give due importance to his mission. When the Khan had been persuaded, or forced, to acknowledge Russian supremacy, two trade caravans were to be despatched—one to the Khan of Bokhara and the other to the Great Mogul of India.

The envoy for India received special instructions from Peter to go 'by water as far up the Amu Daria as possible (or by other rivers which may fall into it) to India, in the guise of a merchant, the real business being the discovery of a waterway to India; to inquire secretly about the river in case progress by water be forbidden; to return, if possible, by the same route, unless it be ascertained that there is another and more convenient way by water; the water-way as well as the land route to be carefully observed and described in writing and to be mapped; to notice the merchandise, particularly aromatic herbs and other articles that are exported from India; to examine into, and write an account of, all other matters which, though not mentioned here, may concern the interests of the empire.' Such were the precise orders given by Peter himself to Lieutenant Kojin, of the Russian Navy, who had been selected as envoy for India. But Kojin appears to have been ill-disposed towards Bekovitch, and even accused the Prince of a treacherous design 'to deliver the Russian troops into the hands of the barbarians.' He was then recalled, and, after being subjected to a court-martial, was imprisoned at St. Petersburg, when Bekovitch, in accordance with orders from the Czar, sent Murza Tevkelef with instructions to proceed to India through Persia, returning to Russia by way of China and Bokhara.¹ But this mission came to nothing, owing to the tragic fate which overtook the over-confident Circassian Prince and his army.

Bekovitch left Astrakhan in June 1717 with a force consisting of 3,500 men, six guns, and a train of 200 camels and 300 horses. He reached the Khivan oasis in the following August, but, falling into a trap cunningly laid by the Khan, he and his officers were killed and mutilated, while his troops were either massacred or reduced to slavery.

While Peter was acting with such vigour in Siberia and against Khiva, he was not neglectful of Russian commercial interests in Persia. He saw that the trade of that state, especially in silk, was by no means inconsiderable, but that Russian merchants had little or no share in it; and he moreover knew that through Persia there was an excellent road to India. He at first resorted to diplomacy, and sent an agent to Ispahan to per-

---

¹ See *Notes on the Intercourse of Russia with Khiva*, by G. Kühlewein, Secretary to Colonel Ignatieff's mission to Central Asia, translated from the Russian by John and Robert Michell.

suade the Shah to turn the Armenian trade in raw silk through Russia. But, although the Shah signed a treaty permitting Russian merchants to trade freely and to purchase raw silk whenever they wished, the agent reported that force would be far more advantageous than diplomacy. A good excuse for such interference was soon obtained. The Lesghians attacked the Persian town of Shemakha and plundered the Russian merchants in common with the other residents. Orders were given for the Russian troops on the Volga to march to winter quarters, from whence they were to advance, *viâ* Astrakhan, in the following spring. But, before the expedition started, Persia had been invaded by the Afghans; and then the Czar, instead of advancing against Persia to punish the attack on his subjects, announced that he was going to assist the Shah against his enemies. This was in 1722. A large Russian army having been collected at Astrakhan under Peter's personal command, advanced against Derbent, and obtained possession of the city without difficulty. Peter then returned to Astrakhan for the winter; but his lieutenant, continuing the operations, captured Baku in the following July; and two months later the representative of the unfortunate Shah Tamasp was compelled to sign a treaty at St. Petersburg by which Mazanderan, Ghilan, and Astrabad were ceded to Russia—very important concessions, which clearly showed that Peter had fully realised the great advantage of obtaining complete control over the shores of the

Caspian, and that he understood the great value of Astrabad.

That the Czar did fully realise the great strategical advantages which would be gained by a Russian occupation of Astrabad is conclusively proved by the words he made use of when at Derbent in 1722. During a conversation he there had with one of his officers regarding the relative advantages of the Cape route and the way to India through Central Asia, Peter remarked: 'Have you ever been in the Gulf of Astrabad? You must know, then, that those mountains' (pointing to the heights on the shore of the Caspian) 'extend to Astrabad, and that from there to Balkh and Badakshan with pack camels is only a twelve days' journey, and on that road to India no one can interfere with us.'

These expeditions of Peter's against Khiva and Persia were the first organised attempts made by the Russians to obtain a permanent footing in Central and Southern Asia.

Having, by the conquest of the Baltic provinces, obtained a footing on the sea, Peter turned his attention to the countries with which the most lucrative trade appeared probable, hoping thus to gain some of the wealth which Russia so sorely needed. He saw that the Portuguese had greatly enriched themselves during the time of Albuquerque, and that at a later period his friends the Dutch, as also the English and French, were obtaining considerable stores of wealth from the East. If such riches could be gained by nations which were separated from India by imperfectly explored and dangerous seas, Peter might reasonably have expected to be able to gain an equal share by means of the shorter and more direct land route through Khiva and Persia. That such was his belief appears to be incontestable, and he was the first Czar to organise and despatch expeditions for this purpose. That any idea of the conquest of India ever entered his mind is, however, highly improbable, and all he wished to obtain for Russia was wealth, which he thought could be more easily gained through the trade with Asia which he hoped to organise.

Mention is frequently made of the apocryphal document called the 'will of Peter the Great,' and many, assuming that document to be genuine, endeavour to prove that ever since Peter's death Russian Czars and diplomatists have steadily pursued a course of policy strictly in keeping with the principles set forth in the so-called will, and which virtually amount to the conquest of the world. But the very existence of such a will is disputed, and its fictitious character, if not actually established, is highly probable. The first mention of this will is contained in a book published by M. Lesur in 1812, entitled, 'Of the Progress of the Russian Power from its Commencement to the Beginning of the Nineteenth Century.'[1] This famous book was apparently written by order of Napoleon I., who at the time ordered the publication in the French newspapers of a series of articles

---

[1] A translation of the will as it appears in M. Lesur's book is given in Appendix I.

wherein he endeavoured to prove 'that Europe found herself in train to become the prey of Russia.' War between France and Russia then appeared inevitable, and Napoleon was anxious to prove that Russia was the enemy of Europe. The will reappeared on several other occasions when it seemed desirable to revive the idea that Russia was bent on obtaining the Empire of the World. But although it is extremely doubtful if Peter left such a will, yet he unquestionably had a very keen sense of the advantages which Russia could obtain by commercial dealings with the Central Asian states, and through them with India; and he undoubtedly initiated a policy which had for its aim the monopoly of—or at all events a share in—the trade with these countries.

For several years after Peter's death, in 1725, Russian affairs in Asia were not conducted with any marked degree of success. There were several reasons for this. The Russians had become imbued with a desire for still further intercourse with European nations, and neglected Oriental concerns; large numbers of foreigners from the West had obtained service in Russia, and were indiscriminately employed in European and Asiatic affairs, to the detriment of the latter; and the fate of Bekovitch had created so great an impression in Russia that 'to perish like Bekovitch' became a synonymous phrase for complete annihilation. It was not long, therefore, before reverses were sustained, which completely neutralised Peter's successes in the Caucasus. When the wretched Shah

Tamasp heard of the disastrous peace which his envoy had signed, he refused to ratify it; and as Turkey at the same time compelled Peter, under a threat of war, to abandon his aggressive schemes south of the Caucasus, the Czar finally came to an arrangement with the Sultan, by which all the Persian provinces which were not in the hands of the Afghans should be divided between the two states. But, after Peter's death, Persia, having under Nadir Shah succeeded in expelling the Afghans, set both Russia and Turkey at defiance, and, after a protracted struggle, regained her lost provinces, which, together with Derbent, were restored to her by the Treaty of Resht, which was signed by the Empress Anne in 1732.

But this defeat was in some measure counterbalanced by the submission of the Kirghiz-Kazaks of the Middle and Lesser Hordes, who inhabited the inhospitable Steppes to the east of the River Ural.

Peter the Great appears to have had some dealings with these people, for in 1722, when in Astrakhan, he said: 'Although these Kirghiz are a roaming and fickle people, their Steppe is the key and gate to all the countries of Central Asia.' Five years after his death (i.e. in 1730) Abdul-Khair, the Khan of the Lesser Horde, being oppressed by the Dzungarians, and harassed by the Bashkirs and Kalmuks, sought the protection of Russia. This act of submission was at the time repudiated by the Kirghiz; but in 1734 both the Middle and Lesser Hordes tendered their submission, and Abdul-Khair bound himself by an agreement to protect Russian caravans, and to secure the Russian borders from molestation.

This event was the cause of much rejoicing in the Russian capital. Peter's words were called to mind, and the Russians thought that by this submission of the Kirghiz they had actually obtained possession of 'the key and gate to all the countries in Central Asia,' and that the wealth of India and the East was within their grasp. They, however, had yet to learn the truth of the axiom set forth by Hyacinth Bitchurin, who said that 'Nomads consider allegiance a bargain with their conscience, in which they expect to win at least four to one; and for that reason, when a favourable case arises, they rival each other in their readiness to declare themselves subjects; but if they be deceived in their hope of winning four to one, they are shrewd enough to repay themselves by pillage, rapine, and murder.' As the Russians found to their cost, this submission of the Kirghiz was due to no anxiety on the part of the nomads to come under the rule of the White Czar, but was merely for the purpose of obtaining protection from their numerous enemies; and by it Russia no more obtained any actual control over the country than she did over Khiva when Peter the Great accepted the allegiance of the Khivans in 1703.[1]

---

[1] The tragic fate of Bekovitch, fourteen years after Peter accepted the submission of Khan Shahmaz of Khiva, shows how little meaning the Khivans attached to their offers of allegiance.

In 1731, also, Colonel Erdberg was sent to Khiva as an envoy from the Empress Anne, but he was attacked on the road and compelled to return.

For the better protection of their new subjects —or, probably, for protection *from* them—the Russians considered it advisable to advance their frontier line, and the fortified town of Orenburg was built in 1735, while at the same time a fortified line of Cossack settlements was established on the banks of the River Ural. These measures, however, failed to keep the Kirghiz in check, although they had a salutary effect on the turbulent Bashkirs, who were cut off from the Steppe, and were thus forced to submit in some measure to Russian control, and to curb their turbulent propensities.

Shortly after this, the Kirghiz chief, Abdul-Khair, was elected Khan of Khiva, but his reign did not last for long. The great Nadir Shah of Persia, then in the zenith of his victorious career, was advancing to subdue the Khanate. In this emergency Abdul-Khair declared the Khanate to be subject to Russia, hoping that by this subterfuge he would arrest Nadir's march. A Russian officer, who was then at Khiva, was even sent by the Khan to meet the Shah and ask for mercy; but his intercession was of no avail, for Nadir continued his advance and captured the Khanate, driving the Kirghiz Khan back into the Steppes.

About this time several attempts were made to establish a Russian post or town at the mouth of the Syr Daria (Jaxartes), and a flotilla on the Sea of Aral; but this could not then be accomplished, owing to the unsettled state of the country; and

Russia was compelled to wait for more than a century before this object was attained.

Though the Empress Anne by the Treaty of Resht lost the provinces which Peter the Great had acquired from Persia, she nevertheless was not blind to the advantages which Russia might obtain through commercial dealings with that state. She therefore, in 1734, granted a concession to British subjects to trade with Persia through Russia on payment of a duty of three per cent. *ad valorem*. Five years later an employé of the British-Muscovy Company, named John Elton, left Astrakhan, and, proceeding to Persia, obtained a decree whereby he was permitted to trade freely throughout the Persian dominions, between the Caspian Sea and River Indus. Elton then returned to Russia, and wrote a letter to the British Minister at St. Petersburg, pointing out the great advantages which British merchants would obtain by means of the trade through Meshed to Bokhara; and in spite of the opposition of the East India Company, an Act of Parliament was passed sanctioning this trade. Permission was received to build two ships for the purpose at Kazan, and an expedition set out from the Volga in 1742. Dissensions, however, arose among the factors, and in the next year Elton took service under the great Nadir Shah as naval constructor on the Caspian. He surveyed the east coast of that sea from the Bay of Astrabad to the ancient mouth of the Oxus, and set to work to build a fleet on the Caspian for the Persian monarch. The Russian Empress, who had no desire to see a Persian fleet established in the Caspian, was greatly incensed at Elton's proceedings, while the English directors of the new Company became alarmed at his neglect of their interests. They ordered him to return, but he found his position too advantageous, and therefore ignored the message; and as matters thus continued in a most unsatisfactory state, the Empress Elizabeth Petrovna issued an ukase forbidding the British to trade on the Caspian. Thus ended the last attempt of the British to obtain a trade route by the Caspian and Khorassan to India and Central Asia.

During the latter half of the eighteenth century Russia made little progress in Central Asia, although some slight intercourse was maintained with Khiva, while Russian officials were also sent from Siberia to Bokhara and Tashkent, for the purpose of examining the countries in the basins of the Oxus and Syr Daria.

In 1750 the Khivans sent an envoy to the Empress Elizabeth with a request that more intimate relations might be entered into between the two states; but this friendly overture was completely neutralised by the pillage of a Russian caravan in the following year.

Again, in 1792, in the reign of Abdulghazi III., the brother of the Inak [1] Ivaz became blind, and

---

[1] An Inak or Inekh was an hereditary governor of Khiva elected from the Kirghiz or Karakalpak chiefs after the death of the Kirghiz Khan Kaip. Khiva at the end of the eighteenth century was ruled by Khans and Inaks, the Khans being the nominal sovereigns, while the actual power was in the hands of the Inaks.

the Empress Catherine II. was asked to send an oculist to cure the disease. Catherine at once complied with this request, and sent 'Doctor or Major' Blankenagel [1] to treat the sick man. On arrival at Khiva, Blankenagel declared the eyes of the patient to be incurable, and this so annoyed the Inak that he called a council to decide how the Russian should be dealt with. It was decided that Blankenagel should be allowed to start for Russia and be put to death on the way. The doctor, however, heard of this plot, and managed to escape to Russia through the assistance of the Turkomans.

The closing years of the reign of Catherine II. were marked by some important events in connection with Russia's dealings with her barbarian neighbours, and were also remarkable for the preparation of the first known scheme for a Russian invasion of India through the Khanates of Central Asia.[2]

This strange form of dual government came to an end on the death of the Inak Ivaz in 1804, when his son drove out the Kirghiz Khan and proclaimed himself sole ruler of the State.

[1] Blankenagel is thus referred to in the *Notes on Russian Intercourse with Khiva*, written by G. Kühlwein, the Secretary to Colonel Ignatieff's mission to Central Asia, and given as Appendix IV. of *The Russians in Central Asia* by John and Robert Michell. It is curious that such a well-informed Russian writer as Kühlwein should throw doubts on Blankenagel's real profession. If Blankenagel was, as Kühlwein almost hints, a military officer and not a doctor, his inability to cure ophthalmia and subsequent rough treatment are easily accounted for.

[2] This scheme is thus referred to by Sir John M'Neill in his pamphlet entitled *The Progress and Present Position of Russia in the East* :—

'It was on this occasion' (i.e. when England, by her league

In July 1774, by the Peace of Kainadji, which was concluded after one of the many wars between Russia and Turkey, Russia finally obtained possession of Azof and some places on the Euxine, and the Crimea was declared to be independent of the Porte. From this time the Crimean peninsula was in a constant state of anarchy. The Sultan, deprived of his temporal sovereignty, still claimed, as the successor of the Khalifs, to be supreme in religious matters; while the people, abandoned to themselves, were divided into two factions—the Turkish and the Russian. In 1775 the reigning Khan, who was devoted to Russian interests, was deposed and replaced by a Turkish adherent, who in turn was dethroned by Catherine, when another Russian puppet, named Schagin Ghirei, was placed on the throne.

What followed is thus described by Sir John M'Neill :—

'But it was the possession, not the tranquillity,

with Prussia and Holland for the preservation of the Turkish Empire, forced the Empress Catherine to make peace with the Porte) 'that the idea of disturbing the British Empire in India was first suggested to the Cabinet of St. Petersburg, as a check on the aggressive power, which the maritime superiority of England enabled her to exert against Russia. The Prince Nassau Siegen presented to Catherine a project for marching an army through Bokhara and Cashmere to Bengal to drive the English out of India. The plan had been drawn up by a Frenchman, and the first step was to be a manifesto declaring the intention of the Empress to re-establish the Great Mogul on the throne of India. This, it was supposed, would secure the concurrence of the intermediate states, and attract to the standard of Russia all the discontented spirits in Hindustan. The scheme, though derided by Potemkin, was favourably received by Catherine, and has never been forgotten in Russia.'

of the Krimea that Russia desired; and, fearing the resistance of the people, she sought and found a pretext for marching an army into the country without opposition. A Turkish pasha had occupied the island of Taman, on the opposite shore of the Cimmerian Bosphorus, and the Russians succeeded in persuading Schagin Geray to demand its evacuation. The fierce Turk put the ambassador to death, and Russia called loudly for vengeance. The Khan, irritated by this barbarous insult, acceded to the proposal of his friends to entrust to them the punishment of the Pasha, and a Russian army entered the Krimea for the purpose of driving the Ottomans from the opposite island; but when it had penetrated to the coast it suddenly fell back, occupied the whole peninsula, seized by stratagem or force all the strongholds, and, at the point of the bayonet, forced the Imams and the people to take the oath of allegiance to the Empress. Specious promises of advantage were held out to all, but the Tartars nevertheless prepared to resist; and Field-marshal Potemkin, informed of their intentions, ordered the principal persons concerned to be put to death. The officer, Prince Proboroffski, to whom his command was first addressed, indignantly refused to execute it; but General Paul Potemkin, a relation of the Field-marshal, and General Suvaroff, were obsequious instruments, and thirty thousand Tartars, of either sex and every age, were slaughtered in cold blood.'

Thus, in a time of profound peace, did the

Empress Catherine gain possession of the Crimea, and so completed the work of Ivan the Terrible by finally subduing and annexing to Russia the last kingdom which recalled the memories of the Mongol yoke and the supremacy of the Golden Horde.

The Sultan at first protested, and threatened a rupture; but he eventually signed the Treaty of Constantinople in 1784, whereby he acknowledged the cession of the Crimea, the island of Taman, and a large portion of the Kuban.

Not content with these important acquisitions, Catherine secretly prepared for nothing less than the partition of the Turkish Empire. The Emperor Joseph II. acceded to her views, and the year 1788 saw Turkey in imminent peril. But England, who had during the previous Russo-Turkish war been fettered by the troubles in America, was now free to resist Russian designs on the Bosphorus, and fitted out a great naval armament for the Baltic. Sweden declared war, and Prussia, after some hesitation, concluded a treaty with the Turks, marched an army into Poland, and, by a convention with Austria, withdrew the Emperor Joseph from his Russian alliance. Europe was in arms against the aggressions of the Muscovites; Catherine was forced to abandon her designs against the Ottoman Empire; and in 1792 a treaty of peace was concluded at Jassy, by which, however, Russia advanced to the Dniester, and obtained the acknowledgment of Turkey to her sovereignty over Georgia.

During the reign of the great Nadir Shah, and for several years after his death, the Russians had abstained from any warlike ventures in Persia; but after the assassination of Nadir, in 1747, troubles ensued which destroyed the integrity of the empire which the Khorassan warrior had built up, left Persia weak and divided, and afforded an opportunity for the outlying provinces to throw off the Persian yoke. Afghanistan and Khorassan became independent, and in 1752 the princes of Georgia (Tamaras and his son Heraclius), being unable to protect themselves against the attacks of the neighbouring mountain tribes, appealed to Russia for assistance. Eight years afterwards Heraclius drove his father from the throne, and the whole of Georgia thus again became united under the rule of one prince, who was completely under Muscovite influence, and who even assisted the Russians in their war with Turkey. In order to protect himself from possible retribution in the event of Persia becoming re-united under a strong ruler, Heraclius, in July 1783, entered into an offensive and defensive alliance with Russia, and signed a treaty whereby he renounced all connection with Persia, and declared himself to be the vassal of the Empress Catherine II., who in turn bound herself and her successors to protect him, and to guarantee the possession of his dominions and such territories as might be acquired by him in future.

Nor was it only in Georgia that Russian intrigue was at work. Persia was distracted by a civil war in which several rival pretenders asserted their claims to the throne. Russian agents seized the opportunity; a Russian *protégé* was supported in his attempt to overthrow Aga Mahommed; and, taking advantage of Persia's helpless condition, the Russians again made an attempt to obtain a permanent footing on the shores of the Gulf of Astrabad.

In July 1781 Count Voinovitch sailed from Astrakhan with four frigates and two armed sloops, having on board the necessary troops and ammunition for a descent on the Persian coast. A landing was made in the Gulf of Astrabad, and the Russians commenced the construction of a fortification about twenty-five miles to the west of Gez, which was to be armed with eighteen guns.

Aga Mahommed Shah, on hearing this, visited the place, congratulated the Russian commander on the result of his labours, dined on board one of the frigates, and, on leaving, invited Voinovitch and the other Russian officers in return to dine with him at his residence in the neighbouring mountains. When they, in response to this invitation, reached the Shah's house on the next day, they discovered that the wily Persian had been merely feigning satisfaction for the purpose of more surely getting the Russians into his power; for no sooner had they arrived than they were placed in irons, and Voinovitch was forced to sign an order directing the commandant of the fort to re-ship the guns and demolish the objectionable buildings. Then, loaded with abuse and exposed to every kind of indignity, the Russians were whipped down to their ships, and thus the second Russian attempt to establish themselves on Persian territory near Astrabad ignominiously failed.

For twelve years after the conclusion of the treaty between Heraclius and the Empress Catherine, the Georgian Prince remained unpunished for his disloyalty to his suzerain, as Aga Mahommed was fully occupied in opposing the rival claimants to the throne of Persia. But in 1795 the Shah, having got rid of his rivals and having received the submission of the southern provinces of Persia, was able to turn his attention to his rebellious subject. He first summoned Heraclius to return to his duty, and to attend at the capital to take the oath of allegiance; but the Georgian Prince replied that he acknowledged no suzerain but the Empress Catherine of Russia. Then Aga Mahommed collected a large army of about 60,000 men; Heraclius was soon afterwards defeated in a pitched battle; Tiflis, the capital, was occupied by the Persian army; and Erivan opened its gates to the victorious Shah.[1]

By this campaign Aga Mahommed regained

---

[1] The fortress of Sheeshah still held out, but was captured by Aga Mahommed in the spring of 1797. This was his last success, for a few days afterwards he was assassinated by two of his servants whom he had condemned to death, but who were allowed to perform their duties while under sentence of death.

complete possession of the Persian provinces in the Caucasus, and he then turned his attention to the subjugation of Khorassan, which district had fallen away from Persia during the troubles which followed Nadir Shah's death; but while so employed the armies of the Empress Catherine were advancing to re-assert Russian prestige, which had been so roughly shaken by the Shah's triumphant campaign in Georgia.

When Catherine II. received news of the attack on her new vassal she at once took steps to recover the territory which had been lost, and to punish the Persian monarch for his temerity in having re-asserted his sovereign rights over a feudatory who had, for a long series of years, paid tribute to the Shahs of Persia, but who, through Russian intrigue, had fallen away from his allegiance. In the spring of 1796 a Russian army, under Count Valerian Zouboff, advanced against Derbent. The outworks were captured, and the town then surrendered; and soon afterwards Baku was also taken, while the island of Sari, near Lenkoran, was occupied, and an unsuccessful attempt was made to capture Enzeli, the port of Resht. In the month of October the Russians took possession of Shemakha, and before the close of the winter two columns had been pushed forward to the frontiers of Azerbijan. But before any decisive results could be obtained, news reached the army of the death of Catherine II., and Zouboff received orders from the Emperor Paul to retire. The Russian general accordingly withdrew his forces, and abandoned the territory which had been occupied, with the exception of the towns of Derbent and Baku, which were retained by Russia. On the death of Heraclius his son Goorgeen, or George, tendered his submission to Futteh Ali Shah, and thus Georgia once again returned to its allegiance to Persia.

CHAPTER III

1800—1828

COLLAPSE OF PROJECTED INVASIONS OF INDIA

Scheme for a French and Russian invasion of India—The Emperor Paul's manifesto—The Sovereignty of Georgia—Russian advance against Persia—French alliance with Persia—India threatened by an Afghan invasion—Treaty of Tilsit—Revival of project for a Franco-Russian invasion of India—Mission of Sir Harford Jones to Persia—Russo-Turkish War—Franco-Russian War—Persian reverses and Treaty of Gulistan—Submission of Turkoman tribes to Russia—The Gokcheh difficulty and renewal of hostilities between Russia and Persia—Treaty of Turkomanchai—M. Griboiedoff's Mission.

The dawn of the present century found Great Britain engaged in a desperate struggle against the power of the First Consul of France. In the previous year (1799), Pitt, finding that England was freed from all dangers in Ireland, and seeing that she had quite regained her naval supremacy by the glorious victories of St. Vincent, Camperdown, and the Nile, revived the coalition with Russia and Austria, lavished enormous subsidies on England's two allies, and made strenuous efforts to overthrow Napoleon.

But the disasters suffered by the Russian troops in Central Europe, and the failure of the Anglo-Russian expedition to Holland brought an angry remonstrance from the Emperor Paul, which appeared in the 'St. Petersburg Gazette,' and he sullenly abstained from any further attack on the French.

This was Bonaparte's opportunity. By dexterous diplomacy he gradually persuaded Paul that England was the common enemy of Europe. By the Treaty of Luneville, France was secured from attacks on the continent, and England stood alone opposed to the increasing power of Napoleon. The Russian Czar saw in the strength of Great Britain the chief obstacle to his designs on Turkey. He claimed Malta, on the ground of his alleged election as Grand Master of the Knights of St. John, and was greatly incensed when the English, who had just captured the island, refused to relinquish it. He daily became more and more imbued with a passion for Bonaparte, surrounded himself with his portraits, and drank his health publicly. The First Consul carefully fostered these sentiments. He offered to hand Malta over to Russia, and, to endorse his friendly feelings towards the Czar, liberated without exchange all the Russian prisoners who had been taken in the war.

Thus the commencement of the year 1801 found the Emperor imbued with strong feelings of friendship, amounting to infatuation, for Napoleon, and preparing to join with Sweden, Denmark, and France in an attack against Great Britain, in the hope of being able to wrest from her the command of the sea.

It was at this time that a second great scheme was prepared for a joint French and Russian invasion of Hindustan for the purpose of driving the English out of their settlements in that country. The French troops still occupied Egypt, and Napoleon still cherished the idea of being able to force the English to abandon India. The Russians also had obtained an advantageous base from which operations against the East Indian settlements might, it was thought, be successfully launched. Since Paul had recalled his troops from the Caucasus, Russian agents had been busily employed in intrigues for the purpose of preparing the way for a final annexation of Georgia. Their efforts were completely successful, for, on September 28, 1800, Prince George XIII. of Georgia renounced his crown in favour of the Emperor of Russia, and thus Paul, without striking a blow, gained possession of a considerable increase of territory, and obtained a more advanced base for the great Indian expedition he was about to undertake.

This Franco-Russian invasion of India was to have been carried out by means of two distinct columns. One of these armies was to be composed of 35,000 French and an equal number of Russians. The French were to descend the Danube, and then to be transported across the Black Sea, in Russian ships, to Taganrog. From thence they were to go up the Don as far as Piati-Isbanskaia, cross to the Volga at Tzaritsin, descend that river to Astrakhan, re-embark on the Caspian in Russian vessels, and on reaching Astrabad would there be joined by the Russian army of 35,000 men—25,000 regular troops of all arms, and 10,000 Cossacks. The combined force, under the command of Massena, was then to advance through Khorassan, Herat, Farah, and Kandahar to the Indus, 'chase the English from India, liberate that rich and beautiful country from the English yoke, and open new roads to England's commercial rivals, and especially to France.' The project entered into the most minute details, and on the margin were scribbled the criticisms of Napoleon with the Czar's replies.

It was calculated by Paul that 'from the Danube to the borders of India the advance will occupy the French army four months, or, avoiding forced marches, five months.'

The armies were to be preceded by commissaries who were to establish stations and halting-places where necessary, and to visit the Khans and great landowners to explain that the expedition was for the purpose 'of driving away the English from the beautiful country which they have subjected—a country formerly so remarkable for its industry and wealth, and which it is now proposed to open to all the world, that the inhabitants may profit by the riches and other advantages given to them by heaven.' The Russian note then proceeded to state:—

'The sufferings under which the population of this country groans have inspired France and Russia with the liveliest interest; and the two Governments have resolved to unite their forces in order to liberate India from the tyrannical and barbarous yoke of the English. Accordingly, the princes and populations of all countries through which the combined armies will pass need fear nothing. On the contrary, it behoves them to help with all their strength and means so benevolent and glorious an undertaking, the object of this campaign being in all respects as just as was unjust the campaign of Alexander the Great, who wished to conquer the whole world. The commissaries are further to set forth that the combined armies will not levy contributions, and will pay in ready money, on terms freely agreed to, for all things necessary to their sustenance; that on this point the strictest rules will be enforced. Moreover, that religion, laws, manners, and customs, property and women, will everywhere be respected and protected. With such announcements, with such honest, straightforward statements, it is not to be doubted that the Khans and other small princes will allow the combined armies to pass without hindrance through their territories. In any case, they are too weak and too much divided by dissensions among themselves to make any opposition. The commissaries will hold negotiations with the Khans, princes, and private landowners about furnishing provisions, carts, and kibitkas. They will subscribe conditions, and according to circumstances will require, or themselves deposit, caution-money.'

Learned and scientific societies were to take part in the 'glorious expedition.' Aeronauts and pyrotechnists were also to accompany the troops, and it was arranged by Paul, 'before the army starts from Astrabad, to hold grand fêtes and perform striking evolutions, in the style of those with which great events and memorable epochs are celebrated in Paris.' The French Government was to send rare objects and produce of national industries, which gifts, 'distributed with tact among the princes of those countries, and offered with the grace and courtesy natural to the French, will enable those races to form the highest idea of the magnificence of French industry and power, and will in consequence open an important branch of commerce.'

Napoleon appears to have doubted the success of the proposed undertaking, and asked, 'Supposing the combined army be united at Astrabad, how do you propose that it should get to India, through countries almost barbarous, and without any resources; having to march a distance of 300 leagues from Astrabad to the frontiers of Hindustan?' Paul, in reply, said, 'The country is not savage; it is not barren. It has long been traversed by open and spacious roads; the soil is like that of Arabia and Libya—not covered with dry sand, rivers water it at almost every step. There is no want of grass for fodder. Rice grows in abundance, and forms the principal food of the inhabitants.' And, after referring to Nadir Shah's march through the same country from Dehli to the Caspian, the Czar ended by saying: 'The French and Russian armies are eager for glory; they are brave, patient, and unwearied; their courage, their perseverance, and the wisdom of their leaders will know how to surmount all obstacles. . . . What a really Asiatic army did in 1739 and 1740, we cannot doubt that an army of French and Russians can do to-day.'

The other army of invasion was composed of 35,000 Russian troops, and was to move by way of Khiva and Bokhara to the upper Indus. That the Russian Emperor was fully determined to carry out this great scheme is shown by the fact that the advanced troops of this northern army had actually proceeded for a considerable distance before the whole scheme collapsed on receipt of the news of Paul's death.

On January 24, 1801, he issued the following orders to Orloff-Denisoff, the Ataman of the Don Cossacks: 'The English are preparing for an attack by land and sea against me and my allies, the Swedes and Danes; I am ready to receive them. But it is necessary to be beforehand with them, and to attack them on their most vulnerable point, and on the side where they least expect it. It is three months' march from Orenburg to Hindustan, and it takes another month to get from the encampments of the Don to Orenburg, making in all four months. To you and your arms I confide this expedition. Assemble, therefore, your men, and begin your march to Orenburg. Thence, by whichever of the three routes you prefer, or by all, you will go straight with your artillery to Bokhara, Khiva, the River Indus, and the English settlements in India. The troops of the country are light troops like yours; you will therefore have over them all the advantage of your artillery.

Prepare everything for this campaign; send your scouts to reconnoitre and repair the roads. All the wealth of the Indies shall be your recompense. . . . Such an enterprise will cover you with immortal glory, will secure you my goodwill in proportion to your services, will load you with riches, give an opening to our commerce, and strike the enemy a mortal blow. I send you maps, as many as I have, and remain your well-wisher, PAUL.

'P.S.—My maps only go as far as Khiva and the River Amu (Oxus). Beyond these points it is your affair to gain information about the possessions of the English and the condition of the Indian population subject to their rule.'

On the same day the following additional instructions were sent: 'India, to which I send you, is governed by a supreme head and a number of small sovereigns. The English possess commercial establishments there, which they have acquired by means of money or conquered by force of arms. The object of this campaign is to ruin these establishments, to free the oppressed sovereigns, to put them with regard to Russia in the same state of dependence in which they now are with regard to the English, and finally to secure for ourselves the commerce of those regions.'

Again, on the next day Orloff is told: 'Be sure to remember that you are only at war with the English, and the friend of all who do not give them help; on your march you will assure men of the friendship of Russia. From the Indus you will go to the Ganges; on the way you will occupy Bokhara, to prevent her going over to China. At Khiva you will deliver some thousands of my subjects who are kept prisoners there. If you need infantry, I will send it to follow in your footsteps. There is no other way, but it will be best if you can be sufficient for yourselves.' And then again, on February 19, comes the pressing note, 'The expedition is urgent; the earlier the better.'

Such were the instructions sent to Orloff-Denisoff, who marched from Orenburg, in the depth of winter, with 22,000 Cossacks and two companies of horse-artillery. The Volga was crossed on the ice, amid great difficulties, and the force had proceeded upwards of 450 miles, when the Ataman received news of the sudden death of the Emperor Paul, which occurred on the night of March 23. On the next day Alexander I. was proclaimed Czar, and peremptory orders were issued for the return of the expedition. Bonaparte's friend and ally was dead; ten days later the Danish fleet was seized at Copenhagen, the League of Armed Neutrality collapsed, and with it the fantastic scheme for the invasion of India fell to the ground.

Although the Emperor Alexander I. put a stop to the expedition against the English settlements in India, he showed no desire to abstain from extending Russian influence in the Caucasus at the expense of Persia. It has been mentioned that in

September 1800 the Prince of Georgia abdicated in favour of the Czar—an act which drew down upon him the hatred and curses of the nobles of his country. The Queen of Georgia, who was ashamed of her husband's weakness, did her best to stir up the people to resistance, and when an attempt was made to seize her in order that she might be deported to Moscow, stabbed the Russian officer who was sent to arrest her. George's younger brother, Alexander, also did his best to raise a general rebellion for the purpose of throwing off the Russian yoke, and sought the aid of the Khan of Karabagh.

But the Czar Alexander had no intention of renouncing his claims to sovereignty over Georgia as the successor of George XIII., and on September 12, 1801, he issued a proclamation to the people of the principality, in which he formally announced his acceptance of the Georgian crown. The following is an extract from this proclamation:—

'It is not for the sake of increasing our power, from no interested motives, nor for the extension of an empire already so vast, that we accept the cares of the Georgian throne; it is only the sentiment of our dignity, honour, and humanity that has imposed on us the sacred duty, not to resist your heart-rending cries, but to relieve you from the evils which afflict you, and to introduce in Georgia a strong Government, capable of administering justice with equity, protecting life and property, and extending to all the ægis of the law.'

General Zizianoff (a Georgian by extraction) was sent as Governor-General of the province, and this officer at once marched into Mingrelia and occupied that province with Russian troops. In the following year the town of Genja was taken by assault, when the garrison was slaughtered amid scenes of the grossest barbarity and ferocity; and from thence Zizianoff advanced to Erivan, being led on by a promise of the governor of the city (Mahommed Khan Kajar) that he would yield it to the Russian general. These proceedings caused the greatest alarm in the Court of Persia. The defection of Mahommed Khan necessitated prompt measures, unless the Shah wished to see Erivan also in the power of the Russian Czar; and a Persian army under the Crown Prince Abbass Mirza therefore took the field early in 1804, and advanced to punish the traitorous governor and to prevent the Russian troops obtaining possession of the city.

After several engagements the city of Erivan was occupied by the Shah's forces, and thus the close of the year 1804 found the Persians once again masters of the surrounding province.

In the following spring the campaign was renewed. Zizianoff gained possession of the province of Shekee, and in July marched into Karabagh, where the fortress of Sheeshah was traitorously handed over to him by the governor; but an attempted descent on the coast of Ghilan at Enzeli was repulsed, and the governors of Kuba, Derbent, and Baku, and the chief of the Lesghians appealed to the Shah for assistance to enable them to throw off the Russian yoke. The Russian general, therefore, marched to reduce Baku, while the Russian squadron from Enzeli steered for the same place.

While conducting the siege, Zizianoff was foully murdered. Threatened with an attack in rear by the Persian forces who were advancing under the Crown Prince from the direction of Ardabil, the Russian general entered into negotiations with the governor of Baku for the surrender of the place. He was invited by the Khan to a conference for the purpose of arranging the terms of the capitulation, and while conversing with the chief under the walls of the fort, was suddenly assailed by a gang of assassins who had been stationed there for the purpose. It was a cruel and treacherous deed, but one which, however reprehensible, can hardly be wondered at, for Zizianoff had throughout his career in the Caucasus rarely shown clemency to those whom he conquered, and was perpetually intriguing with the Persian governors for the surrender of their charges. He thus was in constant communication with traitors of the worst class—men who did not hesitate to commit acts of the blackest treason towards their sovereign and country—and it is not surprising that the men who were thus capable of betraying the charges committed to their trust should sooner or later turn against the instigator of their treachery, and be found ready and willing to commit a cold-blooded murder such as was perpetrated under the walls of Baku.

The death of Zizianoff was a severe blow to the Russians. The news was received in Persia with every sign of satisfaction. The Shah was exultant, and issued a proclamation announcing that a glorious victory had been won, in which the renowned Russian commander had been slain. It was indeed a disaster for the Russians, but reflected little credit on the Persians. Baku was for the time saved from Russian occupation; but the Shah and his ministers fully expected that steps would be taken by their adversaries to avenge the deed, and to prosecute the war with redoubled energy.

But while the campaign in Persia had been dragging on without any decided success having been gained by either of the belligerents, events were taking place in Europe which compelled Russia to turn her attention towards the west, and the war in Georgia became a matter of very minor importance to the Czar Alexander I.

After the death of the Emperor Paul, and the collapse of the League of Armed Neutrality, the war between Great Britain and France continued. On March 21, 1801, General Abercrombie defeated the French army at Alexandria, and, in the following June, French rule in Egypt was terminated by the capitulation of General Hoche.

Both parties now desired peace, and in March 1802 the war was brought to a close by the Peace of Amiens. But Napoleon was resolved to become master of Europe, and it was not long before the pledges given at Amiens were set aside. Piedmont and Parma were annexed to France, and a French army occupied Switzerland. English protests were ignored, and war became inevitable. In May 1803 the British Government declared war against France, and Bonaparte, in the determination to humble his most persistent adversary, formed a gigantic camp at Boulogne and made preparations for the invasion of England. Pitt was recalled to power in this national emergency; by the offer of large subsidies he gained the alliance of Russia, Austria, and Sweden; and thus the terrible struggle on the continent was resumed. The danger which threatened Napoleon from the East compelled him to abandon his dream of crossing the Channel, and all fear of an invasion of England was finally dispelled by the glorious victory off Cape Trafalgar on October 21, 1805.

But two days before this great naval battle the Austrian army had capitulated under Mack at Ulm, and, rapidly following up this success, Bonaparte had inflicted a crushing defeat on the combined armies of Austria and Russia on the field of Austerlitz. It then appeared as if nothing could save Europe from the ambitious designs of the French Emperor; and it was then that Napoleon resolved to lose no opportunity of injuring his opponents, sent Colonel Romieu as an ambassador to the Court of Persia, with promises that if the Shah would repudiate his connection with the English, and enter into an alliance with the French nation, the Persian troops would be subsidised, and a French army would be sent to assist in driving the Russians out of Georgia. Such an alliance would have been to the advantage of both nations, for thereby France could have struck a blow at Russia in a direction far removed from the European theatre of war on which the Czar's whole attention was directed, while the Persians would be freed from the oppression and increasing aggression of their great northern neighbour. But still the Shah hesitated; for had he not already concluded a treaty with the British authorities, and did it not appear most probable that in accordance with that treaty the English would help him in his hour of need?

Seven years before the Government of India had been in a state of the wildest alarm and excitement owing to the invasion of the Punjaub by the Afghans under Zemaun Shah. At that time the people of India had not yet forgotten the great invasion by Afghan hordes under the illustrious Ahmed Shah which culminated in the complete overthrow of the Mahratta Confederacy on the plains of Panipat in January 1761.

It was believed that such another invasion was imminent; and when it became known that several Indian princes had sent invitations to the Afghan ruler, and had promised to aid him in the effort to free Hindustan from the British yoke, Lord Wellesley determined to despatch a mission to Persia, to secure the friendship of the Shah, and thus to obtain an ally who could, by a diversion against Herat, prevent Zemaun Shah from molesting the territory of the East India Company. The presence of the French in Egypt, and French intrigues in India, rendered such a course still more imperative; and in 1800 Captain Malcolm left India as envoy to the Court of Persia. But, even before Malcolm reached the Persian capital, the Shah for his own purposes, and without any inducement from the Indian Government, had carried out the very movement which was to ensure the security of the English in India. Khorassan had been invaded by Persian armies, and Zemaun Shah had been obliged to abandon his ambitious designs on India to save the western province of his kingdom.[1]

[1] Two years before Malcolm went to Persia a Persian nobleman naturalised in India, named Mahdi Ali Khan, had been sent to Teheran by the Governor of Bombay, with instructions ' to take measures for inducing the Court of Persia to keep Shah Zemaun in perpetual check (so as to preclude him from returning to India), but without any decided act of hostility.' This envoy found, on his arrival, that the Shah was disposed to assist the two refugee Afghan Princes, Mahmoud and Firoz-ud-din, without the additional inducement of an English subsidy, which he had been authorised to offer. He therefore took upon himself a considerable amount of responsibility, and by suppressing his credentials, and by leaving well alone, had the satisfaction of seeing the Afghan princes marching towards Herat, supported by Persian troops. This expedition failed, and shortly afterwards Zemaun Shah sent an imperious message to the Shah of Persia, demanding the cession of Khorassan. Futteh Ali Shah replied that it was his intention to restore to Persia the territories which it had possessed in the time of the Sefavean kings; and following up the threat by action, he in 1799 took the field in person, and marched into Khorassan. By this movement Zemaun Shah, threatened with the loss of his western provinces, was forced to withdraw from Lahore. This expedition, however, lasted but a short time, and when Futteh Ali Shah returned to his capital in the autumn of 1799, the Afghan ruler once more turned his attention towards the East. In the following spring, however, the Shah of Persia again marched into Khorassan, and Zemaun Shah was again obliged to move westwards to watch Herat. Thus, when Malcolm reached Teheran, he found that Persian ambition had done all that was required to save India from the danger of an Afghan invasion.

In the following year Malcolm concluded two treaties with the Shah—one political and the other commercial. The Shah engaged to over-run Afghanistan with a great army, in the event of any attempt being made by the Afghans to invade India, and to conclude no peace with that state unless it was accompanied by a solemn promise to abstain from attacking the English. A remarkable clause was also inserted whereby it was provided that, 'should an army of the French nation, actuated by design or deceit, attempt to settle, with a view of establishing themselves on any of the islands or shores of Persia, a conjoint force shall be appointed by the two high contracting parties, to act in co-opera-tion, for their expulsion and extirpation, and to destroy and put an end to the foundation of their treason; and if any of the great men of the French nation express a wish or desire to obtain a place of residence, or dwelling, in any of the islands or shores of the kingdom of Persia, that they may raise the standard of abode, or settlement, leave for their residing in such a place shall not be granted.' The Shah believed this treaty to constitute a complete offensive and de-fensive alliance between Great Britain and Persia, and, therefore, when the French envoy appeared in Teheran, he was coldly received. Persia already possessed a powerful ally, who, she believed, would defend her interests, and who had taught her to consider the French a dangerous and deceitful people; and Colonel Romieu therefore found, in spite of his large suite, handsome presents, and still more tempting promises, that Futteh Ali Shah still looked to the English for aid.

But the British Government viewed Malcolm's treaty in a different light. It is true an offensive and defensive alliance had been concluded against France, but the Shah wanted assistance against the Russians who were not referred to in the compact, and who were then allies of the British Government. Thus, when Futteh Ali in his distress sent Mirza Nubbi Khan as an envoy to ask for assistance from the Governor-General of India, help was denied to him; and then, when the Shah through English inaction was forced to realise that he could expect no support from Great Britain, he threw himself into the arms of the very people whom he had been taught by England to shun. In the summer of 1806 Mirza Reeza was despatched post haste with instructions to proceed to the camp of the French Emperor, and there to enter into negotiations for the purpose of obtaining French aid against the Russians, who were referred to as being 'equally an enemy of the kings of Persia and France, and whose destruction accordingly became the duty of the two kings.' The Persian envoy was also instructed to inform the Emperor that 'if the French have an intention of invading Khorassan, the king will appoint an army to go down by the road of Kabul and Kandahar.'

What fairer terms could Napoleon desire? Persia was thus spontaneously offering to him an alliance whereby an opportune diversion could be made against the Russians, while at the same time assistance would be provided in furthering his ambitious designs on India. A treaty was drawn up and ratified by Napoleon at Fenkenstein in May 1807, and Monsieur Jaubert was at once sent to Teheran to announce to the Shah the terms of the agreement, and to confirm the friendly relations which had been entered upon. This envoy was soon afterwards followed by a more brilliant embassy under General Gardanne. The Persian troops were drilled by French officers, French counsels were predominant in the Shah's council chamber, and the hopes of the Persian Government were centered in the French alliance.

But while Futteh Ali Shah was congratulating himself on thus having gained a new and powerful ally, by whose aid he could beat back the tide of Russian invasion, a great change was occurring in the relations between the European courts which were most interested in Persian affairs. The bloody and indecisive battle of Eylau had been followed by the great French victory at Friedland, which broke down the resistance of Russia and forced the Czar Alexander to seek peace. On July 7 the two sovereigns met on the famous raft at Tilsit, and there arranged the terms of a peace which put an end to the war between France and Russia.

At the conference then held, the two Emperors fully discussed the Eastern question. Bonaparte revived the project for an invasion of India by a Franco-Russian army; Sebastiani urged the Porte to grant permission for the passage of French troops through Constantinople and Asia Minor; and Lucien Bonaparte, the most capable of Napoleon's brothers, was destined for the Teheran mission, to continue the negotiations which Gardanne had so successfully inaugurated, to organise the Persian forces and to persuade the Persian Government to take an active part in the projected invasion.

When these facts became known the British and Indian Governments were filled with consternation, and became possessed with a sense of unreasoning and exaggerated alarm. Simultaneously they both decided to take steps to avert the new danger which threatened India; and each, unknown to the other, determined to send an embassy to the Court of Teheran. Brigadier-General Malcolm, the envoy from India, sailed from Bombay in April 1808, a few days before the British ambassador, Sir Harford Jones, reached that port. The latter, in accordance with the instructions he had received, remained at Bombay awaiting the result of Malcolm's proceedings, while the Indian diplomatist, continuing his journey, reached Bushire on May 10.

But at that time French influence in Teheran was supreme; Gardanne, though debarred by the Treaty of Tilsit from opposing Russian advances in Georgia by force of arms, nevertheless was using his influence to prevent further encroachments; and thus, when Malcolm for the second time set foot on Persian territory, he found that he was coldly and even discourteously received. The mission was a complete failure, and in July the ambassador from the Governor-General of India was forced to re-embark without having even received an audience.

As soon as Lord Minto heard that Malcolm had withdrawn from Persia, he requested Sir Harford Jones to proceed there with the utmost despatch, and on October 14 the ambassador from the Court of St. James reached Bushire. At first he encountered the same irritating opposition and insolence that had caused Malcolm to quit Persian territory; but he steadfastly continued his onward progress, and succeeded in reaching Teheran, where he was well received. Gardanne withdrew on his approach, the British ambassador having stipulated that he would only advance to the capital on the condition that the French envoy received his passports. A remarkable change had indeed taken place in the sentiments of the Persian ruler and his advisers. The French had completely overreached themselves, and were now discredited. When the Shah first heard of the Peace of Tilsit, and realised that he could expect no armed resistance from the French against Russian aggression, his faith in his new allies was sorely shaken. Nevertheless, Gardanne still promised much, and Futteh Ali Shah still believed that through French mediation he would recover Georgia and Karabagh. But after the lapse of many months spent in anxiety and fruitless negotiations, it was seen that the inexorable Muscovites retained their position in spite of French promises, and even threatened further encroachments; and then all faith in the French alliance vanished. Sir Harford Jones reached Bushire when this reaction was setting in, and he skilfully took advantage of it. Gardanne had, in the early days of his mission, impressed on the Persian ministers that the true friend of Persia was the nation which was Russia's enemy. At that time France was at war against England and Russia, and the argument was all in favour of the French. But the Treaty of Tilsit altered the conditions. England now was the enemy of France and Russia,[1] and Gardanne's doctrine therefore afforded a good reason for an alliance with Great Britain. The British envoy with consummate skill took up the French line of argument, and, by utilising Gardanne's own precepts, drove him off the field. On March 12 a preliminary treaty was signed wherein it was stipulated that 'in case any European force had invaded or should invade the territories of the King of Persia, his Britannic Majesty should afford to the Shah a force, or in lieu of it a subsidy, with warlike ammunition, such as guns, muskets, &c., to the amount that might be to the advantage of both parties, for the expulsion of the force so invading'; while the Shah on his part agreed that 'every treaty or agreement which the

---

[1] For in the previous November (1807) the Emperor Alexander I. had declared war against Great Britain.

King of Persia might have made with any one of the Powers of Europe became null and void, and that he would not permit any European force whatever to pass through Persia either towards India or towards the ports of that country.'

Sir Harford Jones's conduct has by many writers been severely criticised, but he unquestionably was very successful in his negotiations, and by his skilful diplomacy restored British credit in Persia, and put an end to foreign intrigue. He appears to have been one of the first English diplomatists who recognised that the greatest external danger which threatened British India was to be found, not in French intrigues at Teheran, nor in the possibility of an invasion by the wild hordes of Afghanistan, but in the steady but insidious encroachments of Russia beyond her European frontiers. English statesmen at that time only perceived one danger, which sprang from the inordinate ambition of the French Emperor, and which threatened to overwhelm the whole of Europe. What cared England for Persia and its troubles, while the very existence of the British nation was at stake? With their scanty knowledge of the history and geography of Asiatic states, how could they realise that the subtle movements of Russia were infinitely more dangerous to India than the stratagems of the French? So long as the French occupied Egypt, and while their fleet in the Mediterranean remained undefeated, the safety of the British settlements in the East was undoubtedly seriously endangered; but at no time did the danger lie through Persia; and when the French had been driven out of Egypt and the English fleet had regained undisputed supremacy in the Mediterranean, then all dangers to India from the French disappeared.

To Sir Harford Jones must be given the credit of having first recognised that another great European power was stealthily advancing towards Hindustan; advancing, it is true, at that time slowly and with uncertain steps, but nevertheless gradually moving forward, at one time by force of arms, and again by means of intrigues and cunning; rarely receding from a position once taken up, and ready to seize every opportunity for further territorial acquisitions.

The preliminary treaty was conveyed to England by Mr. Morris and Hadji Mirza Abul Hassan Khan, was then duly ratified, and Sir Harford Jones was confirmed in his appointment as Minister at the Persian Court.

In 1810 the Indian Government again despatched General Malcolm to Persia, and with him were sent several officers who were employed in drilling the Persian troops and in exploring the country.

Meanwhile the war between Russia and Persia had been continued, the Persians being organised and led by British officers. Baku, Shirwan, Shekee, Genja, Talish, and Mugan were occupied by the Russians, and an unsuccessful advance was made against Erivan.

But Russia was still occupied in the war with Turkey, and was eagerly watching the movements in Western Europe. Alexander I. had, it is true, made peace with Napoleon, but he nevertheless watched with growing anxiety the gradual extension of the French Empire. In 1810 Hanover, Westphalia, and Holland had been annexed by France, and in the following year Hamburg shared the same fate. It was necessary for the Russians to be prepared to face any sudden change in the political situation, and their troops could not be spared to strike a crushing blow in Persia. In 1812 matters reached a crisis. The suspension of all trade with England proved irksome to Russia, and even threatened the Russian landowners with ruin. Napoleon insisted that England should be completely isolated, and became irritated when the Czar refused to entirely suspend all commercial relations with Great Britain. Both nations now began to prepare for the struggle which appeared imminent; a great movement of the French troops began, whereby the armies of the First Empire were drawn from the West and concentrated on the frontiers of Russia, while Russian columns were hurried westward. On May 28 the Czar made peace with Turkey, and concluded the Treaty of Bucharest, whereby the Porte regained possession of Wallachia and Anapa, Russia merely gaining Bessarabia as the fruits of a long and arduous campaign.

But the safety of the Russian Empire depended on the results of the war which was about to commence, and it was necessary that the entire military resources of the state should be utilised to beat back the tide of French invasion. On June 22 Napoleon declared war, and two days later crossed the River Niemen. In September the hosts of France and Russia met on the bloody field of Borodino, where, though terribly shaken, the French troops once again forced their brave enemies to fall back; and the ancient capital of Russia was shortly afterwards occupied by Napoleon.

The outbreak of hostilities between France and Russia naturally brought about a reconciliation between the latter power and England. Under these circumstances British officers could no longer be permitted to lead the Persian armies, and Sir Gore Ouseley, who relieved Sir Harford Jones in the summer of 1811, therefore ordered them to take no further part in the military operations against Russia; though at the earnest entreaty of the Crown Prince and his ministers, Captain Christie[1] and Lieutenant Lindsay with thirteen sergeants were permitted to remain with the Persian army.

But the war now was drawing to a close. The Persian army had marched to the Araxes, and remained for ten days at Aslandooz without taking the most ordinary precautions to guard against surprise. On the morning of October 31 a Russian force consisting of 2,300 men and six guns suddenly

[1] The gallant Christie lost his life during the surprise of the Persian camp at Aslandooz, at daybreak on November 1, 1812.

attacked the camp and caused the Persians to fall back to a position about half a mile distant. There the Crown Prince's army was again surprised on the following morning and completely destroyed by a Russian force of comparatively insignificant strength; all his guns were lost; and his camp, with everything it contained, fell into the hands of the victors.

This disaster was followed by the loss of Lenkoran, which was captured by the Russian General Kotlareffsky in the following January; and although the Persians were able to check the Russian advance on the Araxes, and even made preparations for assuming the defensive, a rising among the Turkomans caused the Shah to lend an ear to the counsels of Sir Gore Ouseley, who had been strenuously endeavouring to re-establish friendly relations between the two powers. The British Ambassador's efforts had, up to that time, proved unsuccessful, as the Russians would make no concessions, while the Persian Government refused to accept any settlement which was based on the actual state of possession of territory. But new dangers having arisen, the Shah was persuaded to accept the Russian conditions, which, though hard, were the best that could be obtained through the good offices of Sir Gore Ouseley.

On October 12, 1813, a treaty of peace was signed at the Russian camp near Gulistan, whereby the Shah acknowledged 'the sovereignty of the Emperor of Russia over the provinces of Karabagh and Georgia, now called Elizabeth Paul, the districts of Shekee, Shirwan, Kuba, Derbent, Bakoobeh' (Baku), 'and such part of Talish as is now possessed by Russia, the whole of Daghestan, the tract of Shoorgil, Achook, Bash, Gooreea, Mingrelia, Abtichar, the whole country between the boundary at present established' (by article 2) 'and the line of the Caucasus, and all the territory between the Caucasus and the Caspian Sea.' It was also agreed that the 'Russian flag shall fly in the Russian ships of war, which are permitted to sail on the Caspian as formerly; *no other nation whatever shall be allowed ships of war on the Caspian*'; and thus, by the Treaty of Gulistan, Russia gained possession of a large slice of some of the most fertile districts of Persia, and converted the Caspian into a Russian lake.

The conclusion of this treaty necessitated certain modifications in the understanding between Great Britain and Persia. On March 14, 1812, Sir Gore Ouseley had signed a treaty based upon Sir Harford Jones's preliminary one; but before it was finally ratified still further changes in its conditions were made by the British Government. After Sir Gore Ouseley's departure from Teheran, Mr. Morier, his Secretary, was left in charge of the Mission, and in 1814 Mr. Henry Ellis was sent out from England for the purpose of obtaining the Shah's assent to the alterations which were required by England. On November 25, 1814, the treaty, modified to meet the wishes of the British Government, was concluded at Teheran by Messrs. Morier and Ellis. It was very similar to the one which had been signed by Sir Gore Ouseley, and its most noticeable features were:

(1) The suppression of a clause whereby England had engaged to supply naval officers, sailors, and artificers, if the Shah should at any time desire to establish a naval force on the Caspian.[1]

(2) The Persian Government bound itself not to permit an European army to enter Persia for the purpose of invading India, and even agreed that 'should any European Powers wish to invade India by the road of Kharezm' (Khiva), 'Tartaristan' (Kashgar), 'Bokhara, Samarkand, or other routes, his Persian Majesty engages to induce the kings and governors of those countries to oppose such invasion, as much as is in his power, either by fear of his arms or by conciliatory measures.'

(3) If the Afghans were at war with the British, the Persian Government undertook to send an army against them; but if war should be declared between the Afghans and Persians, the English Government agreed not to interfere with either party, unless their mediation to effect a peace were solicited by both parties.

(4) In the event of Persia being invaded by an European nation, the British Government engaged either to supply a force to assist in repelling the invasion, or, in lieu thereof, to pay an annual

---

[1] The Treaty of Gulistan had rendered such an agreement between England and Persia devoid of meaning, as by that treaty the Shah had abrogated his right to maintain vessels of war on the Caspian.

subsidy of 200,000 tomans on the understanding that such subsidy would be withheld, if the war with the European nation was brought about by any act of Persian aggression.

Thus the close of the year 1814 found Persia, though deprived of some of her fairest provinces, at peace with Russia and in close alliance with Great Britain: an alliance carefully described in the treaty as being of a strictly defensive character, but, nevertheless, one which bound England to protect her from any further Russian attacks so long as Persia was not the aggressor. But the Government of the White Czar has never wanted astute politicians who were able to gain their ends by means of statecraft and intrigue without risking open hostilities with powerful nations; and it will be seen how Persia *was* invaded by an European Power, and was obliged to undertake a disastrous campaign without the support of England, because Russia, through unwarranted acts of encroachment, forced the Persians to strike the first blow.

During the long peace which followed the final overthrow of Napoleon Bonaparte, Russia displayed increased activity in Asia, and was able to carry out a policy of aggression and conquest, which is remarkable for the undeviating perseverance with which it has been pursued, for the skilful manner in which each new advance has been planned and carried out, and for the vast additions of territory which have thus been incorporated into the Russian Empire.

The Treaty of Paris had not long been signed

when orders were issued for the despatch of Russian officers to the eastern shores of the Caspian, for the purpose of selecting a suitable site for a fort, to enter into negotiations with the Turkomans, and if possible to penetrate to Khiva itself.

Some years previously, certain of the Turkoman tribes are said to have made overtures to the Russian authorities, asking for protection; and in 1803 the Abdal tribe were granted a document which declared that they were the vassals of the White Czar. It is also said that, in 1811, two deputations repaired to Astrakhan, asking for similar protection, and that these overtures were repeated two years later. From the subsequent attitude of the Turkomans it is highly probable that if such deputations actually did reach Astrakhan, they cannot have represented any considerable section of the people, and that they merely claimed Russian protection to escape attacks from Persia and Khiva. Nevertheless, the opportunity thus presented was a favourable one for renewed explorations in the direction of Khiva; and Captain Mouravieff accordingly set out with Major Ponomareff in 1819, carefully reconnoitred the south-eastern shores of the Caspian, selected two suitable sites on which forts could advantageously be erected, and entered into friendly negotiations with the Yomud tribe of Turkomans, who are said to have again applied for Russian protection. Mouravieff then, escorted by a few Yomuds, crossed the desert and succeeded in reaching Khiva, where, however, he was thrown into prison; and though subsequently released, was forced to hastily quit the Khanate.

Attempts were also made to introduce order into the Kirghiz Steppes. The greatest disorder and unrest prevailed throughout that region, and it became absolutely necessary that some steps should be taken to induce the wild nomads to abstain from their reckless acts of outlawry and violence. Since their submission, the Kirghiz had been nominally under the rule of Khans who were the descendants of Abul-Khair, the Russians having, in 1734, agreed to recognise the sovereignty of Abul-Khair's descendants, in return for their submission and the protection of Russian boundaries and trading caravans. But, although this system of government lasted for nearly a hundred years, it was a most pernicious one; for the people ignored the titular Khans thus placed over them, and became more violent and unruly under the nominal rule of Russia than they had been previously. In 1824, therefore, the Khanate was abolished, and the Steppe was divided into three rayons, each of which was to be governed by a Sultan-Regent, nominated by the Russian authorities. This change, however, did little good, for raiding and disorder still continued; and, as will be seen, gave Russia a pretext for sending a large expeditionary force, not against her Kirghiz vassals, but against the ruler of one of the Central Asian Khanates, who was made a scapegoat for the offence of the Czar's own subjects, thus demonstrating the truth of Peter's saying: 'Although the Kirghiz are a roaming and fickle people, their Steppe is the key and gate to all the countries in Central Asia.'

Although by the Treaty of Gulistan Russia had gained very material concessions from Persia, it was not long before fresh difficulties arose, which were due to certain portions of the new frontier having been inaccurately defined. For several years after the ratification of the treaty no steps were taken to remove this obvious source of danger, and when eventually commissioners were appointed to settle the disputed points, no agreement could be arrived at.

The district of Gokcheh, which unquestionably belonged to Persia, was the chief cause of the quarrel, while further disputes arose over the possession of Guni, Balakloo and Kapan. Since the conclusion of the previous war, Russia had gradually strengthened her position in her Caucasian provinces, and she was able, if necessary, to force the Shah to accept her reading of the treaty. All attempts to arrive at an understanding were therefore met by a persistent refusal on the part of the Russian agents to reduce any of their demands, while the Persian Government, feeling that they had right on their side, stoutly contested the Russian claims.

Twice a satisfactory settlement appeared to have been arrived at, but on both occasions the negotiations fell through at the last moment; and finally, in 1825, when a third effort proved unsuccessful, a Russian force occupied the district of

Gokcheh. This step, which was an unwarranted act of aggression, and one which clearly showed that Russia was determined to provoke war, occurred at a time when the Shah's subjects were in a highly excitable state. The Persians had not yet forgotten the previous war by which they had lost so many rich provinces, and their anger against the Russians was greatly increased by the accounts that reached them of the manner in which their co-religionists in the ceded districts were treated by their new masters. The popular excitement was fostered by the priests, who preached a religious war from the pulpits of the mosques, and thus, when the Russian forces occupied Gokcheh, the Shah found it almost impossible to avoid hostilities.

One hope, however, still remained. In 1826 the Persian Court received news of the death of the Czar Alexander and accession of his brother Nicholas, and it was also known that Prince Menchikoff was on his way to Teheran as ambassador from the Russian Emperor. Futteh Ali still believed that peace could be maintained, and negotiations were re-opened as soon as the Prince reached the Shah's summer camp. But Menchikoff had been sent to Teheran for a very different purpose. His mission was to endeavour to divert the attention of the Shah and his people from the north-west towards the east, and, by encouraging an attack on Herat, to simultaneously destroy the Anglo-Persian alliance, to enable Russia to quietly gain possession of the disputed provinces, and still further to advance her interests in the direction of India.

The fanatical frenzy of the people, however, had become far too great for any such schemes to succeed. The populace, excited by the appeals of the mullahs, demanded the evacuation of Gokcheh; the Shah, threatened with the forfeiture of the joys of Paradise, pledged himself to vindicate the claims of his subjects; and nothing else would satisfy the nation.

When, therefore, Menchikoff declined to consent to the withdrawal of the Russian troops, the negotiations were broken off, and hostilities commenced.

From all parts of the kingdom thousands of armed men flocked to the standard of the Crown Prince, and the entire Persian nation united in the effort to avenge the long course of insult and indignities to which they had been subjected.

The Russian authorities on the frontier were completely taken by surprise at the suddenness of the Persian attack. Although by their action they had been steadily provoking war, they did not believe the Persians to be capable of any prompt and united action. When, therefore, the people, carried away by religious fervour, invaded the Russian frontier provinces, they carried everything before them, and forced the Russians to evacuate nearly all the territory which had been acquired by the Treaty of Gulistan.

But, as was inevitable, the tide of Persian successes soon slackened, and then followed a series of disasters which speedily swept the Shah's armies out of Russian territory, and forced Futteh Ali to conclude another humiliating treaty of peace.

As soon as the war commenced, the Persian Government applied to Great Britain for the assistance which had been promised in the last treaty which had been signed by Mr. Ellis. The Shah fully expected that such assistance would be forthcoming, either in troops or money; for, although the Persians had fired the first shot, and struck the first blow, such action had been forced on them through the unprovoked invasion of their territory by the Russians. Nevertheless, England, as represented by her ministers, did not intend to enter into a war with a great European Power to save Persia, and therefore preferred to adopt an interpretation of the treaty which would enable her to escape from the engagements which had been contracted; and thus when a reply was sent to the Persian Court, it was to the effect that ' the occupation by Russian troops of a portion of uninhabited ground, which by right belonged to Persia, even if admitted to have been the proximate cause of hostilities, did not constitute the case of aggression contemplated in the Treaty of Teheran.'

It is needless now to criticise this action on the part of the British Government,[1] but there is

---

[1] For an impartial discussion of this question, see pages 40 and 41 of *England and Russia in the East*, by the late Sir Henry Rawlinson.

no doubt that before the next ten years had elapsed, they had good cause to question the prudence of so having deserted their ally.

Left thus to her own resources, it was inevitable that the war should end in the discomfiture of Persia, and a further advance on the part of Russia.

The conflict, which continued until the spring of 1828, was an unvaried Russian triumph; and at last, when the Persian disasters had culminated in the loss of Erivan and Tabriz, the Crown Prince Abbass Mirza once again appealed to the British Ambassador, through whose good offices peace was restored by the signature of the Treaty of Turkomanchai on February 21, 1828. By this treaty the Shah lost possession of the provinces of Erivan and Nakhtchivan, and agreed to pay a war indemnity of ten crores of tomans, or thirty millions of silver roubles.

After this treaty had been concluded, it became again necessary to modify the terms of the understanding between England and Persia. The Shah's appeal for assistance had placed the British Government in an awkward position, and they then realised the dangers contained in the subsidy articles of the Treaty of Teheran. Taking advantage, therefore, of the Shah's necessities, the British Ambassador offered to pay 250,000 tomans towards the liquidation of the war indemnity, if the subsidy engagements were cancelled; and subsequently, after a bond to this effect had been passed, the necessary erasures were obtained by payment of four-fifths of the amount; a transaction which has been sufficiently condemned by the able author of 'England and Russia in the East.'[1]

The reconciliation of Russia and Persia had scarcely been effected when an event occurred which would undoubtedly have led to a renewal of hostilities had the Emperor not then been engaged in a war against Turkey. In October 1828, M. Griboiedoff, the poet diplomatist, arrived at Tabriz as envoy extraordinary and minister plenipotentiary from the Czar to the Court of Persia. Continuing his progress, the Russian Ambassador proceeded to Teheran, and was there received with every mark of respect and consideration. But the Persians had not yet recovered from their fanatical outburst against the Muscovites; and irritated by the blustering conduct of the Ambassador's Cossack escort, they became still more incensed when M. Griboiedoff haughtily refused to grant redress for the wrongs committed by his followers. Error followed error, and instead of conciliating the people, the Ambassador imperiously put forward demands which tended still further to widen the breach. A eunuch of the royal seraglio was granted protection in the Russian Embassy on the plea of his being a native of the district of Erivan, now a Russian province, and finally a demand was made for the surrender of two Armenian women, who had been drafted from the ceded provinces to the harem of the Asef-Ed-Dowleh. After some hesitation the

[1] See pages 41 to 43 of *England and Russia in the East.*

women were given up and conveyed to the Embassy. The infuriated Persians could stand no more; the people rose, and after obtaining the sanction of their priests, flocked to the Russian Embassy to deliver the women from the hands of the infidels. The offer then made to restore the ladies to their master came too late; the Embassy was sacked, and the ill-advised Ambassador with all his staff and escort slain. The Shah was filled with dismay, and an envoy was sent in haste to St. Petersburg to offer reparation. The Czar, however, had no desire to resume hostilities against Persia; for Russia was then engaged in a war against the Ottoman Empire, and it was necessary that Persia should take no part in the contest. When therefore Khosroo Mirza, the Persian Envoy, obtained an audience of the Czar, and, presenting the handle of his sword to the Emperor, declared himself willing to give his life for that of the Russian Ambassador, he was informed that it would be sufficient if the plundered property were restored, and the persons concerned in the tumult were punished.

CHAPTER IV

1829—1840.

ATTACKS ON HERAT AND KHIVA

Growth of Russian influence in Persia—Russo-Turkish war, and Treaty of Adrianople—Russia incites Persia to attack Herat—Russian intrigue in Afghanistan—Mission of Burnes to Kabul—Persia's withdrawal from Herat—Lord Auckland's expedition to Afghanistan, the Simla Manifesto, and the restoration of Shuja-al-Mulk—Russian expedition for conquering Khiva—Russia and the Kirghiz—Failure of Russian advance upon Khiva.

THE Treaty of Turkomanchai marks a turning point in Persia's relations with Great Britain and Russia. On the one hand the Shah had on more than one occasion felt the weight of Russia's power, and was aware that his great northern neighbour was in a position to inflict still greater humiliation on Persia whenever coercion might be considered desirable; while, on the other hand, he, rightly or wrongly, considered that he had been deserted by England, and his bitter resentment was not appeased by the method adopted in obtaining the cancelment of the subsidy engagements. Moreover, the Persians began to believe that England was unable or unwilling to defend them from their enemies, and this impression speedily gained ground when the English Government, with remarkable capriciousness, abandoned their previous forward policy, and entered upon a course of studied indifference to Persian concerns. Thus Russia, triumphant after her successful campaigns, became emboldened, and took up a position of commanding and almost offensive superiority; while England, hastily arriving at the conclusion that Persia was useless as a barrier against Russian advance towards India, took but little interest in Persian affairs, and permitted Muscovite influence to gain complete ascendency at the Court of Teheran.

But some years elapsed before the full effect of these changed conditions became apparent. Russia had gained much by her recent wars with Persia, and her interests could best be served, not by open hostilities, but by taking advantage of her newly acquired ascendency in exerting moral pressure on the feeble ministers of the Shah, thus causing them to become the tools whereby her aggressive schemes could be carried out. The war with Turkey also, for a short time, caused Persian affairs to assume but a secondary place in Russia's Eastern policy. Six years before the Treaty of Turkomanchai had been signed, the Greeks had revolted against the Porte, and declared their independence. A bitter struggle ensued, and after it had lasted for some years, the despatch of an Egyptian expedition to the Morea, with orders to devastate the country and carry off the people into slavery, forced England, France and Russia to interfere. On October 20, 1827, the combined squadron of the allies, under Codrington, destroyed the Turko-Egyptian fleet at Navarino, and the Greeks were saved from their oppressors. But Russia remained unsatisfied. Canning, who had skilfully arranged the joint action of the Powers against the Porte to keep Russia in check, died without seeing the Greek question settled, and his successors were unable to prevent Russia from using the troubles of the Greeks as a pretext for attacking the Porte.

As soon as peace was restored between Russia and Persia, the Czar, joining his personal grievances to the claims of Europe, declared war against Turkey. Paskievitch, the first Count of Erivan, wheeled his army and entered Asia Minor, while Witgenstein crossed the Pruth. The Russian troops crossed the Danube under the eyes of their Czar, and captured Brailof and Varna; while in Asia the Turks were defeated in a bloody battle near Akhaltsykh, and that town and the fortress of Kars fell into the hands of the renowned Paskievitch. England and Austria became alarmed, but Russia had the encouragement of France, and so the war continued. Diébitch, the successor of Field-Marshal Witgenstein, defeated the Grand Vizier near Pravady, and forced him back on Schumla; Silistria capitulated, the Balkans were crossed, and Adrianople occupied by a Russian army; while in Asia, Paskievitch, continuing his victorious career, twice defeated the Turkish armies in the field and captured Erzeroum. At last Turkey, defeated in Europe and Asia, and without allies, was forced to yield, trusting to the good offices of England and France to obtain for her the best terms possible after her humiliating overthrow. On September 14, 1829, a treaty of peace was signed at Adrianople, whereby Russia, in addition to a large war indemnity and certain concessions in Europe, gained in Asia the districts of Anapa, Poti, Akhaltsykh, and Akhalkalaki, thus rounding off her possessions south of the Caucasus.

After the conclusion of this war with Turkey, the Russians once more turned their attention to Persia, and began to urge the Shah's Government to undertake aggressive movements towards the East. The disorders which prevailed in Afghanistan at this period gave the Russian Ambassador an excellent opportunity for exciting the ambition of the Persian monarch; and after the Crown Prince Abbass Mirza had concluded a successful campaign in Khorassan,[1] it was decided that an attack should be made on the city of Herat, which was then under the independent rule of the Suddozai Prince Kamran.

For a brief space, however, the project remained in abeyance. Abbass was summoned to Teheran, his son Mahommed Mirza being appointed governor of Khorassan in his stead, and Persian reinforcements were marching eastwards to take a part in the war which was to be conducted by the young

---

[1] During this campaign, Abbass Mirza destroyed the Salor Turkoman fort of Old Sarakhs, which stood on the right bank of the Heri-Rud, within a few miles of the Persian town of the same name on the opposite side of the river. The place was razed to the ground by the Persians, the garrison was massacred, and 5,000 slaves were captured, but were afterwards ransomed by the Khan of Khiva for 50,000 tomans.

grandson of the Shah, when Mr. M'Neill, in defence of British interests, threw the whole of his energies into the task of averting the projected invasion. His efforts were in a measure successful, for the attack was delayed. But, though postponed, the idea had not been abandoned. The Czar's agents, by their intrigues, which had been too long unopposed, succeeded in thoroughly rousing the ambition of the Persians, and in the autumn of 1833 Prince Mahommed Mirza crossed the eastern frontier of Persia, and advanced upon Ghurian, a strongly fortified place, about forty miles west of Herat. The inhabitants of that place, however, obstinately refused to surrender, so the Prince left it in his rear, and marched forward to the attack of the capital of Prince Kamran. Here also he encountered a stubborn resistance. The Vizier of the Suddozai prince was a man named Yar Mahommed, who had no desire to see Herat turned into a Persian province, as he would thereby lose much of his power and dignity. The Heratis, under the guidance of this chief, prepared for a vigorous defence, and there was every prospect of a long struggle, when Mahommed received the news of his father's death. Abbass Mirza, anxious to take command of the Persian army, had, contrary to the advice of his physicians, returned to Meshed; but after his arrival there, the disease from which he suffered rapidly grew worse, and he died in the Holy City of Khorassan. This event caused his son to abandon the siege of Herat, and return to Persian territory; and thus the aggressive designs of Persia and the deeply laid plots of Russia were for a time defeated.

On the death of Abbass, the Shah nominated Mahommed Mirza as his heir, and appointed him to the governorship of Azerbijan—the province which had for many years been ruled by his father. But the young prince, who was at this time twenty-eight years of age, did not long remain at Tabriz, for his aged grandfather, the Shah, died on October 23, 1834, and the British and Russian representatives each hastened to be the first to congratulate the new sovereign on his accession to the throne. Rival claimants, however, soon appeared in the field, and while the Russian Ambassador was offering armed resistance, the English Minister took prompt action to overthrow the pretenders. Sir Lindsay Bethune—who had formerly served in Persia as an artillery subaltern—had once again been sent out from England for the purpose of drilling the Persian troops, and a large number of officers and sergeants were at the same time sent from India with the same object, while arms and ammunition were also transmitted for the use of the Shah's army. The presence of these officers enabled the British Ambassador to adopt very effective measures to ensure the succession of Mahommed Mirza, and thus rendered it unnecessary for Russia to supply the military force which had been offered for the purpose. Colonel Bethune had under his command a force far superior, both in arms and organisation, to any which the pretenders could bring against him, and by his prompt march from Tabriz to Teheran, and from thence to Shiraz, he speedily silenced all opposition and secured the throne to Mahommed.

It was a service which should have secured the gratitude of the new Persian 'King of Kings;' but, unfortunately, Mahommed had for many years lived under the shadow of Russian influence, and merely looked upon the action of Sir Lindsay Bethune as an effort made by the English to prevent his being placed on the throne by the aid of the Russians. The abandonment of the siege of Herat, which had been caused by his father's death at a time when his ambition had been thoroughly aroused, had continually rankled in his mind; he had sworn a solemn oath to return to the attack on the first opportunity, and he brooded sullenly over his disappointment. Thus after Mahommed Shah was crowned King of Persia, on January 31, 1835, his first thoughts were turned towards Herat, and his first utterances in public durbar were full of references to the great campaign which he was about to undertake, to humble the pride of the Afghans and the Usbegs, and by means of which Persia was once more to regain possession of the territories which had been subject to the princes of the Sefavean dynasty.

The year 1835, however, passed without any advance being made, and the best part of the next year was also spent in unsuccessful operations against the Turkoman settlements on the Gurgen River; but in the autumn of 1837, as Shah Kamran steadfastly resisted the Persian pretensions to sovereignty over his State, Mahommed once more set out towards the east, fully determined to break down the independence of Herat.

Mr. M'Neill, who by this time had returned to Persia as British Ambassador, found that British credit had sunk to the very lowest ebb, and that there was then no chance of preserving the peace. Nothing short of the armed intervention of Great Britain would suffice to turn Mahommed Shah from his purpose; and how could England possibly interfere without violating her treaty engagements? For had she not, in the ninth article of the Treaty of Teheran, agreed that, ' if war shall be declared between the Afghans and Persians, the English Government shall not interfere with either party, unless their mediation to effect a peace shall be solicited by both parties.' Persia, in pursuit of her ambitious schemes, did not desire British mediation, and when such counsel was voluntarily tendered, it was rejected. And thus the English, who had formerly urged the Persians to invade Afghanistan for the purpose of shielding India from an Afghan invasion, now had the mortification of seeing a Persian army repeating the invasion, not in defence of British interests, but in furtherance of the aggressive designs of a Power whose advances in Asia were—and still are—made for the purpose of threatening the very stability of British rule in Hindustan.

Early in November 1837, the Persian troops crossed the Herat frontier; by the middle of that month the strong fortress of Ghurian had surrendered, and a week later the advanced guard of the invading army took up a position before the capital of Shah Kamran. It is not the intention here to enter into a description of the long siege which followed, as every Englishman who takes an interest in the gallant doings of his countrymen has, or should have, read of the stubborn defence made by the Afghans, encouraged thereto by the unfailing constancy and unflinching courage of the young artillery subaltern, Eldred Pottinger. Nor is it necessary to describe at length how the Persians during their ten months' investment of the fortress were aided by a Russian regiment of so-called deserters: how their operations were directed by Russian officers; and how the crowning assault of June 24, 1838, which, it was confidently believed, would result in the capture of the place, was planned by Count Simonitch, the Russian Ambassador himself, who, 'while Mr. M'Neill was appealing to the prudence and the reason of the Shah, was exciting the ambition and inflaming the passions of that sovereign.'

Mr. M'Neill, leaving Teheran on March 10, 1838, reached the Shah's camp on the 6th of the following month, and from that moment did everything that was possible to induce the Shah to raise the siege. But the Russian Ambassador arrived a fortnight later, and systematically set to work to thwart all the efforts of the British Envoy to bring about a settlement of the differences between the contending parties. 'Whilst the one was preaching moderation and peace, the other was inciting to war and conquest; and whilst the one pointed out the difficulties and expense of the enterprise, the other inspired hopes of money and assistance.'

Such was the state of affairs in Persia during the summer of 1838. The British Mission had fallen into contempt, and the British Ambassador was treated with marked discourtesy, while the Czar's agents were triumphantly witnessing the successful results of their long course of intrigue.

The Russian Government, however, did not confine their attention only to Persia; it was intended that Russian influence should be extended far beyond Herat, and right up to the borders of the British settlements in Hindustan. Persia, it is true, was to be the principal agent for the furtherance of Russia's designs, and the chief interest in Russia's doings at that time centred in the siege of Herat, because in that event the result of Russian machinations was most clearly discernible. But the siege of Herat was only the first move in the great game which was to end in the establishment of Russian influence on the threshold of India. The next move was an attempt to gain the alliance of the Barakzai rulers at Kabul and Kandahar. This was necessary for the complete success of the Russian project; and for this purpose a Russian captain named Vitkievitch was sent on a mission to Afghanistan. When it became evident that Mahommed Shah had definitely determined to attack Herat, Vitkievitch was despatched from Orenburg to Teheran; there, in September 1837, he received from Count Simonitch his final instructions, and set out for Kabul as envoy from the Emperor Nicholas to the Amir Dost Mahommed, bearing with him letters from the Russian Ambassador and from the Czar himself.

The following is a translation of the Emperor's letter:—

'In a happy moment the messenger of your Highness, Mirza Hosan, reached my Court with your friendly letter. I was very much delighted to receive it, and highly gratified by its perusal. The contents of the letter prove that you are my well-wisher and have friendly opinions towards me. It flattered me very much, and I was satisfied of your friendship to my everlasting Government. In consequence of this, and preserving the terms of friendship which are now commenced between you and myself in my heart, I will feel always happy to assist the people of Kabul who may come to trade into my kingdom. On the arrival of your messenger, I have ordered him to make preparations for his long journey back to you, and also appointed a man of dignity to accompany him on the part of my Government. If it please God, and he reaches safe, he will present to you the rarities of my country which I have sent through him. By the grace of God, may your days be prolonged. Sent from St. Petersbourg the Capital of Russia, on April 27, 1837, A.D. and in the twelfth year of my reign.'

Vitkievitch first visited Kandahar and succeeded in winning over the Barakzai brothers to the Russo-Persian alliance,[1] and having thus satisfactorily carried out the first part of his mission, he proceeded to Kabul, and arrived there on December 19, 1837. But Captain (afterwards Sir Alexander) Burnes was then in the Afghan capital, and Dost Mahommed fully realised that a complete understanding with his near neighbours the British would be far more advantageous to him than an alliance with the Russians, and he cherished the hope that the English, in order to secure his friendship, would induce—or compel—the Sikhs to restore Peshawar to the Afghans. The Amir considered the Sikhs to be his greatest enemies, and his policy at that time was to secure an alliance with any State which would help him to overthrow Runjeet Singh, and recover the provinces which had been lost to Afghanistan.

Burnes arrived at Kabul on September 20, 1837, in charge of a so-called 'commercial mission' which had been sent by Lord Auckland 'to work out the policy of opening the River Indus to commerce,' and to establish commercial relations with the Afghans. But he had not been many days in the Afghan capital before the real object of his mission became apparent. His duty was to

---

[1] A treaty was prepared and sent to Persia for the Shah's signature, and when signed, it was returned to Kandahar through the Russian Ambassador, who, in forwarding it to the Sirdars, wrote:—'Mahommed Shah has promised to give you the possession of Herat; I sincerely tell you that you will also get Ghurian on my account, from the Shah. . . . When Mahommed Omar Khan arrives here, I will ask the Shah to quit Herat, and I will remain here with 12,000 troops, and when you join we will take Herat, which will afterwards be delivered to you.'

ascertain the exact power which the Persian party in Kabul possessed over the politics of Afghanistan, in order that the Indian Government might know what steps to take to effectually prevent the Amir from becoming a party to the Russo-Persian Alliance.

Dost Mahommed saw in the arrival of this Embassy a possible opportunity of regaining possession of Peshawar, and he received Burnes with great pomp and splendour. Every possible honour was paid to the British Envoy, and the Amir displayed the greatest anxiety to enter into an alliance with the Indian Government. Thus, when Vitkievitch reached Cabul, he found that he had been forestalled; his reception was of a most discouraging nature; and, for many weeks after his arrival in the Afghan capital, he experienced great difficulty in even obtaining an audience of the Amir.

But after many months spent in negotiations, the only promise which Dost Mahommed could obtain as the price of his complete abstention from intercourse with Russia and Persia, was that the English would restrain Runjeet Singh from attacking the Amir's dominions. Such a promise completely failed to satisfy the ruler of Kabul. He feared no aggression from the direction of Lahore, but on the contrary desired to attack the Sikhs himself. He was promised protection from a danger which only existed in the minds of Lord Auckland and his advisers; while no guarantee was given that his dominions should be defended against the Russians and Persians, although he was to risk incurring the enmity of these Powers by abstaining from all intercourse with them. He, however, made one further attempt to secure the friendship of the Indian Government, and his brother, Jubbar Khan, who was notorious for his friendly feelings towards the English, strove hard to obtain from Burnes some hope that more advantageous terms would eventually be conceded. But the Envoy had received precise instructions, and could make no concessions, and although he remained at Kabul for a short time longer, and had many friendly interviews with the Amir, it became daily more apparent that there was no hope of bringing matters to a favourable issue.

Vitkievitch, who in the meanwhile had been quietly watching the course of the negotiations between Burnes and the Amir, and had also commenced a correspondence with the Sikh Maharaja Runjeet Singh, was then sent for, and was accorded a reception which fully compensated for the previous neglect with which he had been treated. Dost Mahommed, abandoning all hope of concluding an advantageous treaty with the English, threw himself into the Russo-Persian Alliance. Vitkievitch promised everything that was asked of him, and when Burnes turned his back on the Afghan capital on April 28, 1838, the Barakzai ruler of Kabul had become an avowed ally of the Persian Shah, and therefore the enemy of Great Britain.

Russian diplomacy had thus gained a remarkable series of triumphs. The Shah of Persia, apparently in pursuit of his own ambition, but actually for the furtherance of Russia's aggressive designs, was besieging Herat; the Kandahar Sirdars, at the instigation of a Russian agent, had flung themselves into the Russo-Persian alliance; and finally the Amir of Kabul, by promise of Russian money and assistance, had been drawn into the same net. A Russian army was also being prepared for an advance against Khiva, whenever such a movement might be necessary to give a finishing touch to the great design which had been planned with so much care and craftiness.

It was, however, but a short-lived triumph. The Persian army before Herat was unable to break down the resistance of the gallant defenders, and the Shah's ministers, sheltered under the wing of the Russian eagle, at last overreached themselves, when England intervened, and the attack on Herat collapsed.

The influence of the British Minister in Persia had long been steadily declining, and at last it reached such a low ebb that the Persians began to show their contempt for the Mission in petty annoyances and insults. A courier of the Mission had been stopped, seized and ill-treated in October 1838, when the Persian army was advancing towards Herat,[1] and although Mr. M'Neill had

[1] This messenger was on his way from Herat to Teheran with letters from Yar Mahommed and Pottinger to Mr. M'Neill, and having passed through the Persian camp, had arrived near to Meshed, when he was seized by horsemen who had been sent after him, and was forced to return to the camp, where he was placed in custody.

repeatedly demanded reparation for this grievous insult, no redress was offered, and the Persian Government declared that they had the right to punish, or even put to death, any Persian employés of the British Mission, without reference to the Ambassador. The Governor of Bushire also had used offensive language and threats towards the British Resident at that port, and in this case also Mr. M'Neill's demands for redress were studiously ignored; while, in addition to these direct affronts, the Shah, though pledged to the conclusion of a commercial treaty with England, put forward many frivolous excuses, whereby the long promised settlement was indefinitely postponed.

Any one of these offences was sufficient in itself to have caused a rupture with the Persian Court; but Mr. M'Neill had still remained at his post, in the hope of inducing the Shah to abandon the attack on Herat, and believing that the Persian Government would eventually accede to the British demands. As time passed, however, it became

'He succeeded, however, in making his way to the tent of Colonel Stoddart, and was by that officer conducted to the Prime Minister, who, after he had been informed by Colonel Stoddart that the man was in the service of the Mission, again placed him in custody, while Hadji Khan, an officer of the rank of brigadier in the service of the Shah, not only used offensive language in addressing Colonel Stoddart in presence of the Prime Minister, but after the messenger had been released by order of His Excellency, seized him again in the midst of the camp, stripped him to search for any letters he might have concealed about his person; took from him Lieutenant Pottinger's letter, which was sent to the Prime Minister; used to the messenger the most violent threats and the most disgusting and opprobrious language; and took from him a portion of his accoutrements.'

daily more obvious that nothing less than a complete cessation of diplomatic intercourse would turn Mahommed Shah from his wild scheme of aggression, and show the Persian Court that, even though they were aided by Russia, Great Britain had the power to enforce compliance with her just demands, and was resolved to uphold her dignity and defend her interests. Mr. M'Neill therefore wrote a letter to the Persian Government, in which all the British demands were clearly set forth. The Shah then began to shuffle and prevaricate. He did not desire that matters should be brought to a crisis, and he therefore first offered to comply with all the demands excepting the abandonment of the siege, if the question of Herat was treated separately; but shortly afterwards he changed his mind, and said that he would only adopt that course if Lieut. Pottinger was ordered to quit the city, and if no further reference was made to Herat affairs.

It thus became clear that Mahommed had no intention of withdrawing from before Herat, unless compelled to do so by a display of force, or unless the English purchased the safety of the place by the payment of a large sum of money. Mr. M'Neill, however, objected to any half measures, and declared that, unless the whole of the British demands were acceded, he would quit Persia. As the Shah still refused to raise the siege, he, on June 3, announced his intention of leaving the camp on the following day, and demanded permission to proceed to the frontier. The Shah then pretended not to understand what was required of him, and stated that no insults had been offered to the members of the British Embassy. M'Neill however, reiterated his demands, and insisted on their compliance—excepting the conclusion of the commercial treaty—within three days; and, as this was not done, he left the Persian camp on June 7.

In the meantime the Indian Government had tardily resolved to make a demonstration in the Persian Gulf. For this purpose some war vessels were sent with the steamers 'Semiramis' and 'Hugh Lindsay' conveying detachments of the 15th, 23rd, and 24th Regiments and Marine Battalions with a couple of field guns. This insignificant expeditionary force reached the island of Karrack on June 19, when the troops were at once landed and took possession of the island. Orders were at the same time sent to Mr. M'Neill, instructing him to inform the Shah that the British Government would view the occupation by Persia of Herat, or any portion of Afghanistan, in the light of a hostile demonstration against England. He was also directed to refer to the despatch of the expedition to the Gulf, and state that, if Mahommed Shah desired the suspension of hostilities, he must at once withdraw from Herat. M'Neill received these instructions when he was at Shahrud, on his way to Teheran, and he at once ordered Colonel Stoddart to return to the royal camp and deliver the message.

Stoddart reached the camp on August 11, and on the following day had an interview with the

Shah, when he found the Persian King more disposed to listen to reason. The great assault which had been planned by Count Simonitch had already failed, and the Shah had begun to grow weary of the long siege. Moreover the news of the occupation of the island of Karrack had already reached the Court, where it was believed that an English army had landed at Bushire, and was advancing through Shiraz to the Persian capital. While the British officer was delivering his message, the Shah interrupted him with the remark: 'The fact is, if I do not leave Herat there will be war. Is not that so?' Stoddart replied, 'It is war; all depends on your Majesty's answer, and may God preserve your Majesty.' Whereupon Mahommed Shah, taking the English message into his hand, said, 'It is all I wished for.' Two days later Stoddart was called before the King, and was then informed by the Shah that he would comply with all the demands of the British Government.

But before the Persian army could retire, it was necessary that baggage animals should be collected for the transport of the Shah's camp and the large force which been assembled before the city. Thus some delay occurred; and Count Simonitch seized this opportunity to try and bring about an arrangement which would enable the Persians to withdraw with some appearance of success. He sent a letter into Herat offering to mediate between Shah Kamran and Mahommed Shah, and an attempt was made to persuade Shah Kamran to visit the Persian camp and pay homage to the Persian army. But the wary Vizier, Yar Mahommed, supported by the advice of Eldred Pottinger, declined to be drawn into the trap, and thus the Russian diplomatists failed to secure for their ally even the faintest semblance of victory.

British interference had compelled the Persians to withdraw from before Herat; this fact was well known throughout the length and breadth of Persia; and the Shah's proclamation that he had raised the siege 'in sole consideration of the interest of our faith and country, and from a due regard to the welfare of our troops and subjects,' did not lessen the humiliation. By September 9, 1838, the Persian army was in full retreat, and on the morning of that day Colonel Stoddart reported to Mr. M'Neill that 'the Shah has mounted his horse "Ameerij," and is gone.'

Some time before Mahommed Shah advanced against Herat, the British ambassador in Persia had earnestly exhorted the British Government to make some movement in Afghanistan which would counteract the ambitious projects of the Persian King, and thwart the designs of his Russian confederates. The Indian Government had long mistrusted the Barakzai Sirdars, and when the Persian army invested Herat, and it became known that the Kandahar chiefs were intriguing with Persia, Lord Auckland began seriously to consider the expediency of reinstating Shuja-ul-Mulk on the Afghan throne. As the dangers in the West began to thicken, this idea gained a stronger hold on the mind of the Governor-General, and he eventually decided to send a mission to the Court of the Sikh Maharaja Runjeet Singh for the purpose of ascertaining on what conditions a Sikh army would advance to Kabul in support of the exiled Suddozai. In accordance with this resolution Mr. Macnaghten was sent from Simla to the Court of Lahore, accompanied by Captains Osborne and Macgregor and Dr. Drummond. The Mission reached Adeena-nuggur on May 31 1838, and there received a cordial and gracious reception from Runjeet Singh.

It is unnecessary to enter into details of the subsequent negotiations, which resulted in the signature of the Tripartite Treaty of Alliance between Maharaja Runjeet Singh and Shah Shuja-ul-Mulk —a treaty executed with the approbation of, and in concert with, the British Government, and by which it was agreed that a Sikh army should march on Kabul from Peshawar, while Shuja-ul-Mulk advanced through Shikarpur and Kandahar, the Indian Government aiding the movements with their moral support and pecuniary assistance. Nor is it necessary to describe how the ideas of the Indian Government gradually expanded until in August 1838 it was decided that a large English force should be employed to depose Dost Mahommed and reinstate Shuja-ul-Mulk on the Afghan throne; how Lord Auckland met Runjeet Singh at Ferozepore amidst the roar of artillery and braying of military bands, while the British and Sikh armies were reviewed and fought mimic battles to display their prowess and to add importance to the occasion; how the famous 'Simla Manifesto' was published, setting forth the reasons which had led the Government to despatch a British army across the Indus; and how Lord Auckland still persisted in his fatuous design of invading Afghanistan with British troops, even after he had received news that the Persian army had retired from before Herat, and when it thus became known in India that there was no longer any immediate danger to be expected from Persian aggression or Russian intrigue. Herat was safe; but still the Barakzai Amir of Kabul had to be deposed and the feeble Suddozai puppet placed on the Afghan throne, and for this purpose the British army, though somewhat reduced in numbers, moved forward across the Indus.

The combined columns from Bengal and Bombay, with Shah Shuja's contingent, reached Quetta on April 4, 1839, and three weeks later appeared before the walls of Kandahar, when Kohundil Khan and his brothers fled towards Persia, and the city was occupied without resistance. On May 8, a grand review of the entire force was held on the plains outside the city, and Shah Shuja was there installed as King of the Durani Empire. On June 27 the march was resumed towards Kabul; Ghuzni was captured at daybreak on July 23; and Dost Mohammed moved out of Kabul towards Maidan—about twenty-seven miles to the southwest of Kabul—where he intended to dispute the British advance. But the news of the fall of Ghuzni paralysed the Afghan defence, and one by one the

Amir's adherents went over to the enemy; the Kizilbashes traitorously deserted, their example being quickly followed by the greater part of the Afghan troops; and, finally, Dost Mahommed was forced to take refuge in flight, without being able to strike one blow in defence of his crown. The news of his flight soon reached the British camp, and Captain Outram, with 500 horsemen, eagerly started off in pursuit. But the fugitive had a day's start of his pursuers, and, aided by the treachery of an Afghan Sirdar named Hadji Khan Khakur, who accompanied Outram, succeeded in escaping across the Hindu Kush into the dominions of the Usbeg ruler of Kunduz. On August 7 the British army entered Kabul, and the Suddozai king was again seated on the throne from which he had been driven twenty-nine years before.

Thus was the restoration of Shuja-ul-Mulk accomplished. The chief cities of Eastern Afghanistan were occupied by British garrisons; the Barakzais had been overthrown, and forced to fly from the country; and in the first flush of success it appeared as if a great triumph had been achieved. It was believed that a friendly Government had been permanently established in Afghanistan, and it was confidently expected that in a short time the British troops might be safely withdrawn, and the Suddozai ruler left in firm possession of the country.

But shortly afterwards vague rumours began to circulate that a Russian army was advancing southwards, across the wild unknown Steppes of

Central Asia. These indefinite reports gradually began to assume a fixed shape, and at last it was known for certain that the Czar had despatched an army to conquer Khiva.

This expedition had been planned some years previously, at the time when the Czar's agents were striving to induce the Persian Government to attack Herat. The Russian Government had prepared a gigantic scheme of attack, which was to make Russian influence supreme throughout the whole of Western Asia. Persia was to conquer Herat; by means of the alliance with the Barakzai Sirdars, Russian influence was to be pushed forward to the Indus; and while this portion of the programme was being carried out, a Russian army was being prepared at Orenburg, from whence it was to be pushed forward to Khiva, whenever a demonstration against that Khanate could be made with the most telling effect. Such was the scheme prepared by the Russians—amazing in its audacity, and preposterous because of the enormous difficulties in the way of its realisation. In the early years of the nineteenth century the Czar Nicholas and his advisers tried, by one great stroke, to secure a position on the borders of India which their successors have not yet gained after an interval of threescore years spent in constant warfare, and unceasing interference and aggression. The time for such a move was not yet ripe; the intervening countries were unknown and unexplored; the characteristics of their inhabitants had not been studied; and, above all, it was not realised that

Russia, with her frontiers at Orenburg and on the River Araxes, was quite unable to establish any permanent influence in the countries bordering India, or to destroy the stability of British rule in Hindustan. The Czar's government, however, felt that something had to be done to neutralise the effects of the retreat from Herat, and as a counter-stroke to the British occupation of Afghanistan, and it was therefore decided that the invasion of Khiva should be carried out as speedily as possible. A plausible pretext for this readily obtained. Russian subjects were languishing in horrible dungeons on the banks of the Oxus, and the Kirghiz Steppes were the scenes of constant disturbances, which were said to have been due to Khivan instigation.

It has already been related how the Kirghiz-Kazaks were gradually driven westwards by the Dzungarians, until in 1723 the tribes of the Middle and Lesser Hordes, settled in the Steppes to the east of the River Ural. In 1734 these tribes tendered their submission to the Czar, in order to obtain Russian protection from their numerous enemies, but with little intention of bowing to Russian authority. The Russians then advanced their frontier line, and built the town of Orenburg, while at the same time a fortified line of Cossack settlements was established on the banks of the River Ural. These measures, however, failed to keep the Kirghiz in check, and from that time they continued to carry on a system of raids, in which no respect was paid to Russian caravans.

The methods which the Russian authorities adopted for governing these people were ill-advised, gave rise to the greatest discontent, and tended to create opposition rather than to pacify the district. This misgovernment was due to the complete ignorance of the Russians concerning the customs, ideas, passions, and even language of the Kirghiz. At first, although these nomads were in name the subjects of the White Czar, they displayed but little respect for their masters; and the Russian settlers on the banks of the River Ural considered it a matter of some good fortune if the Kirghiz did not break through the line of fortified posts, ravage their villages, and carry off the people into slavery. But when the Russian position on the Ural became strengthened, and their settlements behind the fortified frontier line were no longer exposed to attacks, they then began to devise measures for the purpose of turning the Kirghiz from nominal into actual subjects; and then their ignorance in all matters concerning these nomad people became abundantly evident. For many years all correspondence was carried on in the Tartar language, because it was believed that the Kirghiz were of the same race as the Volga Tartars—a method of communication which was about as useful and intelligible to the Khans as a letter written in Spanish would be to an Italian. Then, again, it was believed that the Kirghiz were Mahommedans, and they were treated as such; when, as a matter of fact, they were really Shamanists, and have only become Mahommedans through the Mussulman religion having been forced on them by Russia. But their chief mistake was in considering that, so long as the Khans were friendly, the people also would be obedient; and this error was the cause of most of the troubles which followed. These mistakes, combined with others, tended to increase the already wide-spread discontent which was still displayed in constant pillage and disorder. Caravans were plundered; Russian subjects were carried into slavery; and, whenever an opportunity arose, the people gathered round some trusted leader and openly rebelled against Russian authority.

Such being the condition of the Kirghiz who were under Russian protection, it can readily be imagined that the independent tribes of the adjoining states were not loth to take advantage of these continual disturbances in order to enrich themselves. Thus the Khivans and Khokandians were at one time accused by the Russians of inciting the Kirghiz to make forays, while at another time they were charged with attacking these same Kirghiz and preventing them from living quiet, peaceable lives. Both charges had, no doubt, a considerable substratum of truth; but had the Russian authorities adopted a more popular system of government among their Kirghiz subjects, and endeavoured to make them take to a more settled mode of life, one great reason for the frontier troubles would have been removed; and, although the Russians could not have entirely prevented the traffic in slaves at Khiva without invading that Khanate, it is probable that the

Khivans would have, to a great extent if not altogether, been obliged to obtain their chief supplies of slaves through the Turkomans from Persia.

Instead of doing this, however, 'the authorities at Orenburg,' according to a Russian writer,[1] 'tried formerly, by every possible means, to prevent the wandering Kirghizes from adopting a settled mode of life and pursuing agriculture, being afraid that cattle-rearing would be neglected.' And thus, rather than risk any neglect of cattle-rearing, the Russian authorities prevented the Kirghiz from settling down, and so indirectly caused that very condition of disorder throughout the Steppes which resulted in incessant raids, and the capture of Russian subjects who were sold as slaves in the markets of Central Asia.

During the course of about fifteen years (from 1820 to 1835) Russia despatched several small expeditions against the Kirghiz tribes; but her wars with Persia and Turkey, the revolution in France, which drove Charles X. from the throne, and the insurrection in Poland, compelled her to abandon for a time the idea of conquering Khiva.

In 1834 the Russians constructed the fort of Novo Alexandrovsk at the head of the Mertvii-Kultuk bay on the east coast of the Caspian, for the protection of the Emba fisheries against the Turkoman pirates;[2] and they also commenced the

---

[1] *The Russians in Central Asia*, by Captain Valikhanoff, M. Veniukoff, and other Russian travellers; translated by John and Robert Mitchell, p. 482.

[2] This fort was abandoned in 1846, when a new one, bearing the same name, was erected on the Mangisblak Peninsula.

erection of a continuous rampart, somewhat like the Chinese Wall but on a smaller scale, which was to connect Orsk on the River Ural with Omsk on the Irtish. This bulwark was actually commenced and about twelve miles were completed in 1836, when it was abandoned.

But matters remained in an unsettled condition. The Kirghiz continued to carry on their 'barantas,' or forays, and displayed on every possible occasion their discontent with the Russian administration. They received support from the Khivans, who found the traffic in slaves to be most advantageous; while the Russian authorities, instead of endeavouring to find a remedy by means of a more satisfactory government of the Kirghiz tribes, and by encouraging, or if necessary forcing, them to adopt a more settled mode of life, continued to misgovern them, whereby their discontent and predatory instincts were fostered; and then the whole blame was thrown on Khiva. The acquisition of Khiva had long been coveted by the Russians, and the Khan was therefore made the scapegoat for all the offences of the Kirghiz.

When Mouravieff returned to Russia in 1822 from his mission to Khiva, he wrote an account of his journey in which there is the following paragraph :—' Khiva is at this moment an advanced post which impedes our commerce with Bokhara and Northern India. Under our dependence Khiva would have become a safeguard for this commerce against the attacks of populations dispersed in the Steppes of Central Asia. This oasis, situated in the midst of an ocean of sand, would have become a point of assembly for all the commerce of Asia, and would have shaken to the centre of India the enormous superiority enjoyed by the rulers of the sea.' Mouravieff's words expressed the opinions of all Russian politicians and soldiers from the reign of Peter the Great downwards, and until Khiva became a Russian possession in 1873.

Ever since the time of Peter the Great the Russians endeavoured to obtain a footing on the Oxus, as they believed that river to afford the easiest route to the heart of Central Asia. But in order to obtain control over this water-way, it was necessary to subjugate Khiva, and the acquisition of that State has therefore been steadily kept in view. The importance to Russia of a successful campaign against Khiva had, in 1839, become doubly great. It was necessary that the Russians should take immediate steps to minimise the effects of the failure of their intrigues in Persia, and the advance of the British troops into Afghanistan, and this could be best done by an advance on Khiva. What better reason for the movement could be desired than the suppression of the horrible and degrading traffic in slaves? England herself had been for years engaged in the suppression of the slave trade, and it surely was part of the duty of Holy Russia to take her share in the crusade! No one could deny that Khiva was one of the centres in which this abominable trade was carried on, but how many persons were aware that among the most prominent offenders in this respect were Russia's own subjects the Kirghiz, who should first have been brought into subjection and encouraged to lead peaceable and settled lives before the crusade was carried further afield.

On March 24, 1839, when the British troops were toiling through the Bolan Pass, the Czar approved of the following recommendations of a special committee :—

I. To commence at once the organisation of an expedition against Khiva, and to establish the necessary depôts and stations on the route without delay.

II. *To conceal the real object of the expedition, which was to be given out as a scientific expedition to the Aral Sea.*

III. To postpone the departure of the expedition until the settlement of English matters in Afghanistan, in order that the influence and impression of the Russian proceedings in Central Asia might have more weight, and that England, in consequence of her own conquests, might no longer have any right to trouble the Russian Government for explanations; on no account, however, to delay the expedition later than the spring of 1840.

IV. In the event of the expedition terminating successfully, to replace the Khan of Khiva by a trustworthy Kazak Sultan; to establish order and security as far as possible, and to give full freedom to the Russian trade.

V. To assign 425,000 silver roubles and 12,000 gold ducats for the estimated cost of the expedition, and to supply the detachment with arms and the indispensable material, and to allow the Governor-General of Orenburg to avail himself of the assistance of the local artillery and engineer force.

On October 10, 1839, final orders were issued regarding the Russian operations which were to be carried out after the capture of Khiva, and a document was prepared for the guidance of the new Khan, in which his relations towards Russia were clearly set forth; and finally, on November 26, a manifesto was published at Orenburg, stating the causes and objects of the proposed expedition, wherein it was said that 'just and reasonable considerations have induced His Majesty the Emperor to send a military force against Khiva, in order to secure by force of arms the rights and interests of Russian subjects, to put an end to pillage and rapine, to liberate prisoners then in Khiva, to inspire the respect due to Russia, and to establish the influence indisputably belonging to her, and which is the only guarantee for the maintenance of peace in that portion of Asia. Such is the object of the intended expedition against Khiva.'

Meanwhile preparations for the advance had been pushed forward. Large stores of provisions and forage were purchased and collected at Orenburg, and every possible want was anticipated and provided for. As the expedition would have to march through an almost waterless Steppe, the great difficulty which was to be expected was the absence of sufficient water for the large force which it was proposed to send. It was known from Kirghiz reports that wells existed on the Ust-Yurt plateau, but these only gave a sufficient supply for small caravans, and were totally insufficient for the requirements of large parties. It was therefore considered advisable that the advance should be made in the winter; and this decision was the cause of the disasters which followed. The troops were saved from the distress and dangers of marching through the desert in the burning heat of summer, but they had to face an exceptionally severe winter, which paralysed their movements and eventually necessitated a retreat.

As the stores were received at Orenburg they were sent forward to the intermediate depôts which it was intended to establish at various points along the line of march, and for this purpose 7,750 carts were obtained from the Bashkirs.

On June 30, 1839, the first detachment, consisting of a small force of infantry with 400 mounted Bashkirs and 2 howitzers, marched out of Orenburg, under Colonel Heke, for the purpose of establishing advanced posts. The last portion of his march was attended with the greatest hardships, owing to the great heat and scarcity of water; but on July 27 he arrived at Ak-Bulak, and there commenced the construction of a fortified post. Convoys of stores were then sent forward, and by the end of October the preparations for the general advance had been completed. Early in

November a detachment was sent forward under Colonel Danilevski, who was ordered to await the main army at a post which had been constructed on the River Emba.

At the end of November 1839, the main body commenced its advance under General Perovski, who had been entrusted with the command of the expedition. The total strength of the army (including the detachments which had been sent forward in advance) amounted to 5,325 men, with 22 guns and 4 rocket stands. It was divided into five columns, four of which were to advance from Orenburg, while the fifth marched from the Kalmykovski Fort on the lower Orenburg line direct to the River Emba, where it was to effect a junction with the remainder of the army.

But intense cold, frequent snowstorms, and terrible hardships decided the result of the expedition, and by the time the columns reached Ak-Bulak, during the first week in February, it was evident they could go no further.

General Perovski, who had remained at Fort Emba till the whole of the troops had left, and who passed the columns on their march to Ak-Bulak, and thus saw the enormous difficulties and hardships they had to contend against, then began to realise that a continuance of the advance would probably lead to the total loss of the force. He therefore consulted his commanding officers, who unanimously decided that it would be madness to go on.

On mustering his force the General also found

that it had been sadly thinned through sickness and death, and that the loss in camels had been so great that even if the weather had been more favourable it would have been impossible to reach Khiva.

The effective force of men available only amounted to 1,856.

No alternative now remained but to retreat, and Perovski was therefore reluctantly compelled to issue a general order, thanking the troops for the unflagging devotion and energy they had displayed, and ordering the return of the expedition.

Thus the second organised Russian invasion of Khiva was a miserable failure, and little short of disaster. Snow and pestilence had done their work, and Khiva was delivered, not by the valour of its people, but through its peculiarly isolated situation, surrounded as it is on all sides by hundreds of miles of barren, pathless, and waterless deserts.

When it became known that Perovski's force would not be able to reach Khiva, and had been compelled to retreat, steps were at once taken to repair the catastrophe, and great preparations were made for the despatch of a new expedition: orders were issued for strengthening the Orenburg Corps by six more battalions; and Admiral Korsakoff was sent to report on the number of vessels on the Volga and Caspian available for transporting troops to the eastern shores of the Caspian, in order that the new expedition might follow the route taken by Prince Bekovitch Tcherkasski.

But it was found that there were not sufficient vessels for the purpose, and arrangements were therefore made for the new expedition to again use the Orenburg-Ak-Bulak line, the advance being, however, so timed that the whole force might be concentrated at Ak-Bulak during the autumn, and thus have only to cross the Ust-Yurt plateau in the early winter. But fifty years ago there were no railways in Russia, by means of which troops and stores could be rapidly pushed forward to Orenburg, and before the preparations for a renewed attack on Khiva were completed, the English, by obtaining the liberation of the Russian captives, deprived Russia of all excuse for making war against the Khan.

In June 1839, Major d'Arcy Todd, an artillery officer, was despatched on a special mission to Herat, and on his arrival there he sent a Mahommedan priest, named Mullah Hussan, to Khiva with a letter of friendship to the Khan. This messenger arrived in the Khanate at the time when the people were in a wild state of alarm on account of the Russian advance, and he was therefore cordially received, as England was the only nation which could save Khiva from falling into the hands of Russia. Mullah Hussan on his return reported the successful results of his mission, and was accompanied by a Khivan ambassador bearing letters from the Khan full of declarations of friendship. Major Todd therefore despatched Captain Abbott to Khiva in order to improve the friendly relations which had been entered upon, and he was also instructed to persuade the Khan to liberate the Russian prisoners, in order that Russia might have no further excuse for invading the Khanate. Abbott obtained permission for a Russian official to visit Khiva and take away any Russian captives who wished to return; and he then set out for the Caspian, but was robbed and cruelly treated on the way, and only reached Astrakhan with difficulty. Meanwhile Major Todd heard that Abbott was dead, and he therefore sent Lieutenant Shakespeare to complete the work which Abbott had been sent to perform. Shakespeare obtained the release of all the Russian prisoners, to the number of 416, and in the summer of 1840 accompanied them across the Steppe to the Caspian, and handed them over to the Commandant of the Russian fort of Novo Alexandrovsk, when the Russians, in their turn, released many Khivan subjects whom they had previously captured and detained as hostages.

CHAPTER V

1840—1845

TROUBLES IN AFGHANISTAN

Dost Mahommed's attempt to regain his throne—Outbreak in Kabul, and murder of Sir Alexander Burnes and Sir William Macnaghten—Fate of General Elphinstone's army—The only survivor of the army—Disaster to Colonel Palmer and his troops—Critical situation in Afghanistan—Stoddart's and Conolly's missions to Khiva and Bokhara—Failure of Russian mission to Khiva—Russian mission to Bokhara—Russian occupation of Ashurada.

IF events in Afghanistan had turned out differently, there is no doubt that the Russian Government would have found some fresh pretext for pushing forward. But even while Shakespeare was marching across the desert toward the Caspian with his little band of liberated slaves, events were occurring in Shah Shuja's dominions which were shortly to culminate in an appalling disaster to the British arms, which completely dwarfed the failure of Perovski, and rendered it quite unnecessary for Russia to think of invading Khiva for the purpose of resisting British advances into Central Asia. From the very moment that Shuja-ul-Mulk, supported by a British army, had been reseated on the Afghan throne, it was evident that he had no hold over his subjects, and that he would be unable to maintain his position once the British troops were withdrawn. His installation on the plains of Kandahar, when only about a hundred Afghans assembled to do honour to their sovereign, should have plainly warned the British authorities that their policy was inherently weak and ill-advised. But Mr. Macnaghten, the British envoy, shut his eyes to facts which were patent throughout the army, and continued in his firm faith in the popularity of the Suddozai Shah. He believed that there would be no further trouble in Afghanistan, and fixed his attention on affairs far beyond the frontiers of the kingdom of Kabul. He urged that Herat should be attacked and annexed to the dominions of Shuja-ul-Mulk, and even considered the advisability of despatching a force to Balkh and far distant Bokhara. He had a firm belief in the success of the British policy, and believed that 'a beautiful game' could be played by pushing the British armies far beyond the position they then occupied. But while he was thus engaged in the contemplation of grand operations which were to place 'the safety of British interests on a firm and solid basis,' and 'effectually frustrate the designs of Russia,' everything was going wrong in the dominions of the effete Suddozai king. The British were standing on a mine which was shortly to explode with terrible results.

When Dost Mahommed fled from Argandeh in August 1839, he took refuge in Bokhara, but was there ill-treated by the Amir Nasrullah Khan. He therefore fled to Shahr-i-Sebz, and from thence went to Khulm, where he was well received by the Wali, who assisted him to raise an army for the purpose of recovering his throne. By the autumn of 1840 he was in a position to take the field, and advanced to Heibak, a fort about 150 miles north of Bamian, which latter place was then occupied by a small British detachment. In September he forced the British to evacuate the advanced posts of Saighan and Bajgah, but reinforcements under Brigadier-General Dennie were hurried forward from Kabul to Bamian, and on September 18 he, with his small force of about 1,500 men and two guns, inflicted a severe defeat on the Amir's army, which was said to be 40,000 strong. Dennie then advanced to Saighan, destroyed that place, and forced the Wali of Khulm to make terms. Dost Mahommed meanwhile fled to the Nijrao valley, in the Kohistan north of Kabul, where Brigadier-General Sale had been sent with a column, to chastise some chiefs who refused to acknowledge Shah Shuja.

After several skirmishes, Sale on November 2 approached Parwan, a small village on the southern slopes of the Hindu Kush. He there saw the enemy evacuating the village and neighbouring forts, and flying to the hills; and the British cavalry was pushed forward in pursuit. But when they had advanced about a mile in advance of the column, Dost Mahommed, at the head of 200 Afghan horsemen, rode forward and prepared to meet his assailants. Uncovering his head, he called upon his adherents to follow him in the name of God and the Prophet, or he would be a lost man; and then, placing himself at the head of his small band of followers, he rode forward to drive the infidels from the field, or perish in the attempt. Captain Fraser formed the Light Cavalry into line and sounded the charge; the British officers rode steadily forward, believing that their men were following; but the native sowars held back, and then fled in confusion before the Afghan horsemen. Of the five British officers who rode in the charge, three—Lieutenants Broadfoot and Crispin, and Dr. Lord—were cut to pieces, while the other two, Fraser and Ponsonby, were severely wounded.

But Dost Mahommed's triumph did not last long. The British infantry, coming up, quickly recovered the lost ground and, driving the Afghans away from the hills overlooking the Parwan Pass, forced them to retreat towards the Panjshir Valley. Dost Mahommed had made one last gallant attempt to save his cause, and had failed. He now clearly saw that it was hopeless to continue the struggle against the British, and on the next day he rode into Kabul, there surrendered to Sir William Macnaghten, and within ten days was on his way to India under a strong escort.

During the next twelve months there were many signs that the affairs in Afghanistan were by no means satisfactorily settled. Early in 1841 a serious rising of the Duranis took place in the Zemindewar to the north-west of Kandahar; Yar Mahommed, the Vizier of Herat, was doing his utmost to destroy British influence, and to stir up the Duranis against the unbelievers; British troops were twice repulsed by the Khakars of Sibi in an attack on the village of Kojak; and a British column was busily employed in coercing refractory tribes in the neighbourhood of Jalalabad. During the summer troubles arose at Kalat-i-Ghilzai, fresh disturbances broke out in the Zemindewar, and a trifling outbreak in the Kohistan had also to be suppressed. In October Brigadier-General Sale started for India with his brigade, and had some sharp fighting in the passes. Before the end of that month the Kohistanis were again in open revolt, and news was received that Dost Mahommed's son, Mahommed Akbar Khan, had left his asylum at Bokhara and reached Bamian.

At last the storm broke. On November 2 a tumult arose in the city of Kabul. The mob, acting in accordance with a preconcerted plan, attacked the house of Sir Alexander Burnes, murdered him, his brother, and Lieutenant William Broadfoot of the Engineers, and then looted the Treasury. It is needless to repeat the oft-told tale of the follies which were then committed; of the hesitation and vacillation of the infirm General in chief command, and of the impracticable temper and perversity of his second in command. Mistake followed mistake, and the army rapidly became so demoralised, that when Sir William Macnaghten was traitorously murdered on December 23, 1841, by Mahommed Akbar Khan, during a conference held within 400 yards of the British cantonments, no attempt was made to rescue him or to avenge the deed; his body was permitted to remain on the plain in full view of the force, and to be carried thence by the Afghans, and paraded about the streets and bazaars of the city.

After Macnaghten's death, political matters were entrusted to Major Eldred Pottinger, the gallant defender of Herat, and he appealed to the military chiefs to continue the struggle and to occupy the Bala Hissar, which, with a determined garrison under competent leaders, might have been defended until reinforcements arrived from India. But his exhortations were unheeded, and on January 6, 1842, the British army, commanded by General Elphinstone, commenced its retreat from Kabul in accordance with the terms of a treaty of capitulation, which had been ratified five days previously. What followed is well known. Out of an army which numbered 4,500 fighting men and 12,000 camp followers, one solitary Englishman alone succeeded in reaching Jalalabad, where Sale had entrenched himself on hearing of the disasters in Kabul.

'On January 13, when the garrison were busy on the works, toiling with axe and shovel, with their arms piled and their accoutrements laid out close at hand, a sentry on the ramparts, looking out towards the Kabul road, saw a solitary white-faced horseman struggling on towards the fort. The word was passed, the tidings spread. Presently the ramparts were lined with officers, looking out with throbbing hearts through unsteady telescopes, or with straining eyes tracing the road.

Slowly and painfully, as though horse and rider both were in an extremity of mortal weakness, the solitary mounted man came reeling, tottering on. They saw that he was an Englishman, on a wretched, weary pony; clinging as one sick or wounded to its neck, he sat, or rather leant forward; and there were those who, as they watched his progress, thought that he could never reach unaided the walls of Jalalabad. A shudder ran through the garrison. That solitary horseman looked like the messenger of death. Few doubted that he was the bearer of intelligence that would fill their souls with horror and dismay. Their worst forebodings seemed confirmed. There was the one man who was to tell the story of the massacre of a great army. A party of cavalry were sent out to succour him; they brought him in, wounded, exhausted, half-dead. The messenger was Dr. Brydon, and he now reported his belief that he was the sole surviver of an army of some sixteen thousand men.'[1]

After this fearful disaster to the Kabul force, only Ghazni, Jalalabad, Kalat-i-Ghilzai, and Kandahar remained in the hands of the British. Ghazni was, however, lost shortly afterwards. Towards the end of November, 1841, the enemy appeared in force before the place, but withdrew on hearing of the advance of a brigade under Maclaren from Kandahar *en route* for Kabul. But Maclaren only went two marches north of Kalat-i-Ghilzai and

[1] *History of the War in Afghanistan*, by John William Kaye, F.R.S. Vol. ii., pp. 358 and 359.

then retraced his steps, when the Afghans collected again round Ghazni and completely invested the place. Colonel Palmer, the commandant, had omitted to expel the inhabitants from the city, and they made a passage under the walls by which the besiegers entered the town on December 16. The garrison then retreated to the citadel, and there held out for several weeks. But, on March 6, Palmer and his troops opened the gates and marched out of the citadel, trusting to the Afghan promise of safe conduct to Peshawar. It is needless to state that this promise was not kept. On the following day the troops were suddenly attacked while they were cooking their dinners, and after three days of hard fighting those who survived the slaughter were carried off into an apparently hopeless captivity.

Thus, in the spring of 1842, the British position in Afghanistan appeared to be well-nigh hopeless. Incompetence and vacillation on the part of the military commanders had brought about a condition of affairs such as a British army had never before experienced. Kandahar, Kalat-i-Ghilzai, and Jalalabad alone remained in British hands, and the defence of the two latter places were the only bright spots during this terrible crisis.

While fresh armies were being collected and hurried forward to avenge the disasters which had occurred in Afghanistan, a dark tragedy was being enacted far north of the Hindu Kush. Shortly after the close of the siege of Herat, Mr. M'Neill sent Colonel Stoddart on a mission to Bokhara to counteract the machinations of the Russians, who were known to be intriguing in that state; and to remove a possible excuse for Russian interference by obtaining the liberation of such Russian subjects as were in slavery there. In 1820 a Russian embassy had been sent to Bokhara under M. Negri. In 1834 another mission was sent under M. Demaison, who adopted the disguise of a Tartar Mullah. In 1835 Lieutenant Vitkievitch—who afterwards appeared in Kabul—visited the Khanate disguised as a Kirghiz-Kazak; and since that time several Bokharan envoys were sent to Russia, their visits being returned by the despatch of Russian agents. It was, therefore, time that England took steps to prevent the Amir Nasrullah from falling completely under Russian influence. Stoddart arrived in Bokhara at the close of the year 1838, but on his arrival there he foolishly refused to conform to the customs and etiquette of the Bokharan Court, and within three days of his arrival he found himself a prisoner. He was suddenly seized in the minister's house, thrown to the ground, bound with cords, and shortly afterwards cast into a filthy and noisome pit, where he remained with criminals for his companions, 'covered with vermin and surrounded by reptiles, in killing which they were constantly occupied.' At the end of two months he was released from this fearful dungeon and removed to the house of the chief of the Bokharan police, but two days later he was informed that he would be put to death unless he consented to become a Mahommedan. Exhausted in body and mind by the terrible ordeal he had passed through, he reluctantly consented to conform to the rites of the Mahommedan faith—an act which he bitterly repented of throughout the remainder of his miserable existence. From that time he was treated with less brutality, as the Amir had heard of the British successes in Afghanistan, knew that British troops had advanced across the Hindu Kush to Bamian and Saighan, and feared that a force would be sent across the Oxus to avenge his cruel treatment of the British ambassador.

In September, 1840, Captain Arthur Conolly was sent on a similar mission to Khiva and Khokand. He first went to Khiva, where he was well received, and thence to Khokand, which state was then at war with Bokhara, Madali Khan, the ruler of Khokand, having invaded Bokharan territory and captured the strong fortress of Ura Tepé. Nasrullah believed that Conolly had advised this movement, and he therefore determined to get the British officer into his power. He accordingly invited him to visit his Court, and prevailed upon Stoddart to use his influence to persuade him to do so. Conolly, in spite of the advice of the Khan of Khokand, accepted the invitation and arrived in Bokhara in November, 1841.

For a short space all went well; but soon after his arrival news reached Bokhara that the Afghans were in revolt against Shah Shuja-ul-Mulk, that Burnes had been murdered, and that the British army had been defeated, and were closely besieged in their cantonments outside Kabul. This was Nasrullah's opportunity. The British envoy who, according to his belief, had incited the Khokandians to invade his dominions, and the other Feringhi who had defied him and insulted his minister, were both in his hands, and he could now punish them as he willed without fear of consequences. Stoddart and Conolly were both seized and imprisoned in the house of the Topshi-Bashi, or chief of the artillery, in Bokhara, where they remained for more than six months in a condition of the most abject and heart-rending misery. The rain leaked freely through the mud-roof of the miserable hut in which they were confined; the very clothes they wore rotted from off their bodies, and they suffered indescribable torments from the attacks of vermin, while ague and fever sapped their strength and reduced them to the condition of mere living skeletons.

But the end came at last. The Bokharan Amir, after some delay, had collected an army for the invasion of Khokand, and after a short but successful campaign, returned to his capital in triumph. Intoxicated with his success, the cruel tyrant remembered his Feringhi captives, and gave orders for them to be put to death. On June 24, 1842, the two Englishmen were taken out of their prison and conducted to a small courtyard close at hand, where Stoddart was first put to death in the presence of an assembled crowd of natives. Conolly was then offered his life on the condition that he adopted the Mahommedan faith; but he scornfully rejected the proposal, saying:—'Stoddart and Yusuf, my servant, turned Mahommedans, and yet you have killed them; I have no confidence in your promises; I will not turn from my faith; I am prepared to die; finish your work.' The tragedy was finished. Arthur Conolly was speedily put to death; and thus died two brave British officers who, taking their lives in their hands, went cheerfully into unknown lands and there laid down their lives in their endeavours to add to the glory of their dearly-loved country, and to thwart the designs of England's enemies.

While Stoddart and Conolly were in Central Asia, Russia was not idle. As the Khan of Khiva had released the Russian prisoners and issued a proclamation abolishing the trade in Russian slaves, the Czar's Government decided to reopen negotiations with him, and Captain Nikiforof was therefore sent on a mission to Khiva in 1841, accompanied by an escort of twelve Cossacks. On his arrival he behaved in much the same way as Stoddart had done at Bokhara, refused to yield to the demands of Khivan etiquette, treated the Khan's officials in a contemptuous manner, and generally assumed a bold and defiant demeanour. Fortunately for the Russian envoy, Allah Kul was not an inhuman monster of the type of Nasrullah of Bokhara; the Khivan Khan, moreover, had not forgotten the alarm occasioned by Perovski's advance; and the British officers, Abbott and Shakespeare, had been advising him to abstain from any act which might give Russia an excuse for a fresh attack on the

Khanate. Nikiforof, therefore, experienced no unpleasant results from his overbearing conduct. His mission, however, was completely unsuccessful, for he was unable to secure any trade concessions, and the Khan declined to enter into any treaty.

In the following year another Russian agent, named Colonel Danilefsky, was sent to Khiva. During his stay in the Khanate, Allah Kul Khan died, and Danilefsky succeeded in persuading his son and successor, Rahim Kul, to sign a treaty engaging not to undertake hostile acts against Russia or to permit robbery or piracy.

An important embassy was also sent to the Court of Nasrullah Khan of Bokhara. In 1840 the Amir began to fear that his dominions would be invaded by a British column from Kabul, and he therefore sent an influential envoy named Mukin-Beg to St. Petersburg, with letters and presents for the Czar, besides gifts for various other Russian authorities. The Russian Government seized this opportunity, and despatched a mission under Colonel Butenelf, charged with the collection of 'positive and reliable information concerning the Khanate of Bokhara and neighbouring countries, and with the arrangement of terms for regulating the mutual relations between Bokhara and Russia.' In the instructions which he received from the Russian Minister of Foreign Affairs, he was also directed to observe the effect produced on Bokhara by the recent events in Afghanistan, as the acquisition of this information would enable him 'to suggest the best means for strengthening the political influence of Russia and for developing Russian trade in this part of Asia.'

Buteneff, accompanied by Captain Bogoslovski, M. Lehmann, M. Khanikoff, and a small staff of miners and topographers, left Orenburg in May, 1841, and reached Bokhara on August 17, having been escorted as far as the Syr Daria by a detachment of 400 Ural Cossacks. Shortly before he crossed the Russian frontier, Lord Palmerston had directed the British ambassadors at St. Petersburg and Constantinople to enlist the sympathy of the Russian and Turkish Governments in the cause of the captives in Bokhara, and both the Sultan and Czar did what they could to obtain the release of Stoddart and Conolly.

When the officers of the Russian mission reached Bokhara, they received a very favourable reception, and Buteneff lost no time in exerting his influence for the purpose of obtaining Stoddart's release.[1] As a result of his friendly efforts, Stoddart was permitted to live in the house occupied by the Russian mission, where he received great kindness from the Russian officers; and the Amir even promised to permit him to leave the country. But Stoddart had been sent on his mission to Bokhara by the British Government, and he considered it to be his duty to remain until recalled, and thus the opportunity of escape was lost. Conolly soon afterwards arrived; news of the British disasters reached Bokhara, and the two British officers were closely confined until their death.

[1] Conolly had not then arrived in Bokhara.

The British defeat in Afghanistan had also a very marked effect on the Amir's behaviour towards the Russian embassy. So long as the British armies remained at Kabul and Bamian, he was afraid that an advance would be made against his dominions, and he therefore was anxious to be on friendly terms with the Russians; and thus for the first few months of their stay in the country the Russian mission was treated well, and the members of the embassy were permitted to visit the eastern and less known portion of the Khanate. But as soon as the British evacuated Kabul, and all danger of invasion from the south was removed, Nasrullah began to show his disinclination to have any dealings with the infidel—whether Russian or English—and from this time the position of the Russians became daily more and more difficult. Buteneff, however, remained in hopes of being able to effect the release of Stoddart and Conolly, and of the many Russians who were detained in slavery; and he also tried hard to obtain the Amir's signature to a treaty with Russia. But Nasrullah clearly showed that he no longer wished to come to any arrangement; the Envoy's requests were ignored; and the members of the mission were in danger of sharing the fate which had overtaken the British ambassadors. Nothing remained but to quit the inhospitable and treacherous Court. On the night of April 19, 1842, Buteneff and his companions started on their way back to Russia, the negotiations having been completely unsuccessful. But great acquisitions to science were made during their eight months' sojourn in the country, and—what was of more advantage to Russia—extensive surveys of the Khanate had been made by Khanikoff and the topographers, which proved of much assistance when the Russians made their great advance a quarter of a century later.

While these events were occurring in Afghanistan and the Khanates of Central Asia, Russia did not remain inactive in Persia. By the Treaty of Gulistan, and again by the Treaty of Turkomanchai, Persia had renounced her right of maintaining war vessels on the Caspian, and thus was unable to check the piracy of the Turkomans, who infested the shores of the sea between Krasnovodsk and the Gulf of Astrabad, and carried off hundreds of Persian subjects into slavery. As the Shah was thus unable to repress the piratical Turkomans, he in 1836 pointed out to the Russian Government the difficulties of the situation, and foolishly applied for their assistance. The Czar's Government were not slow to comply with the request, and in 1837 and 1838, vessels were sent from the Russian naval station at the island of Sari, to cruise off the south-eastern shores of the Caspian Sea, while at the same time the island of Ashurada (at the mouth of the Gulf of Astrabad) was quietly occupied. This step alarmed the Persians, and a request was made that the Russian naval commander should either be placed under the orders of the Governor of Astrabad, or failing this, that naval aid might be withheld. The Russians, however, had no intention of withdrawing, as they had managed to get hold of an excellent and long-coveted *point d'appui*, from which they could threaten Astrabad and Khorassan.

This first landing on the island attracted but little attention, and was apparently merely a temporary occupation; but in 1841 Ashurada was permanently taken possession of, for the ostensible purpose of protecting Persian trade against the Turkoman pirates. Sir John M'Neill reported the matter to the British Government in 1842; and in 1849, as Persia was unable to induce the Russians to evacuate the island and had petitioned England for aid, Lord Aberdeen applied to Russia to withdraw. But they had meanwhile been strengthening their position; extensive buildings had been erected; and negotiations were opened from thence with the Turkomans. The English representation, therefore, had no effect, and Ashurada has since remained in Russian hands.

This seizure was an act for which no possible excuse can be found. Ashurada was as much a portion of Persia as Hayling Island is of England; its permanent occupation by Russia was therefore an unprovoked violation of the Shah's dominions, which admitted of no justification. But the Czar's Government knew that the thoughts of everyone in England were then turned towards Afghanistan, where the avenging armies were moving forward to Kabul to wipe out the disgrace which had sullied the British reputation; and that it was not likely that much attention would be given to the occupation by Russia of a small sandy islet in the

Caspian. Persia, unaided, could do nothing more than expostulate, and thus Russia was able to quietly take up a position from whence she can, when desirable, move forward to the mainland, and gain possession of the narrow neck of fertile country which connects the province of Khorassan with the remainder of Northern Persia, and which thus forms one of the most valuable strategical positions in Southern Asia.

CHAPTER VI

1846–1858

RUSSIAN ADVANCE ACROSS THE KIRGHIZ STEPPES

Russian Frontier-line at the beginning of the Nineteenth Century—Operations in the Sea of Aral and Construction of Fort Raim—Subjection of the Southern Kirghiz to Russia—Founding of Kopal—Collisions between Russians and Khivans—The Aral Sea Flotilla—Khokandian attacks on the Russians—Siege of Ak-Mechet and its capture by the Russians—Khokandian Expeditions for retaking Ak-Mechet—Further Russian Aggression across the Ili—The Crimean War—Two Russian Plans for the Invasion of India—Herat again besieged by Persia—British Force despatched against the Shah—Intrigues and Insurrection of Izzet Kutebar—Ignatieff's Missions to Khiva and Bokhara—Further Russian Explorations of Central Asia—Khanikoff's Mission.

At the commencement of the present century, the Russian frontier from the Caspian to Eastern Siberia was defended by a continuous line of fortified posts, which protected the Russian settlements from the attacks of the wild tribes which inhabited the Steppes of Central Asia. This frontier line commenced at Guriev, at the mouth of the River Ural, and followed the left bank of that river as far as the town of Orsk; from thence it ran to Troitska, and then across the Ishim Steppe, past Petro-Paulovsk to Omsk on the Irtish; the line then followed the left bank of that river to Semipalatinsk and Buktarminsk on the borders of

China. But, although this frontier was a good one for defensive purposes, being on the northern extremity of vast, barren, and sparsely populated Steppes, the Russians had no intention of treating it as a permanent line beyond which they should not advance.

It has already been shown how they endeavoured on more than one occasion to get a footing on the great River Oxus, the main waterway into the heart of Central Asia, and how their attempts had failed. The disastrous failure of Perovski's expedition, together with the lessons which had been derived from the previous attacks on Khiva, taught the Russians that the time was not yet ripe for the conquest of that Khanate, and that they could not yet acquire control over the navigation of the Oxus.

But some distance to the north of that river there is another great stream, the Syr Daria, or Jaxartes, which rising in the Thian Shan Range, appeared to offer a line of advance almost as favourable for their purpose; and the Russians therefore began to turn their attention in that direction.

Even before the failure of Perovski's expedition they had determined to examine this line of advance, and in 1837 the Asiatic Committee decided to despatch a so-called scientific mission to the north-eastern shores of the Sea of Aral, and up the Syr Daria. But this mission was indefinitely postponed on account of the serious events which were occurring in Persia and Afghanistan, followed by Perovski's abortive attempt to reach Khiva. Then troubles broke out among the still discontented Kirghiz, and a serious rebellion of these turbulent subjects had to be suppressed; so that it was not till 1846 that steps could be taken to carry out the recommendation of the Committee. In that year, however, General Obrucheff, who was Governor-General of Orenburg, obtained permission to occupy a point on the shores of the Sea of Aral; and for this purpose Captain Leo von Schultz was despatched to survey the mouth of the Syr Daria, and to select a suitable site for a fort. As a result of his investigations a fort, which became known as Fort Raim or Fort Aralsk, was constructed in 1847 at the mouth of the river, while at the same time three other forts were built, as links in the chain connecting the old Orenburg line with the Syr Daria. These intermediate posts were Kurabutakski and Uralski on the River Irghiz, and Orenburgskoi on the River Turgai.

While the Russians were gradually pushing forward from Orenburg, in order to gain a footing on the Syr Daria, they were also throwing forward their left flank in the direction of Little Bokhara or Kashgar. Thus, after the lapse of more than a century, they commenced a series of movements precisely similar to those which had been initiated by Peter the Great. Peter, at the commencement of the eighteenth century, had invaded Persia, attacked Khiva, and sent an expedition to gain possession of the gold mines of Little Bokhara; while his successors in the present century also invaded Persia on two occasions, tried to conquer Khiva, and pushed forward towards Kashgar.

As has already been mentioned, the town of Omsk was founded in 1716 by Buckholtz on his retreat from Lake Yamyshef. Two years later the first fortress was built at Semipalatinsk, and in 1720 Ust-Kamenogorsk was founded by Likhareff on his retirement from Zaisan Nor. The Orenburg and Irtish forts were connected in 1752 by the New Siberian line of posts across the Ishim Steppe, and in 1760 the Buktarminsk Fort was erected as an advanced post against possible attacks from the Chinese. At this time the country round the headwaters of the Irtish was populated by the Kalmuks, but in 1758, the Chinese having conquered Dzungaria, set to work, and indiscriminately massacred the Kalmuk inhabitants of the province. The Kirghiz-Kazaks of the Middle Horde then hastened to occupy the vacant pastures, and thus became the neighbours of the Russians. These people, however, coquetted with both the Chinese and the Russians, and at first gave some trouble, but in 1760 their Khan, Sultan Abdul Faiz, sent an ambassador to St. Petersburg asking the Czar to take him under his protection, and promising to protect Russian caravans trading with the states of Central Asia. This request was granted, and thus all the Kirghiz-Kazaks between the Irtish and Orenburg became the nominal subjects of the White Czar. Those to the south of the Irtish, however, behaved in exactly the same way as their kinsmen to the west had done. Caravans were plundered and the

Steppes were the scenes of continual disorder and violence. At the commencement of the present century the Russian authorities began to adopt measures for enforcing order among these unruly subjects. Each caravan proceeding southwards was escorted by a small detachment of Cossacks, and between 1808 and 1819 a considerable force was employed under General Glasenap, for the purpose of completely subduing the marauders. These operations were crowned with success, and the Kirghiz on the Irtish Steppes were so reduced to subjection that solitary travellers could traverse the country in complete safety.

But the Russians were determined to advance southwards, towards the unknown lands from whence continual reports were received of the great stores of mineral wealth which lay hidden in the mysterious regions to which but few Europeans had yet penetrated. The Kirghiz were again to be made the excuse for aggression, and once again were Peter's words to be verified:—'The Kirghiz are a roaming and fickle people, yet their Steppe is the key and gate of all the lands and countries of Asia.' In 1827 Cossacks were stationed at Kokchetaf and Karkaraly; in 1831 the town of Sergiopol was founded; and in the following year Akmolinsk and Baian-Aul were made the headquarters of sub-districts. At this time, a portion of the Great Horde of Kirghiz tendered their submission, and the relations of the Russians with their Kirghiz subjects became much more satisfactory. But still the advance was continued.

Scientific officers and topographers were sent forward to make surveys and to report on the mineral resources of the countries visited; and in 1846, the town of Kopal was founded by Prince Gortchakoff, the Governor-General of Western Siberia, on a fertile plateau at the base of the Ala-Tau range.

Such was the condition of affairs at the eastern end of the Orenburg-Siberian line when Fort Raim was built at the mouth of the Syr Daria. The Russians, advancing beyond their line of fortified posts, had thrown forward their right and left flanks — ostensibly for the subjugation of the Kirghiz, but really in the deliberate pursuit of a well-matured scheme of aggression. The extremities of these two arms which were thus thrown forward were far in advance of the old fortified line, and were separated from each other by many hundreds of miles of barren Steppes and unexplored mountain ranges. The position for a time was a weak one; but the Russians soon began to consider the best means of closing the long undefended gap between Fort Raim and Kopal. With this object it was considered necessary that the whole of the Steppes between the two advanced flanks should be annexed, and that a new line of fortified posts should be constructed along the southern limits of the territory so appropriated.

The Russian Government professed to believe that by doing this their Kirghiz subjects would be brought under proper control, and protected from the attacks of the Khivans and Khokandians; but they ignored the fact that by abandoning their old defensive line, and taking up a new position at the southern edge of the Steppe, they ran the risk of collisions with the Khivans and Khokandians, which would necessarily prove far more troublesome than the worst raids of the Kirghiz, and inevitably involve Russia in constant warfare with the Central Asian Khanates.

The Khokandians and Khivans naturally considered the Russian occupation of the mouth of the Syr Daria to be an unwarranted act of aggression. The former had, early in the century (about 1817), constructed the forts of Yani-Kurgan, Julek, Ak-Mechet, Kumysh-Kurgan, Chim-Kurgan, Kosh-Kurgan, and others, and had since that time regularly levied taxes on the Kirghiz who settled on the banks of the river; and in 1830, the Khivans, who considered that their authority extended throughout the Kizil Kum desert to the south of the Syr Daria, had also erected several forts on the left bank of the Kuvan Daria (a branch of the Syr).

But the Khokandians were at this time engaged in a bitter civil war, and could therefore offer but slight opposition to the Russians; while the Khivans could do little or nothing at such a distance from their capital. During 1847 and 1848, however, the Khivans made repeated inroads into the country round Fort Raim, and there were frequent collisions between them and the Russian detachments which were sent against them. The Russians were almost invariably successful in these encounters, and eventually the Khivans were obliged to give up the struggle, and contented themselves with merely demanding the evacuation of the fort.

When the Russians built the Raim fort, they at the same time commenced the formation of the Aral Sea flotilla. In 1847 two sailing vessels were built at Orenburg. One of these, the *Nikolai*, was a war vessel intended for surveying purposes; while the other, the *Mikhail*, was a merchant ship for establishing fisheries. These vessels were transported in pieces to Fort Raim and were there put together and launched. The *Nikolai* at once put to sea, but owing to the lateness of the season could do little in the way of surveying. However, in the spring of 1848 the whole of the northern coast of the Aral Sea was surveyed, and another and larger war-vessel, the *Constantine*, having meanwhile been sent from Orenburg, Lieutenant Butakoff commenced in the following autumn to make a thorough survey of the whole of the Sea of Aral—a work which was satisfactorily completed in two years.

In 1850 two steamers were ordered from the Motala Ironworks in Sweden, for the navigation of the Syr Daria. These steamers, the 'Perovski' and the 'Obrucheff,' reached Fort Aralsk in November, 1852, and were there put together, being ready for work by the end of the following May.

At this time the Governor of Ak-Mechet was a man named Yakoob Beg, who had gradually been making a name for himself in the troubled Khanate of Khokand, and who some years later, as the Atalyk Ghazi of Kashgar, occupied a prominent position in Eastern politics, and became known as the most powerful sovereign in Central Asia. In 1845 he was Chamberlain to the newly-appointed Khan Khudayar; shortly after he was made a 'Pansad Bashi,' or commander of 500 men; in 1847 he married a Kipchak lady of Julek—a Khokandian post some miles east of Ak-Mechet—and towards the close of that year he was raised to the rank of 'Kush-Begi,' and entrusted with the command of Ak-Mechet and the surrounding Khokandian district on the banks of the Lower Syr Daria.

Yakoob Beg appears to have been imbued with strong feelings of hatred towards the Russians, and as soon as he arrived at Ak-Mechet he began to adopt measures for the defence of his district. The establishment of the Russians at Fort Raim constituted a standing menace to the Khokandian posts higher up the river; and Yakoob anxiously watched the preparations which were being made for a fresh advance. The Khokandians did not realise that their best policy was to abstain from attacking the Russians, and thus to have given them no excuse for further encroachments. They had no idea of the strength of the great Power which had now become their neighbour. They only knew that the troops of the White Czar had advanced across the wild Kirghiz Steppes, and had without provocation seized upon a portion of Khokandian territory, where they had established themselves, and were making preparations for a further advance against the other Khokandian forts along the banks of the river. Yakoob believed that unless the Russians were driven out of Fort Raim his district would inevitably be lost to Khokand, and he therefore organised a series of raids against the fort and the adjoining Russian settlements. These attacks, however, gave the Russians an excellent excuse for a further advance; and in 1851, Major Engmann, the Commandant of Fort Aralsk, attacked a party of Khokandians who had advanced to the neighbourhood of the fort, and pursuing them along the banks of the river, captured their fort Kosh-Kurgan.

But the Russian preparations for a general advance were not then complete, and until the following year no decisive measures could be taken to drive the Khokandians from their strongholds higher up the river.

In April, 1852, however, a surveying party was despatched up the Syr Daria, but on reaching Ak-Mechet was very naturally stopped and turned back. This act was denounced as a piece of intolerable interference, and General Perovski, the Governor-General of the Orenburg district, resolved to despatch a strong force to curb the insolence of the Khokandians, and to reduce their chief stronghold, Ak-Mechet. Accordingly, on July 3, 1852, a detachment left Fort Aralsk, consisting of 12 officers and 420 men, with 2 guns, and accompanied by 36 irregulars.

This small column was placed under the command of Colonel Blaramberg, who received the following orders :—

(1) To survey the right bank of the Syr Daria as far as Ak-Mechet.

(2) In the event of an encounter with the Khokandians, *or in case they should make any uncalled-for demands*, to attack them immediately.

(3) Without touching at any fortifications lying nearer to Aralsk, to proceed direct to Ak-Mechet, and there act as circumstances might require. If Ak-Mechet lies within Russian limits, to endeavour to raze it ; but, *under all circumstances, to notify to the Khokandians that the fort must not remain on its actual site.*

Warned of the enemy's approach, the Khokandians destroyed the dam which diverted the waters of the Syr into Lake Ber Kazan, and thus flooded the adjacent country. But the Russians, in spite of this obstacle, managed to safely cross five branches of the river, and eventually arrived before the fortress on July 19. Here Blaramberg found that the capture of the place was not such an easy task as had been expected. He found that the defences consisted of an outer wall, within which there was a strong citadel, the ramparts of which were composed of hard clay, about 25 feet high and 10 feet thick. His force was unprovided with scaling ladders, the whole country was inundated, and a considerable rise in the water was by no means improbable. Moreover, he heard that a strong Khokandian reinforcement was daily expected. Under these circumstances he decided to attack the outer portion of the fortress, and to destroy all that lay between the exterior walls and the citadel; and he therefore commenced a preliminary bombardment of the place on the night of July 19. The Khokandians at once returned the fire, but by daylight on the 20th their guns had been dismounted, and the outer gate of the fortress had been destroyed.

Blaramberg then formed his small force into two columns, and assaulted the place; while one party forced an entrance through the broken gateway, the other scaled the wall by the aid of pickaxes and hatchets. In less than ten minutes the Russians obtained complete possession of the whole space between the outer walls and citadel, and advanced to the foot of the ramparts of the keep. But here their progress was stopped; it was impossible to make any impression on the massive walls, and without scaling ladders the place could not be stormed. The Russian Commander therefore decided to abandon the attempt, and to retire to Fort Aralsk. Before retiring he, however, set fire to all the buildings outside the citadel, and completely destroyed everything of value. The conflagration lasted the whole night, during which many of the garrison who endeavoured to save their property were killed.

On July 21 the retreat commenced, and on the way back to Fort Aralsk, Colonel Blaramberg destroyed the small forts of Kumysh-Kurgan, Chim-Kurgan, and Kosh-Kurgan.

Thus the first serious advance which the

Russians made along the Syr Daria was repulsed; but Perovski determined to renew the attack on Ak-Mechet as soon as possible, and to employ such a formidable force as would render success certain. Preparations were accordingly pushed forward, every possible precaution being taken to insure the success of the undertaking; and in the spring of 1853 a force of 2,168 men, with 12 guns, left Orenburg under the command of the Governor-General of the district in person. The force marched in two columns and concentrated at Aralsk.

Although one of the reasons for the Russian advance along the Syr is stated to have been for the purpose of protecting the Kirghiz from the oppressions of the Khokandians, yet Perovski appears to have been afraid that these Russian *protégés* would, instead of affording assistance to their deliverers, attack the convoys; and he therefore gave orders to the Sultan rulers to remove their followers into the Steppe, and prohibited them from encamping during the summer near to the road leading from Orenburg to Aralsk. This order was carried out; but the Kirghiz openly displayed their unfriendliness by refusing to supply camels for the expedition.

Towards the end of June the force detailed for the attack on Ak-Mechet marched out of Aralsk. It consisted of 1,500 infantry, 750 cavalry, and 10 guns, and was accompanied by 780 waggons and 1,150 camels, besides numerous baggage-horses and oxen.

Meanwhile the Khokandians had not been idle. As they fully expected that the Russians would renew the attack on their stronghold, they had set to work to improve its defences. The *débris* of the old outer fortification and buildings was removed, and the citadel was greatly strengthened. The plan of the place had been improved, the walls made thicker, and the gates carefully screened by outworks. Three guns were mounted on the ramparts, and lumps of sun-dried clay, called 'kisiak,' were prepared in readiness to hurl down at the assailants.

As soon as Perovski arrived before the fort he sent a messenger under a flag of truce demanding its immediate surrender; but when this man arrived within gun-shot, the Khokandians opened fire on him, and he was obliged to return.

On July 21 the bombardment commenced, but its effect was found to be very unsatisfactory, and Perovski therefore determined to advance by means of common saps, and to form a breach by mining. Systematic approaches were accordingly started on July 22 and were steadily pushed forward; but the slowness of this form of attack caused considerable discontent among the troops, who had expected that the fort would be taken by storm immediately after their arrival.

On July 25 a Khokandian prisoner was sent to the fort with the following summons to surrender:—

'From the Governor-General of Orenburg to the Commander of the Fortress of Ak-Mechet.

'By order of my Sovereign, the Emperor of All

the Russias, I have come to take Ak-Mechet, erected by the Khokandians on Russian territory for the purpose of oppressing the Kirghiz subjects of His Imperial Majesty.

'Ak-Mechet is already taken, although you are inside it, and you cannot fail to perceive that without losing any of my men, I am in a position to destroy every one of you.

'The Russians have come hither, not for a day, nor yet for a year, but for ever; they will not retire.

'If you wish to live, ask for mercy; should you prefer to die in Ak-Mechet you can do so; I am not pressed for time, and do not intend to hurry you. I here repeat that I do not come to offer you combat, but to thrash you until you open your gate.

'All this I would have told you on the first day of my arrival, when I approached the walls of your fort unarmed, had you not traitorously opened fire on me, which is not customary among honourable soldiers.'

In the evening the messenger returned with a reply that while the Khokandian Government declined to be answerable for the acts of oppression committed by the Kipchaks, the Commandant was willing to evacuate the fort if he were allowed fifteen days for the purpose, during which time the Russians were to retire from under the walls; otherwise the garrison would resist 'so long as the gunbarrels remained in their stocks, or their sword-blades and spear-handles were unbroken, and the supply of "kisiak" was unexhausted.' At the same time the Commandant explained that the first Russian messenger had been fired upon because the Russians had invaded Khokandian territory and approached the fort without any declaration of war, or explanation of their reasons for so acting. The attack was therefore continued, and on July 27 the approaches had reached the ditch, which was shortly afterwards crossed by a covered sap, and a mined gallery was driven under one of the bastions.

At three o'clock in the grey dawn of August 9, three rockets were discharged in rapid succession; a few moments later the earth trembled, and with a dull roar a great black mass of earth was seen to rise in the air and then settle down into two confused heaps on the ground. The mine had been sprung, and a great opening was formed in the walls more than thirty feet wide. Ak-Mechet was enveloped in dense clouds of smoke and dust, which for a time concealed the breach from the Russians; but the piercing shrieks and cries which rose from behind the walls proved to the besiegers that their work had been well done. The Russian batteries at once opened a heavy fire of grape on the spot where the breach was known to have been made, and the storming parties rushed forward to the attack. But the Khokandians were not taken by surprise, for before the smoke and *débris* from the explosion had cleared away they had lined the breach, and, although exposed to a heavy fire from the Russian guns, poured a continuous fire of musketry into the advancing troops. The Russians were twice driven back, and it was only after they had received reinforcements that their third assault proved successful. At half-past four all resistance had ceased, and the Russians became masters of Ak-Mechet, which had been the chief barrier against their advance towards the Kara-Tau Mountains.

Yakoob Beg appears to have left the fort during the siege, and his successor, Mahommed Wali, was killed, while out of a garrison of 300 men, 230 were found dead in the ditch or inside the fort, which proves the desperate bravery with which the Khokandians defended their stronghold. The Russian loss consisted of 13 men killed, and 8 officers and 52 men wounded.

The loss of Ak-Mechet was a severe blow to the power of Khokand, as it was the chief bulwark of that State on the Lower Syr Daria, and it was not long before the Khokandians began to make efforts to recapture it. But Perovski had taken steps to render his position as strong as possible. During his advance up the river he had given orders for the construction of two forts, which were to connect Ak-Mechet with Fort Aralsk. One of these forts was built on the Kazala branch of the river, and became known as the Kazala Fort, or Fort No. 1, while the second was built higher up the Syr at the Karmakchi settlement, and became known as Fort No. 2. The Khokandian fort of Kumysh-Kurgan, which had been abandoned by its garrison during the siege of Ak-Mechet, was also occupied by the Russians, and named Fort

No. 3. These three forts, together with forts Aralsk and Ak-Mechet (which was re-named Fort Perovski), formed the new line of the Syr Daria.[1]

At the end of 1853, Fort Perovski contained a garrison of 1,055 men, with 14 guns and 5 mortars, and was supplied with provisions for eighteen months.

Early in September, 1853, the commandant of Fort Perovski received intelligence that a force of about 7,000 Khokandians had arrived at Julek, and were advancing against him. But they were speedily routed by the troops despatched by the Commandant.

Undaunted by this failure, a fresh Khokandian force of about 13,000 men with 17 guns left Tashkent in November, 1853, under Yakoob Beg, for the purpose of driving the Russians out of their posts on the Syr, and messages were sent to the Kirghiz, inciting them to join in the attack. But this expedition also entirely failed. More than 2,000 Khokandians were killed, whilst the Russian loss only amounted to 18 killed and 49 wounded.

This affair completely put an end to the Khokandian attempts to recover possession of Ak-Mechet, for although there were several rumours of further attacks being meditated, the Russian posts on the Syr Daria were not interfered with.

While these events were occurring on the Syr Daria a similar advance was being made far away in the East. The town of Kopal was originally

---

[1] Fort Kumysh-Kurgan was abandoned by the Russians in 1855, and in the same year Fort Aralsk was removed to Fort No. 1.

supposed to have been built for the protection of the Great Horde of the Kirghiz-Kazaks, the majority of whom had become Russian subjects some few years previously. But this town was situated on the northern confines of the tract which was inhabited by the Horde, and a new advance was soon said to be necessary for the purpose of protecting these people from the Kara-Kirghiz, or Dikokamenni-Kirghiz, who frequented the mountainous districts further to the south. It was merely a repetition of the old story. The Kirghiz were once more to be put forward as an excuse for further aggression. It is doubtful whether any Government has displayed such an amount of solicitude and thoughtful consideration for any section of its subjects as the Russians have manifested with regard to these unruly Kirghiz. But this anxious solicitude for the welfare of these people was unfortunately only displayed when an excuse could thereby be obtained for fresh aggression. For many decades after these nomads tendered their submission to Russia, no steps were taken to improve their mode of living, or to introduce among them any of the blessings of civilisation. They have always been wild, reckless barbarians, living in the most primitive manner, and but little has ever been done to better their condition. But whenever the Russians have established themselves in an advanced position, and have completed their preparations for a further forward movement, it has invariably been found that some tribe or state has been molesting the Kirghiz, and must therefore be punished. And so the game has continued; the Russian frontiers meanwhile having been pushed forward many hundreds of miles, until the extreme limits of the country occupied by the Kirghiz-Kazaks have been reached, and the excuse no longer needed.

Thus, a few years after the building of Kopal, it was decided that a new advance should be made across the River Ili, and that the whole country between that river and Lake Issik Kul should be occupied, in order that the Great Horde might be defended from its enemies, and that permanent peace might be obtained by making the Russian frontier conterminous with the borders of the Chinese Empire. Such were the motives which are said to have induced the Russians to push southwards across the River Ili; and it will be seen in the sequel how utterly erroneous it was for them to imagine that by advancing far into the wilds of Central Asia, they would be able to secure peace.

In 1853 a Russian detachment crossed the River Ili, but instead of being welcomed as the saviours of a down-trodden and oppressed race, they were violently attacked by strong bodies of the very people whom they had come to deliver. A considerable section of the Great Horde had not submitted to the Russians, and now stoutly opposed their advance. Their chief stronghold was the Fort of Tuchubek on the Kaskalan River, from whence they boldly attacked the Russian troops, and clearly showed that they had no desire to become subjects of the White Czar.

But in the following year a larger force was sent across the Ili, Tuchubek was destroyed, and the Kirghiz were compelled either to submit to Russian authority, or to take refuge in Khokandian territory. Many preferred the latter alternative, and either fled to the Naryn Valley or settled down on the banks of the Talas River. The Russians wintered on the banks of the Tolgar (a small tributary of the Ili), and in the following year, 1855, advanced to the northern slopes of the Ala-Tau Mountains, and there founded the town of Vernoye or Almaty, on the banks of the little Almatinky stream. Thus, while the Russians were extending their right from Orenburg towards the Syr Daria, the left flank was also pushed forward to the borders of Eastern Turkestan, then a province of the Chinese Empire; and preparations were made for a simultaneous movement from both flanks towards the centre, which would round off the Russian possessions to the south of Siberia, and extend Russian authority to the very borders of the Khanate of Khokand.

But in the meanwhile events had occurred in Europe which forced the Czar Nicholas to abandon further military operations on the frontiers of his vast Asiatic dominions. The peace which had been maintained in Europe for so many years was now drawing to its close. On Dec. 2, 1851, Louis Napoleon, taking advantage of certain unpopular acts of the Republican deputies, overthrew the Republic which he had sworn to defend, and a year later assumed the title of Emperor of the

French. The European Governments viewed this change with considerable apprehension, as it was generally expected that the new Emperor would endeavour to strengthen his position by aggressive enterprises against his neighbours. The Russians also had been, as usual, intriguing in Turkey, and finally demanded that the Sultan should acknowledge the Czar's right to protect the Christian subjects of the Ottoman Empire. The Sultan refused to agree, and England and France supported the Porte. Napoleon was desirous of going to war to divert the thoughts of his people from home affairs, and the English Ministry failed to make the Czar understand that a Russian attack on the Porte would mean war with England. In July, 1853, Russian troops occupied the Danubian Principalities; the Sultan declared war in the following October; and by the end of March, 1854, Great Britain and France had formed an alliance, and the Crimean war began.

While this great war was in progress, two schemes for the invasion of India were laid before the Emperor Nicholas. After the failure of the siege of Herat, and the British invasion of Afghanistan, the Russian Government did their utmost to allay the commotion which had been caused through their intrigues on the borders of India. Vitkievitch was therefore disowned; and Count Simonitch was recalled from Persia, as he was said to have exceeded his instructions. Simonitch was succeeded at Teheran by General Duhamel; and when the Crimean war began, this officer presented a memorandum to the Czar, wherein he recommended that a Russian force should be sent against India, in order that the English might be alarmed for the safety of their East Indian possessions, and thus be unable to concentrate the whole of their attention on the struggle which was being fought out in Europe.

In this project General Duhamel stated:—

'When, towards the close of the last century, an army corps was quartered on the Eastern borders, by order of the Czar Paul, for the purpose of attacking India, the English people, although not certain of the fact, were greatly startled when they received reports of the concentration. Since then British writers have never ceased to point out, in various ways, the dangers of a possible Russian invasion of India, and their Parliament has often discussed the question.

'The present war, which is to be fought out to the bitter end, imposes on Russia the duty of showing how she can attack England in her only vulnerable point, in India, and thus force her to assemble so great a force in Asia as to weaken her action in Europe. History teaches us that nearly all the Powers which conquered India found their way to it through Central Asia and Persia, and that the roads by which Alexander the Great, Genghiz Khan, Tamerlane, Baber, and, finally, Nadir Shah broke into India are still open. They traverse Khorassan and Afghanistan, whether they lead from Persia or from the river Oxus. The cities of Kandahar and Kabul are the gates of India.

'The first route leads from Orenburg over the Ust-Yurt plateau to Khiva, and thence through Merv and Herat to Kandahar and Kabul.

'The second goes from Orsk or Orenburg to Fort Aralsk, and thence to Bokhara, Balkh, Khulm, and Kabul.

'The third leads from Orsk or Troitska, through Fort Aralsk and Ak-Mechet to Tashkent; or goes direct to Petro-paulovsk, and thence on to Khokand, Khulm, Bamian, and Kabul.

'The fourth is by water from Astrakhan to Astrabad, and thence, through Kabushan (Kushan' or Shahrud, to Meshed, Herat, Kandahar, and Kabul.

'The fifth and last route leads from the frontier on the River Araxes to Tabriz, Teheran, Meshed, Herat, Kandahar, and Kabul.

'The first three roads lead through the desert where it is widest, and by these, even if the oases of Khiva and Bokhara were made use of, many thousands of camels would be required for transport purposes. The last two routes lead through a country where there are no deserts, and which in some places is very fertile, and inhabited by a sturdy race of people. These two lines of advance do not traverse any such inaccessible points as are met with in the Hindu-Kush Mountains, nor are there any impassable rivers, such as the Oxus, between Bokhara and Balkh. When once the necessary transport vessels are collected on the Caspian Sea, then the Astrakhan-Astrabad line is to be preferred to all the others, for it is the shortest. Once in Astrabad, a footing in Khorassan can easily be obtained, and the remaining distance to Kabul is only 1,870 versts. The infantry, guns, and ammunition would be carried across the Caspian Sea, while the cavalry and train marched from Circassia through Persia.

'A march through Turkestan would be a dangerous operation, for the Khans and their tribes would have to be fought, and, even when defeated, they would attack our rear, and thus cut our communications. The march through half-civilised Persia would, however, be comparatively easy, for that State is so bound by treaties as to be incapable of offering any serious opposition, and is moreover threatened from all sides (especially from Circassia), and thus rendered powerless. What more, then, can be wanted? Active co-operation on the part of Persia involves active co-operation on the part of Afghanistan, on account of the deadly hatred which exists between the two peoples; and this is the *conditio sine quâ non* of an attack against Hindustan. . . . Naturally England would take steps to prevent all this; but even if she had time and means for despatching an expedition to the Persian Gulf, and occupied the island of Karrack and Bunder Bushire, or raised up a rebellion among the tribes of Southern Persia, it would be of little avail if Russia guaranteed to the Shah the secure possession of his throne and dominions, and still less should she promise the restoration of the Turkish provinces of Baghdad, Kerseldi, and a part of Kurdistan, thereby kindling a war between Persia and Turkey. The route through Persia is therefore for many reasons to be preferred to those through Turkestan.

'There are three roads from Afghanistan to India:—(1) from Kabul, through Jalalabad and Peshawar to Attock; (2) from Ghazni to Dehra Ismail Khan; (3) from Kandahar, through Quetta and Dadur to Shikarpur.

'These three roads lead through defiles which are easily defended, but which are all more exposed to a successful attack from the west than from the east. The best, shortest, and most healthy, is the first; although in 1839 the English adopted the third. From Attock it is easier to reach Lahore and Delhi, which are the principal objectives. The selection of this route would give rise to a rebellion in the very heart of the English possessions, and cause all the Mahommedan races to rise against them. This line also offers to the Afghans the most tempting prospects of plunder and extension of territory. If the Sikhs were also won over so much the better, but the friendship of the Afghans is of the most vital importance. Once this is gained all is won; for we invade India not to make conquests, but to overthrow the English, or at all events to weaken England's power. To effect this but a small force is required to form the nucleus of the attacking force, round which all the conquered races would gather, and which might even be gradually reduced as a general rebellion brought fresh recruits to the invading army.'

Such was the scheme submitted by General Duhamel in 1854, and in the following year General Khruleff prepared another project for a Russian invasion of India. This was very similar to the one which had been drawn up by the Russian Minister in Persia. It was proposed that an army of 30,000 men should advance from Ak-Kala, near Astrabad, to Kandahar, viâ Bujnurd, Kushan, Meshed, and Herat; that when Kandahar had been occupied an embassy should be sent from thence to Kabul, to gain the alliance of the Afghans; and that then India should be invaded, the people incited to rebel, and the English driven out of the country or so weakened that they would be forced to abandon the war in Europe. Khruleff considered that for such a scheme to succeed it was indispensable that Persia should observe perfect neutrality, and that the Afghans should co-operate in the invasion. He explained how the friendship of Persia could be obtained, stated that the Afghans would welcome the advent of a Russian army, and 'be gratified at our endeavour to overthrow the English'; and then proceeded to discuss the precautions which would be necessary to guard against possible attacks from the Khivans and Turkomans. Then, after explaining the proposed method of invasion, the Russian General continued:—'I am deeply imbued with a conviction of the possibility of carrying it into execution, and of this the English are more assured than we are. A large army would be embarrassing; we should try to raise a native force; our own should merely form the reserve. We should instruct the people in our methods of opposing the oppression of the English, whose army in India consists of only 25,000 European soldiers. The Indian army, according to Major Everest, consisting of some 300,000 men, is dispersed over an area of 1,076,590 square miles, and is called upon to defend a frontier 707 miles in length, being at the same time commanded by only 7,343 European officers, which was the establishment in 1847. There have been many instances in which these troops have retreated before compact masses of England's native enemies when the officers have been killed. The advent of a long desired army of 30,000 men would rouse the natural hatred of the Afghans towards the English, and will shake the power of the British in India. We may make compromises with our other enemies, but England's bearing towards us, which tends to weaken our power, does not justify us in leaving her in peace. We must liberate the people who are the sources of her wealth, and prove to the whole world the might of the Russian Czar.'

But these schemes were never carried out, and the Russians were unable to prove the might of their Czar before the whole world. Their forces had been defeated in the field, and their most powerful stronghold in the south, though bravely defended, was closely besieged by the armies of the Allies; the Baltic ports were bombarded, and their commerce destroyed; whole divisions while marching to the front perished on the frost-bound

Steppes, and defeat and ruin stared them in the face. They had no time to devote to wild ventures in the inhospitable countries of Central Asia, and were forced to concentrate the whole of their energies on the struggle in Europe.

It may be asked why, when Russia was contemplating an attack on India at the time of the Crimean war, did not England take advantage of her enemy's crippled condition, and commence operations in Asia which would have driven the Russians back to the northern extremities of the Kirghiz Steppes, and forced them to abandon their conquests south of the Caucasus? An English corps operating in Georgia, with the aid of Turkey and Persia, and backed by Schamyl and his hardy mountaineers, would certainly have driven the Russians beyond the Caucasus; while a little assistance to the Khivans and Khokandians would have raised such a convulsion in Central Asia that the Russians could not possibly have maintained their isolated posts in the Steppes, and would have been forced back to the frontiers they occupied at the commencement of the century.

Such schemes *were* laid before the British Government, but found no favour for several reasons. Just as the English people suspected that they had been dragged into the war in order that the popularity of the new French Emperor might be enhanced, so the French believed that they had been drawn into the quarrel to advance English interests in the East. Any attempt on the part of England to carry the war into Asia would, therefore, have been viewed with the greatest suspicion in France, and might even have caused a rupture between the Allies. Then, again, England had not forgotten the last movement beyond the Indus; and although the avenging armies successfully performed their task, and in a great measure re-established British credit, still the entire nation had become possessed with an intense dread of any interference with the States of Central Asia, and shrank from the very idea of despatching troops beyond the Indus. It was not understood that the Kabul massacre had been due to the utter incompetence of the military commanders, and would never have occurred if even an average amount of decision and military capacity had been displayed. The disaster had been of such an appalling nature that the very judgment of the English people appeared to have been affected. Instead of appreciating the true causes which led up to the catastrophe, it was erroneously imagined that the country was so inaccessible, and its inhabitants of such a formidable and even terrible character, that any new movement beyond the Indus would inevitably result in renewed defeat and disaster. No British Ministry would therefore undertake the responsibility of waging war with Russia in Central Asia; and thus no attempts were made to shake her position on the Syr Daria, while even a hostile demonstration in the Caucasus was abandoned, in order that French susceptibilities might not be wounded.

During the Crimean war the relations between

England and Persia were most unsatisfactory. Mahommed Shah died in 1848 and was succeeded by his son, Nasr Eddin, the present Shah of Persia, who had not long been seated on the throne before he began to meddle with Herat affairs. Yar Mahommed Khan, who had formerly been Shah Kamran's Vizier, but who murdered his master in 1842, and had since been the independent ruler of Herat, died in the autumn of 1851, and was succeeded by his son, Said Mahommed. This prince, on his accession, met with considerable opposition from the chiefs of the city, and appealed to the Shah for support; and Herat would then have become a province of Persia if the British Government had not interfered and insisted on its independence. On January 25, 1853, a treaty was concluded, whereby the Persian Government engaged to abstain from all interference in Herat affairs, and renounced all claims to sovereignty over the State. It was also agreed that no Persian troops should on any account be sent to Herat, unless the place were attacked by troops from Kabul or Kandahar, or from other foreign territory; and the Persian Government also relinquished all claims to the coinage of money, or other sign of subjection on the part of the people of Herat to Persia. This convention was a source of considerable irritation to the Shah, and predisposed him to be influenced by counsels which were hostile to England. When, therefore, late in the autumn of 1853, a Russian army was concentrated south of the Caucasus, for the invasion of the Turkish provinces in Asia Minor, and the Russian Minister (Prince Dolgorouky) suggested that Persia should co-operate with Russia in an attack on Turkey, the Shah was not unwilling to enter into the proposed alliance, and even issued orders for the concentration of 40,000 troops in Azerbijan and 15,000 men in Kermanshah. But the Persian Prime Minister suggested that it would be more advantageous to Persia if the Shah were to throw in his lot with the English and French, as thereby Persia might recover the provinces which she had lost in the previous wars with Russia. Acting on this advice, Nasr Eddin decided to watch the course of events before he committed himself; and the Russian Ambassador shortly afterwards destroyed all chance of a Russo-Persian alliance through an act of unseemly violence. At an interview with the Vizier, Prince Dolgorouky reproached him with the evil counsel which he had given to his master, and warned him of the disastrous consequences that would assuredly follow; and then completely losing control over his temper, he assaulted the Minister with a cane which he held in his hand. Such an act naturally put an end to the projected alliance, and Persia remained neutral throughout the war.

But although the Shah took no part in the great struggle which was being fought out between Russia and the Western Powers of Europe, it was not long before he displayed his enmity towards the English by direct acts of hostility. He first tried to form an offensive and defensive alliance with the rulers of Kabul, Kandahar and Herat; and when this scheme was frustrated by the opposition of Dost Mahommed—who had been restored to the Afghan throne after the first Afghan war—Nasr Eddin tried to bring about a collision between Kandahar and Herat, in order that he might have a pretext for interference. In March, 1855, Dost Mahommed, alarmed by the threatening attitude of the Persian Court, concluded at Peshawar a treaty of perpetual peace and friendship with England; but, at about the same time, Said Mahommed of Herat was deposed by Mahommed Yusuf, a grandson of the Suddozai Prince Firoz-ud-din. This prince had been for many years a refugee in Meshed, and it was believed that he had taken possession of Herat through the instrumentality of Persia. That such was actually the case was soon proved beyond any doubt. In March, 1856, Nasr Eddin threw off the mask, and marched an army across the frontier. The gates of Herat were thrown open, and Mahommed Yusuf openly declared his allegiance to the Shah. But shortly afterwards the people, led by Isa Khan, broke into rebellion, deposed the Suddozai Prince, expelled the Shah's troops from Herat, and prepared to defend the city against the Persians. Herat was once again besieged by a Persian army. But Isa Khan had not the energy and capacity with which Yar Mahommed was endowed, nor was there an Eldred Pottinger within the walls; and after a desultory contest, which lasted for four months, Isa Khan, despairing of receiving any assistance from the Afghans, surrendered the fortress to the Persians on October 25, 1856.

Meanwhile the relations between England and Persia had been daily becoming more strained, and after a long course of studied provocation, Mr. Murray, the British Minister, was forced to suspend relations with the Court of Teheran, and left for Baghdad on December 6, 1855. When, therefore, it was known that in addition to previous insults the Shah had deliberately attacked Herat in spite of the Convention of 1853, the British Government decided to despatch an expedition to the Persian Gulf. On November 1, 1856, a proclamation was issued in Calcutta, declaring war with Persia, on account of the hostile expedition against Herat; on December 4 the Island of Karrack was once more occupied by British troops; five days later the Persians were dislodged from the old Dutch Fort of Reshire, after a short but fierce encounter; and on the next day Bushire was occupied by the invading army. After the arrival of Sir James Outram, on January 27, 1857, preparations were made for striking decisive blows which would speedily force the Shah to sue for peace. On February 8 a Persian force was defeated at Kushab; on March 26 Mohamreh (at the mouth of the Karun River) was bombarded, and the enemy's batteries captured; and by April 1 the British troops had advanced far up the Karun River, and driven the Persians from Ahwaz. But even before Mohamreh had been attacked, the Persian Ambassador at the Court of France had concluded a peace, which was signed in Paris on March 4, 1857. Intimation of this event reached Outram at Mohamreh on April 4, and the treaty was ratified at Baghdad in the following month.

In the meanwhile the Russians were occupied in the suppression of a serious revolt of the Kirghiz, which compelled them to remain inactive on the Syr Daria for some years after the conclusion of the Crimean war.

After several fruitless expeditions, and when the rebellion had lasted for five years, General Katenin, who had succeeded Perovski as Governor-General of the Orenburg district, determined in 1858 to resort to conciliatory measures. Izzet Kutebar, the chief leader in the revolt, was promised complete forgiveness in the event of his submission, and, at the same time, a general amnesty to all the rebel Kirghiz was proclaimed. At first Izzet declined to enter into negotiations with the Russian authorities, but having heard of the arrival of General Ignatieff's mission at the Emba, *en route* for Khiva and Bokhara, he changed his mind, and on June 4 surrendered himself to the Russian Envoy. He begged Ignatieff to inform the Czar of his firm desire to atone for former misdeeds by future loyalty and zealous service, and in order to emphasise his devotion to the Russian Government he sent his son with the mission as far as Khiva.

This mission of Ignatieff's to Khiva and Bokhara was despatched in response to an invitation which had been received from the Amir of

Bokhara. In July, 1857, an envoy from Khiva arrived from Orenburg with a suite of sixteen men, and requested permission to proceed to St. Petersburg for the purpose of delivering letters from the Khan and his Ministers, congratulating the Emperor Alexander II. on his accession to the throne. This Khivan Embassy was followed by the arrival of a similar mission from the Amir of Bokhara, which reached Fort Orsk on August 22. The Bokharan Envoy was the bearer of several presents for the Czar, and a letter from the Amir, in which Nasrullah, after having congratulated the Czar on his accession to the throne, and announced his victories in Shahr-i-Sebz, asked that 'the precious and bright intelligences of the Sovereign might be directed towards the sending of an Embassy from himself.'

These ambassadors went on to the Russian capital in September and October, 1857, and after a short stay there returned to Orenburg in January, 1858, and soon afterwards returned to their respective countries.

The Russian Government determined to accept the invitation which had been given by the Amir of Bokhara, and gave orders for the equipment of a mission which was to proceed to that State under Colonel Ignatieff, who was afterwards Russian Ambassador at Constantinople. Ignatieff was directed to proceed through Khiva, for the purpose of concluding a treaty with the Khan, Said Mahommed,[1]

---

[1] Said Mahommed, the son of Khan Mahommed Rahim and brother of Khan Allah-Kul, succeeded to the Khivan throne in 1856.

one of the chief clauses of which was that Russian vessels should be permitted to navigate the Amu-Daria. He received special instructions to collect information regarding the ancient bed of the Oxus, and to carefully survey the course of that river from its mouths as far as Balkh if possible, and for this purpose the Aral flotilla under Captain Butakoff was to co-operate with the mission. On May 15, 1858, Ignatieff started from Orenburg with an escort of 57 men and 1 gun. But his mission to Khiva was a complete failure; for the Khan, after much hesitation and delay, eventually decided that no Russian vessels should be permitted to remain on the Oxus. The negotiations were then broken off, and Ignatieff was obliged to leave Khiva without having gained permission for Russian vessels to navigate the Oxus, which was the main object of his mission. But, after leaving Khiva, he went on to Bokhara and obtained this privilege from the Amir of that State, although the concession so obtained was of but little use so long as the entrance to the river from the Sea of Aral was barred by the Khivans.

While Ignatieff was thus employed, other Russian agents were busily engaged in exploring the countries of Central Asia. In 1857 and 1858 M. Borshchoff and M. Syevertsoff examined the country lying between the Ural Mountains and the Caspian Sea, and thoroughly explored the Mogadjar Mountains and the Ust-Yurt plateau; in 1859 Captain Golubeff, accompanied by M. Matkof, went forth into the country beyond Lake Balkash and the

River Ili, and surveyed Lake Issik Kul; in the same year Captain Valikhanoff, the son of a Kirghiz Sultan, crossed the Thian-Shan range with a company of traders, spent the winter in Kashgar and its neighbourhood, and collected much valuable information regarding the geography, ethnology, and history of Eastern Turkestan; and at the same time other parties of surveyors mapped some 38,000 square versts on the eastern shores of the Caspian, and gained accurate information regarding the shores of that sea in the neighbourhood of the Kara-Bugaz Gulf and Balkan Bay.

But the most important mission was one under M. Nicholas Khanikoff, which was despatched for the exploration of Khorassan. This expedition started in March, 1858, and travelled through Astrabad, Nishapur, and Meshed to Herat, and then returned by the Lake of Hamun, Kerman, Yezd, and Ispahan to Teheran. When it reached Herat, India was still in the throes of the terrible Indian Mutiny, and Khanikoff therefore turned his attention from scientific pursuits to political intrigues. When Mahommed Yusuf, the ruler of Herat, had been deposed by Isa Khan, he had been sent as a prisoner to Teheran; and after peace was concluded between England and Persia, the Persian Government, knowing that if the Suddozai Prince was restored to his throne, he would feel that he owed its possession to the British, and thus be hostile to Persia, determined to get rid of him and place a ruler on the throne of Herat who would owe his advancement to the goodwill of the Shah's

Government. They accordingly permitted Mahommed Yusuf to be put to death by the relatives of Said Mahommed, and then Sultan Ahmed Khan —Dost Mahommed's nephew and son-in-law—was placed on the throne. This man, who had previously quarrelled with his uncle, Dost Mahommed, and had sought the protection of Persia, was the ruler of Herat when Khanikoff arrived, and the Russian Envoy succeeded in confirming the Barakzai Prince in his dependency on Persia. Nor was he content with this, for he intrigued in Afghanistan, and even proposed that Russian officers should be sent to Kabul and Kandahar, to revive the alliances which Vitkievitch had concluded. But fortunately Dost Mahommed remained true to his friendship with England, and thus the Russian plot failed.

CHAPTER VII

1859-1868

ATTACKS ON KHOKAND AND BOKHARA

Civil war in Khokand—Russian forward movement in Khokand—Capture of Aulie-ata and Hazret-i-Turkestan—Tchernaieff captures Chimkent—British policy of 'masterly inactivity' in India—Prince Gortchakoff's circular—Fall of Tashkent—Russian declarations regarding Tashkent—Russian invasion of Bokharan territory—Capture of Khojent—Capture of Ura-Tepé, and occupation of Jizakh—The 'Steppe Commission'—Formation of the Province of Turkestan—Occupation of Samarkand—Treaty of Peace with Bokhara.

As soon as Russia had recovered from the exhaustion caused by the Crimean war, and had quelled the insurrection of the Kirghiz under Izzet Kutebar, she once more found herself in a position to resume her aggressive movements on the Syr Daria and in the country between Ak-Mechet and Vernoye, and preparations were therefore made for a campaign in Central Asia, which was to be conducted on a far greater scale than any of the previous Russian efforts in that direction.

Khokand had for many years been in a constant state of civil war, and had been subjected to repeated invasions from Bokhara—a state of affairs which sapped the strength of the State, and prevented the people from opposing a solid front to the Russian advance. When the Russians were making their first advance up the Syr Daria, the Khokandian regent, Mussulman Kuli, was fully occupied in his endeavours to subdue the rebellion of the Sarts in Tashkent; and then followed the split between Khudayar Khan and his 'Ming Bashi,' which ended in the execution of the latter and the merciless slaughter of the Kipchaks. Thus, when Perovski attacked Ak-Mechet, the Khokandians were fully occupied with the bitter struggle between the rival factions of the State, and were unable to pay any attention to the advances of their powerful northern neighbour. Ak-Mechet and the other Khokandian forts were thus easily captured, and the Russians were able to consolidate their position on the Syr Daria without encountering any serious opposition from the main Khokandian armies. Even after this, when Russia was fruitlessly struggling against the great Western Powers of Europe, and was subsequently obliged to devote her attention to the restoration of order in the Kirghiz Steppes, the miserable dissensions in Khokand still continued, and the Khokandians thus threw away their last chance of regaining possession of their strongholds on the Jaxartes. The opportunity so lost was gone for ever, for as soon as the Russians had recovered from the exhausting effects of the Crimean war, and had subdued the Kirghiz, they recommenced their career of aggression, speedily captured the chief towns of Khokand, and by rapidly penetrating into the heart of the country, obtained a position from which it was impossible to dislodge them.

It has already been mentioned that the Russian authorities considered it necessary to close the undefended gap between the Orenburg and Siberian lines by a series of forts between the Syr Daria and Vernoye. Just before the Crimean war it had been decided that this new frontier line should run from Fort Perovski (the new name for Ak-Mechet) along the northern slopes of the Kara-Tau Mountains to the Chu River, and then along the course of that river to Vernoye. But the local commanders now strongly urged a reconsideration of the matter, and it was finally determined that the new frontier should start from a point higher up the Syr Daria, and, after including the Khokandian towns of Hazret-i-Turkestan and Aulie-ata, should follow the line of the Talas River and Alexandroffski Range. This decision meant that the Russian Government deliberately determined to seize two important Khokandian towns and to occupy a large portion of Khokandian territory without provocation, and solely because it suited their policy to do so.

The first forward movement in pursuance of this Russian scheme was made in 1859, when the Khokandian fort of Julek was captured and destroyed.[1] In 1861 a Russian fort was built on the site of the old Khokandian post, and in the

[1] This post, which was on the Syr Daria, some seventy or eighty miles above Fort Perovski, was destroyed by General Paduroff in July, 1853, when Perovski was besieging Ak-Mechet; but when the

same year a detachment advanced some fifty miles further up the river and seized Yani Kurgan. In the meanwhile another column, under Colonel Zimmermann, was moving forward from the Irtish, and in 1860 the two Khokandian forts of Pishpek and Tokmak were captured. The Russian force available for operations west of Vernoye was at this time inconsiderable, and after these first successes it was split up into several small detachments for the purpose of watching the extensive frontier. One party was left in a fort on the River Ili to cover the communications with Semipalatinsk; another detachment occupied Vernoye; while the main body was posted in a small fort at the mouth of the Kastek Pass, with a small party at Uzun-Agatch, for the purpose of maintaining communication between Vernoye and the Kastek fort. It was expected that in the event of the Khokandians retaliating, their first attack would be through the Kastek Pass, which offered the easiest line of advance from Khokand to Vernoye, and it was for the purpose of resisting such a movement that Lieutenant-Colonel Kolpakoffsky placed himself at Kastek with the main body of the Russian troops.

It was not long before the Khokandians collected an army of some 30,000 men, and advanced under Khanayat Shah, one of their best generals, to rebuild Pishpek and Tokmak, and if possible to

Russians retired, the Khokandians rebuilt the fort, and held possession of it until 1859, when it was finally destroyed by the Russians.

expel the Russians from their posts south of the Ili. The Khokandian commander knew that it would be useless to attack the Russian force at Fort Kastek; and he, therefore, crossed the mountains by another pass in October, 1860, and with the greater portion of his force fell on the detachment at Uzun-Agatch, hoping thus to cut off Kolpakoffsky from his supports, and to be able then to reduce Kastek and Vernoye at his leisure. The attacking force consisted of some 19,000 men, and as the Russian party at Uzun-Agatch was very small, it appeared almost impossible for them to escape annihilation. They, however, defended themselves with the greatest fortitude, and managed to communicate with Kolpakoffsky, who at once sallied out from Kastek, and attacking the Khokandians in rear, drove them in confusion from the field. It was a brilliant victory, and reflected the greatest credit on Kolpakoffsky and his troops, for with a strength of only 800 men and 6 guns they completely routed a force of vastly superior strength, and demoralised the Khokandian defence.

In 1863 preparations were made for important combined operations from both flanks, by which the long wished-for junction between the Orenburg and Siberian lines was to be effected. But the outbreak of the Polish Rebellion and the threatening aspect of affairs in Western Europe, forced the Czar to defer the attack till the following year, when all danger of a general conflagration in Europe had disappeared. In the summer of 1864 the advance began. Colonel Tchernaieff moved forward from Siberia with a force of 2,500 men, and assaulted the town of Aulie-ata on June 16. The attack was completely successful, and the place was soon occupied by the Russians, who only lost five men wounded, while over 300 Khokandians are said to have been killed in the fight. This town, which stands on the banks of the River Talas, is of insignificant dimensions, and its capture was important only because it is situated in a fertile district about half-way between Fort Perovski and Vernoye, and is at the junction of two important routes which lead to Chimkent in the west and to Namangan in the south.

While Tchernaieff was advancing against Aulie-ata, another column, 1,200 strong, was moving eastwards from Fort Perovski, under Colonel Verefkin, to effect a junction with the Siberian troops. A glance at the map will show that unless Verefkin kept to the north of the Kara-Tau Mountains, he would necessarily pass close to the town of Hazret-i-Turkestan (the most sacred city in that part of Asia), and a collision with the Khokandians would inevitably follow. But it has already been shown that the Russian Government had deliberately rejected the frontier line of the Kara-Tau mountains, and had determined to seize Hazret-i-Turkestan and to absorb the neighbouring Khokandian district; and in accordance with this decision, Verefkin attacked the city in June, 1864. The Khokandian garrison manfully defended the place; but, in order to hasten its fall, the Russian artillery were directed to open fire on the great mosque over the tomb of the Saint Hazret Hodja Achmet Yasavi, a substantial building constructed of well-burnt bricks, which rises to a height of over 100 feet, and is flanked by two massive towers or bastions. The Russian fire did considerable damage to the mosque and had the desired effect. A flag of truce was soon hoisted by the Sheikh-ul-Islam, and shortly afterwards the city surrendered.

By the capture of Hazret-i-Turkestan and of Aulie-ata, the Russian design for closing the gap between the Orenburg and Siberian lines was successfully accomplished; for the two Russian columns shortly afterwards joined hands, the two towns were held by Russian garrisons, and the surrounding country was taken possession of in the name of the White Czar. Verefkin was then recalled, and Tchernaieff assumed command of the united columns.

Tchernaieff, however, was by no means content with the success which had been achieved. Chimkent, which was now the most advanced Khokandian fortress, commanding the main road between Hazret-i-Turkestan and Aulie-ata, was occupied by a garrison of some 10,000 Khokandians who were fairly well provided with artillery; the fortifications were being strengthened, and preparations were made to stoutly oppose any further advance on the part of the Russians. He saw the importance of the place, and determined to attack it before its defences could be completed. It was said to be intolerable that a Khokandian army should be permitted to assemble so close to the Russian frontiers. The stronger Power, Russia, had unprovokedly invaded the territories of a weaker neighbour, occupied its towns, and shot down its inhabitants; but when the outraged people assembled a force to defend the residue of their possessions, it was declared that such defensive measures could not be permitted, and necessitated further punishment. Undoubtedly, where Russian interests are concerned, there is one law for the strong and another for the weak. Chimkent was required by the Russians to cover their communications between Hazret-i-Turkestan and Aulie-ata; and Tchernaieff, therefore, with between 4,000 and 5,000 men, rapidly pushed forward and captured the place on October 3, 1864, with the trifling loss of five men. It was a brilliant affair, well conceived and boldly carried out, and one which stamped Tchernaieff as a leader of great daring and enterprise. By it the safety of the Russian line from Fort Perovski to Vernoye was secured, and a wedge was driven into Khokand by which Tashkent, Khojent, and the capital itself were brought within easy striking distance of the Russian frontier.

When the news of these operations reached England, but little interest was manifested in the Russian movements. Far more momentous occurrences were taking place elsewhere; Denmark had been attacked by Prussia and Austria, and the whole sympathies of the English were extended towards the nation which had just given their fairest Princess to be the bride of the future King of England; a desperate struggle also was being carried on in North America, which caused much distress in Lancashire by its interference with the supply of cotton; while the fitting out of piratical cruisers in British ports in the name of the Southern Confederation gave great annoyance to the Northern States, and threatened to cause a war between England and America. In India also the policy of 'masterly inactivity' was in full swing; and Lord Lawrence, the new Viceroy, was inculcating the doctrine that 'Russia might prove a safer ally, a better neighbour, than the Mahommedan races of Central Asia and Kabul.'[1]

But though the British public displayed but little interest or concern in the annexation by Russia of the northern districts of the Khanate of Khokand, Prince Gortchakoff, the Russian Chancellor, considered it necessary to publicly announce the causes which had induced the Czar to sanction the invasion of Khokand. This explanation was given in the now famous circular of November 21, 1864, to all the Russian embassies and legations in foreign countries,[2] which professed to place the Asiatic policy of Russia in its true light. After explaining the causes of the invasion, Prince Gortchakoff stated that there was no intention on the part of Russia to make any further advances,

---

[1] See p. 41 of *Papers relating to Central Asia and Quetta*, printed by order of the House of Commons, February 25, 1879.

[2] A translation of this interesting document is given in Appendix II.

as they found themselves 'in presence of a more solid, compact, less unsettled, and better organised state; fixing for us with geographical precision the limit up to which we are bound to advance, and at which we must halt, because, while on the one hand any further extension of our rule, meeting (as it would) no longer with unstable communities, such as the nomad tribes, but with more regularly constituted states, would entail considerable exertions, and would draw us on from annexation to annexation with unforeseen complications.'

The specious phrases and plausible arguments contained in this remarkable circular were considered to be fairly satisfactory; for it was now for the first time clearly stated that Russia had been forced to advance in spite of all its efforts to the contrary and in opposition to the wishes of the Czar; that no further aggressive movements were contemplated; and that it was hoped that the day might come when regular relations might, to the advantage of both parties, take the place of the permanent troubles which had, up to that time, paralysed all progress in those countries.

At that time the English had yet to learn that Russian promises are liable to be broken, and that Russian agreements are not always worth the paper on which they are written. The Black Sea clauses of the Treaty of Paris had not been then repudiated; Khiva and Merv had not been annexed, in spite of repeated promises that no such steps would be taken; and Russian agents had not been intriguing in Afghanistan after positive assurances had been given, and reiterated, that Russia considered Afghanistan to be outside her sphere of influence, and that no such envoys would be sent into that country.

But even before this circular was written, hostilities had been resumed on the Syr Daria, and the Russians had begun a new advance which marked the commencement of a series of campaigns which ended in the conquest of Tashkent and Samarkand, and was the stepping-stone to the establishment of Russian influence throughout Central Asia up to the borders of Afghanistan and Eastern Turkestan.

As soon as Chimkent had been captured, Tchernaieff rapidly advanced against Tashkent in hopes of being able to gain possession of that important city by a *coup de main*. On October 15, 1864, he suddenly appeared before the town, placed a battery in position, made a breach in the walls, and then delivered an assault. The attempt, however, failed; and the Russians were forced to retreat to Chimkent. The Khokandians quickly followed up this success, and a considerable force soon marched northwards for the purpose of regaining possession of Hazret-i-Turkestan. On their approach a small force of Cossacks was sent out to the village of Ikan, which lies some eighteen miles to the south-east of Hazret, on the Chimkent road. This party, which was under the command of Captain Serof, only consisted of one sotnia of

Cossacks—120 men—with one field-piece; and when they arrived near Ikan on the evening of December 16, they found the place swarming with Khokandians, who speedily surrounded the small detachment. Serof thus found himself in a position of extreme danger; but the gallant little band of Russians defended themselves with the utmost valour, and absolutely refused to surrender, although they were offered a safe retreat to Hazret. Throughout the evening and night of the 16th, the whole of the next day and night, and until the evening of the 18th, these brave Cossacks held their own, and eventually, after having lost 57 of their party killed and 43 wounded, the few survivors spiked their gun and forced their way back to Hazret. By this splendid piece of bravery the Khokandian attack was broken, Hazret-i-Turkestan was saved, and the Russians were delivered from a very serious danger to their newly acquired position on the Syr Daria.

Tchernaieff's sudden attack on Tashkent in October 1864 greatly alarmed the Amir of Bokhara, who looked upon Khokand as his legitimate prey, and resented the Russian invasion of that State. It has been mentioned that Khokand was constantly invaded by the Amirs of Bokhara; and one such invasion took place when the Russians were advancing against Hazret-i-Turkestan and Aulie-ata, on which occasion Mozuffer-Eddin was supporting Khudayar Khan against the Regent Alim Kuli. After Alim Kuli was defeated, the Amir returned to Bokhara, when the Regent once more took the field, and drove Khudayar out of Khokand. The exiled Khan took up his abode in Jizak, there secretly made preparations for a fresh campaign, and finally persuaded the Amir to again support him in his attempt to regain the throne. It appears that Mozuffer-Eddin's object in marching into Khokand was not merely to reinstate Khudayar, but at the same time to prevent Tashkent from falling into the hands of the Russians. At all events, Tchernaieff viewed the Amir's attitude at this time with the greatest suspicion, and when he heard that a Bokharan army was being assembled at Ura-tepé, he determined once more to advance against Tashkent.

At this time the city—which contained a population of over 100,000 souls and was defended by a garrison of about 30,000 men—was encircled by a hard clay rampart from twelve to fifteen feet high, sixteen miles in circumference, of considerable thickness, well provided with loop-holes and embrasures, and pierced by twelve gateways. The chief water-supply was obtained from the River Chirchik, from whence it was brought by means of a large canal, called the 'Bos-su,' which left the river at a place named Niazbek, some sixteen miles to the north-east of the city, where there was a small fort. This canal had four branches, which conducted the water to all parts of the town.

On account of the great size of the city, Tchernaieff was unable to invest it, and as he did not feel inclined to risk another assault, he first attacked Niazbek in April 1865, and, by the capture of the fort, obtained command over the water-supply. Then he took up a position within six miles of Tashkent, and entered into correspondence with some of the inhabitants of the city, who, being discontented with Alim Kuli's government, were inclined to favour a Russian occupation; and he arranged with them that on May 20, while he made a demonstration against the north-east front of the town, they should attack the garrison and open the gates. This plot was, however, frustrated by the Regent Alim Kuli himself, who on that day entered the city with some 6,000 fresh troops and forty guns. On the following day (May 21) the Khokandians made a determined attack on the Russian position. For a short time the Russians were hard-pressed, and it seemed as if they were about to experience a second reverse before Tashkent; but during the battle Alim Kuli was killed, and the Khokandians were eventually repulsed at all points and forced to take shelter under the walls of the town.

After the Regent's death the inhabitants of Tashkent sent an embassy to the Amir of Bokhara, offering their submission and begging of him to send assistance. To prevent Bokharan interference Tchernaieff occupied the fort of Chinaz on the Syr Daria for the purpose of guarding the ferry at that place, and then, hearing that the Amir's troops had retreated across the river, he returned and took up a position about three miles from Tashkent.

In the meanwhile, Mozuffer-Eddin had informed the Tashkendians that Khudayar's nephew, Said Sultan Khan, who was then in the city, must be surrendered to him as the price of his assistance. Said Sultan, on hearing this, fled on the night of June 21, and a party of Bokharans then marched into the city, while the Amir's troops began to show themselves at various points along the Syr Daria.

Tchernaieff was thus placed in a critical position; but he determined to make a bold bid for success by assaulting the city before the Amir's army could render such a course impracticable. Accordingly, at three o'clock in the morning of June 27, a storming party, under Captain Abramoff, scaled the walls near the Kamelan gate, surprised the guard, and after silencing the guns which were turned on them from the adjoining bastions, opened the gate to the Russian troops. Abramoff then advanced for about six miles along the ramparts, as far as the Kara-Serai gate, while a second column, under Major de la Croix, entered by the Khokand gate and captured that portion of the fortress. Throughout the whole of that day the Russian troops were engaged in incessant street-fighting, and although during the ensuing night there was a pause in the conflict, at daybreak on the next day they found that numerous barricades had been erected in the principal streets and alleys. The whole of the 28th was spent in destroying these obstacles and in subduing the resistance of the garrison; but on the morning of the 29th a deputation of the leading inhabitants waited on

Tchernaieff, and unconditionally surrendered the city to the Russians.

Thus was Tashkent captured and the fate of Khokand sealed. But while these movements were being carried out, and three months after Tchernaieff had cut off the water-supply at Niazbek, and had commenced systematic operations for the reduction of the city, the Russian Government declared that they had no intention of occupying the place. On July 21, 1865 (a month after the city had been taken), the director of the Russian Asiatic Department (M. Stremoouchoff) informed the British Chargé d'Affaires at St. Petersburg that 'the Russian Government hoped, at no distant date, *without occupying Tashkent,* to make that place the great *entrepôt* for Russian commerce with Central Asia.' And again, on September 11 (two and a half months after the city had fallen), Prince Gortchakoff informed the British Ambassador that ' it was the intention of the Imperial Government to insist on the Bokharan troops being withdrawn from Khokandian territory, *and on Tashkent being declared an independent town.*' Such declarations can only have been made for the purpose of misleading the British authorities, for the Russian Government must have been aware of Tchernaieff's movements, which had been commenced in the previous spring; and a month before it was stated that Tashkent would be declared to be an independent town —the Governor-General of Orenburg had actually visited the place and promised the inhabitants that they would be ' admitted to the privilege of becoming subjects of the "White Czar."' General Krijhanoffsky, the Governor of the Orenburg district, visited Tashkent in August 1865; convoked an assembly of the elders of the city, and then accepted their submission; declared Tashkent to be a province of the Russian Empire; and promised to protect the people with his troops, and to respect their manners and customs. This is a fair example of the value of Russian declarations.

The capture of Tashkent greatly incensed the Amir of Bokhara, who wrote to Tchernaieff, calling on him to evacuate Khokandian territory, and threatening in the event of refusal to kindle a religious war against the Russians. In order to emphasise his demands, he also confiscated the property of such Russian merchants as happened to be in Bokhara. Tchernaieff scornfully rejected the Amir's demands, and made reprisals by detaining the Bokharan merchants who were found in Russian territory. Mozuffer-Eddin was at this time engaged in the suppression of a rebellion at Shahr-i-Sebz; and as he had no desire to be drawn into a war with Russia, he despatched a man, named Hodja Nedjm-Eddin, on a mission to St. Petersburg to complain to the Czar of the unprovoked invasion of Khokand. This envoy was, however, arrested on the road and detained at Kazala; and shortly afterwards Tchernaieff sent an embassy to Bokhara, under M. Struvé, to demand the release of Russian subjects. As might have been foreseen, the Amir was not likely, after what had occurred, to treat the Russian embassy with any consideration; and as soon as Struvé's party reached Bokhara they were detained, two of the members of the mission being cast into prison.

When Tchernaieff heard of this he collected a force of 2,000 men and fourteen guns, and, crossing the Syr Daria on February 11, 1866, marched against Bokhara to force the Amir to release the captives. Crossing the 'Golodnaia,' or 'famished steppe'—a barren, waterless desert between the Syr Daria and the Bokharan fortress of Jizakh—the Russian column arrived before Jizakh on February 16, 1866, when it was found that the place was too strongly fortified to permit of its being carried by storm, while regular siege operations were out of the question, on account of the considerable Bokharan army which was close at hand. Tchernaieff was thus unable to capture Jizakh, and was obliged to fall back, his force being surrounded during the retreat by swarms of Bokharan irregulars, who managed to inflict some slight loss on the column. On nearing Tashkent the Khokandians also joined in the attack on the infidels. A large force marched out of the city and attacked the Russian troops, while at the same time the Khokandian garrison of Niazbek opened fire on a Russian detachment as it was marching towards the Chirchik. Although these attacks were quite unexpected, the Khokandians were speedily beaten off and dispersed, and Tchernaieff regained possession of Tashkent without difficulty, when the garrison of Niazbek marched out, leaving 370 prisoners, six guns, and a considerable quantity of small arms and ammunition in the hands of the Russians.

After this failure General Tchernaieff was recalled, and was succeeded by Major-General Dimitri Ilyitch Romanoffsky. The Russian Government stated that Tchernaieff had been recalled because he had exceeded his orders, and had advanced in direct opposition to the wishes of the Czar. The Emperor was, no doubt, annoyed that the promises and explanations contained in Prince Gortchakoff's circular should have been so speedily proved to be nothing more than hollow diplomatic phrases published for the purpose of throwing dust in the eyes of the British public; but it has never been satisfactorily explained why —if Tchernaieff had really advanced in defiance of the Czar's orders—he was not recalled when his first attack on Tashkent became known to the Imperial Government. He assaulted Tashkent in October 1864, but was not recalled; then, again, in April 1865, he advanced against the place and captured it after a three months' campaign, but still he was not recalled, nor were any orders issued for the purpose of moderating his aggressive designs; and it was not till the spring of 1866, when he had failed to capture Jizakh and was forced to retreat before the Bokharan forces, that the Czar's Government thought fit to remove him from his command. When these points have been satisfactorily explained—if such explanation is possible—the English people may be asked to believe that Tchernaieff was deprived of his command because he exceeded his instructions; otherwise they may rest assured that he was recalled, not because he did too much, but because he failed in his attempt to seize Jizakh, and was forced to retreat on the first occasion that Russian troops were brought face to face with the Bokharan forces.

If Tchernaieff had really been superseded on account of his unauthorised advances, it might reasonably be assumed that his successor would have been warned to avoid similar excesses. But, nevertheless, no sooner did Romanoffsky take command than he proceeded to make preparations for a still more serious and unprovoked attack against Bokhara. Large quantities of stores were sent up from Kazala to Chinaz, and in May 1866 a Russian force marched southwards for the invasion of Bokharan territory.

Mozuffer-Eddin had in the meanwhile collected an army of 5,000 regular troops and 35,000 Kirghiz, with twenty-one guns; and numerous petty encounters took place on the banks of the Syr Daria. On May 18 Romanoffsky heard that the Bokharan army was moving in the direction of Tashkent, led by the Amir in person; and although he could only muster fourteen companies of infantry and five sotnias of Cossacks, with twenty guns and eight rocket-stands, he determined, nevertheless, to march against the enemy. Two days later the Russians reached the plain of Irjar, where the Bokharans had taken up a position about two and a half miles in extent, their whole front being covered by swarms of irregular horsemen. After a considerable amount of skirmishing between the Cossacks and Bokharan cavalry, Romanoffsky, towards noon, commenced a heavy artillery fire on the enemy's intrenchments, and shortly afterwards the infantry advanced to the attack. The battle ended in the complete rout of the Bokharans. The Amir fled with a small escort to Jizakh; and the Bokharan troops were scattered in all directions, leaving the whole of their artillery, treasure, and large quantities of stores in the hands of the Russians.

In this battle the Bokharans are said to have lost over 1,000 men, while the Russians' had only between 20 and 30 men killed and wounded—a very trifling loss, considering the great importance of the victory and its far-reaching effects.

After this defeat Mozuffer-Eddin released M. Struvé and his companions, and sent them back to Tashkent loaded with presents. Romanoffsky, however, rapidly pushed forward, and, after capturing Nau, advanced against the city of Khojent. The Russians appeared before the place on May 29, and while part of the force occupied a position about four miles from the city on the Bokhara road, another column took possession of the right bank of the Syr Daria to the north of the town. After two days spent in careful reconnaissances, Romanoffsky commenced the bombardment on June 1. For four days a heavy fire was maintained from eighteen guns and two mortars, and at daybreak on June 5 the assault was delivered. The Russians, taking advantage of the ruggedness of the ground, managed to approach unobserved to within a short distance from the walls, and there planted a battery, which soon silenced the enemy's guns. Then a company under Captain Baranoff rushed forward with scaling ladders, and quickly forced an entrance into the city. But the garrison still held out, and defended themselves from house to house with remarkable vigour, and it was not until the following day that all resistance ceased, and the city of Khojent surrendered at discretion to the victorious troops of the powerful 'White Czar.' In this affair the Russians sustained a loss of 11 men killed or missing, and 122 wounded, while more than 2,500 Khokandians were placed *hors de combat*.

By the capture of Khojent Russia had gained possession of the last important town in the western portion of the khanate of Khokand. Khudayar Khan, panic-stricken and helpless, now found that half his kingdom had been seized, and his chief cities occupied, by the insatiable infidels, who would undoubtedly rob him of his remaining possessions unless foreign help could be obtained. In his distress he appealed to the Khan of Khiva, to Bokhara, and to the rulers of the Usbeg States on the banks of the Upper Oxus, and tried to kindle a holy war against the unbelievers. None of these States, however, cared to incur the wrath of the powerful Muscovites; and when Khudayar found himself left alone opposed to the Russians, he strove to save the remnants of his kingdom by propitiating his enemies. Romanoffsky urged that the whole khanate should be annexed to Russia, and that the capital should be occupied by a Russian garrison. The Government, also, though objecting to such wholesale conquest, desired to occupy the province of Namangan, and thus to limit Khokandian rule to the country south of the Syr Daria. One false step or one aggressive movement on the part of the Khokandians would assuredly have been followed by a Russian occupation of Namangan, and possible annexation of the entire khanate. At this time, however, Khudayar Khan was fortunate in having a shrewd adviser in the person of his Atalyk, or commander-in-chief, Ata Bek; and when he found that he would have to fight the Russians single-handed, he acted on this chief's sound advice, and sent envoys to Romanoffsky to congratulate him on his successful campaign against the Bokharans, and to declare his friendly feelings towards the Russian Government. Thus there was no possible excuse for any Russian movement against Khokand, and the conquest of that khanate had to be postponed.

Romanoffsky, moreover, had not yet sufficiently humbled Bokhara, and further operations towards the south were considered necessary. It was well known that Khokand could be conquered whenever such a step might be considered to be advisable; but the attitude of the Bokharan Amir constituted a standing menace to the Russian position on the Syr Daria. Mozuffer-Eddin, though defeated, was by no means subdued; and although he entered into negotiations with a view to the restoration of peace, it was evident that he had no intention of submitting to the Russian demands. The truce lasted for some months; but eventually, in October 1866, a Russian detachment marched against Ura-tepé, which was defended by one of the strongest citadels in Central Asia. Batteries were established before the place on October 6, and after a close siege for eight days, the fortress was assaulted and captured, after a severe fight, which lasted for about an hour and a half. Abdul Gaffar, the Bek of the place, with most of its defenders, managed to escape to the mountains; but many of the garrison were overtaken in their flight, and hundreds of corpses testified to the severe punishment which had been inflicted. The Russians lost 3 officers and 200 men, but made many prisoners, and among their trophies were 16 guns and 4 standards.

While Ura-tepé was being attacked, another force, under the command of General Krijhanoffsky, moved against Jizakh, which had been greatly increased in strength since Tchernaieff's unsuccessful attempt to reduce it.

After carefully examining the place, and spending some days in constructing siege batteries, Krijhanoffsky commenced the bombardment on

October 28, and at noon on the 30th an assault was ordered. In spite of the natural strength of the place and its strong defences, and notwithstanding the determined resistance of the garrison, the Russians gained a footing within the walls after an hour's fighting. But the enemy for some time refused to surrender, and were slaughtered by hundreds, while some, finding further resistance to be useless, blew themselves up in the powder-magazine. Out of the eighteen Beks who were in the place, only two escaped with their lives, Allayar Bek, the brave commandant, being among the slain. Nearly 6,000 Bokharans were killed, and 2,000 were taken prisoners; while the Russians only lost 6 men killed and 92 wounded. Although the important fortresses of Khojent, Nau, Ura-tepé, and Jizakh had been thus occupied, there still remained one important point which the Russians wished to possess, because it commanded the water-supply of Jizakh, and thus, if held by the Bokharans, would have enabled them to place the Russian garrison of that place in a very critical situation. This was the fort of Yani-kurgan, in the Kara-Tau branch of the Nurata Mountains; and in the spring of 1867 it was seized and occupied by a Russian detachment.

The result of these fresh triumphs was that the Amir, Mozuffer-Eddin, recognising the futility of continuing the struggle alone, was compelled to sue for peace. He first vainly endeavoured to form an alliance with the Amir of Afghanistan.

But the country to the south of the Oxus was then in a very troubled condition on account of the bitter struggle between Dost Mahommed's sons; and although he succeeded in establishing friendly relations with Faiz Mahommed Khan, the Governor of Balkh and half-brother of Shere Ali, he found it impossible to procure Afghan assistance against his vigorous and triumphant enemies. After this he tried to enlist the sympathies of the Indian Government, and sent an envoy to Calcutta to seek the assistance of the British; but England had not yet forgotten the cruel murder of her Ambassadors—Stoddart and Conolly—nor had she yet recovered from her unreasoning dread of interference in Central Asian affairs which had been induced by the Kabul disaster. The Amir's Ambassador was therefore politely snubbed, and Mozuffer-Eddin was left to make the best terms he could with his insatiable foes.

Up to this time the administration of the newly acquired Russian territory had been carried on chiefly through the agency of native officials, and no serious attempt had been made to improve the former methods of government which had been in force under the Khokandian Khans and Beks. But at about the time when Romanoffsky was appointed Governor in supersession of Tchernaieff, a special commission was appointed by the Czar to report on the best means of governing the country. This commission, which is known as 'The Steppe Commission,' consisted of M. Giers, and Colonels Giens, Protsenko, and Dandeville;

and these officers, after careful inquiries, submitted an elaborate report in the spring of 1867, which was submitted for the consideration of a superior committee, under the presidency of the Russian Minister of War, who was assisted by delegates from the Ministries of the Interior, of War, and of Foreign Affairs. As the result of these deliberations, an ukase was published on July 23, 1867, announcing the formation of the Province of Turkestan, which was to be ruled by a Governor-General, who would be appointed by the Emperor, and placed under the orders of the Russian War Office. This new province was to include the whole of the newly acquired territory, together with that portion of the Siberian Province of Semipalatinsk which lies to the south of the Tarbagatai Mountains. Tashkent was fixed as the headquarters of the province, which was divided into the two districts of the Syr Daria and Semiretchinsk, each of which was to be controlled by a military governor nominated by the Ministry of War. The district of Syr Daria included the 'uyezds,' or sub-districts, of Kazala, Perovski, Turkestan, Chimkent, Aulie-Ata, Kurama, Khojent, and the city of Tashkent (which formed a separate sub-district of its own); while the district of Semiretchinsk was divided into the 'uyezds' of Sergiopol, Kopal, Vernoye, Issik Kul, and Tokmak. These orders were not promulgated without a certain amount of opposition. General Krijhanoffsky, the Governor-General of Orenburg, whose authority had hitherto extended over the whole of the newly acquired tracts on the Syr Daria, and under whose orders the military operations had been carried out, was loth to have his power curtailed, and he protested against the proposals of the Steppe Commission, basing his objections on the disadvantages which would result if the Kirghiz were placed under two separate administrations. The correctness of this argument was to a great extent proved by the disturbances which arose among the Kirghiz in 1869 and 1870, when they again revolted, destroyed stations on the postal route, and captured travellers, who were either killed or sold as slaves in Khiva. But Krijhanoffsky was unsupported. The Kirghiz had played their part in the game of Russian aggression, and when no longer useful as an excuse for fresh conquests, were to be permitted to lapse into their former neglected and despised condition. Two of the members of the Commission—viz., M. Giers and Colonel Protsenko—also objected to the inclusion of Semiretchinsk in the new province, on the grounds that the frontier affairs of Siberia and Turkestan required different methods of treatment, and could therefore be best controlled by two distinct sources of authority. These and other minor objections were, however, overruled by the War Ministry, and the new Province of Turkestan was formed on the lines already described. Romanoffsky continued to hold command till the arrival of the first Governor-General in the person of Adjutant-General von Kaufmann, who reached Tashkent on November 17, 1867.

At this time negotiations for peace were still proceeding between the Russians and the Amir of Bokhara. General Krijhanoffsky had drafted a treaty of peace, which had been sent for Mozuffer-Eddin's signature in the previous September—that is, some ten months after the capture of Jizakh and the suspension of hostilities. In this treaty it was stipulated that a part of the frontier line between the new province of Turkestan and Bokhara should follow the crest of the Nurata Range, the Russians being under the impression that there was only one such range, while in reality there are two branches—the Kara-Tau on the north and the Ak-Tau on the south—between which lies the fertile Bekship of Nurata. Before signing the treaty the Amir wished to know which branch of the range was referred to; and thus the negotiations dragged on, the Russians declaring that the point had been raised for the sake of procrastination, and through a desire on Mozuffer-Eddin's part to avoid coming to terms.

In the meanwhile irresponsible bands of Bokharans made raids on the Russian frontier, and a Russian officer (Second-Lieutenant Slushenko) and three soldiers were captured by robbers on the road between Chinaz and Bokhara. A small column, under Baron von Stempel, was sent against the village which was believed to be mixed up in this affair; but although the place was burnt, the villagers fled to the mountains, and so escaped punishment. Kaufmann, however, arrived shortly afterwards, and he at once demanded the release of the captives and insisted upon the immediate signature of the treaty. This action resulted in the release of Slushenko and his companions, but the treaty remained unsigned; and in March 1868 the Russian Governor-General determined to adopt strong measures for the purpose of enforcing compliance with the Russian demands. A force of some 500 Cossacks was accordingly sent to establish a permanent camp close to the city of Samarkand, and to there commence the erection of a fortress. This step naturally roused the anger of the Bokharans, who had not yet forgotten their previous defeats, and were burning to avenge themselves. The progress of the Russians was opposed, and a fight ensued at a place called Uchum, which, of course, resulted in the flight of the native troops. Then, during the absence of the Amir from his capital, the Kazis and Mullahs proclaimed the necessity for a holy war, and roused the people to resist the unwarranted advances of the infidels. Mozuffer-Eddin, knowing that his army was powerless to oppose the troops of the White Czar, tried to pacify the people; but riots took place in Samarkand, and when he returned to his capital he was there ill-treated by the enraged populace.

At this time there were two distinct parties in opposition to the Amir. His eldest son, the Katti-Tiura, was intriguing against his authority, and his nephew, Said Khan, supported by the Beks of Shahr-i-Sebz, Chilek, and Ura-tepé, was also trying to gain possession of the throne. Being aware of the differences between Mozuffer-Eddin and the Russians, Said Khan's party ordered Omar Bek of Chilek to attack the Russian forces near Jizakh, in order that the Russians might be provoked to invade Bokhara, and that Said Khan might thus obtain a chance of seizing the throne during the disturbances which would follow a foreign invasion. This attack was made, but Omar Bek was easily repulsed and fled to Shahr-i-Sebz, lest he might be punished by the Amir for having thus afforded the Russians an excuse for attacking Bokhara.

A few days before this affair, Iskander Khan, an Afghan prince, deserted to the Russians with some 2,000 followers. This prince had been driven out of Afghanistan by Shere Ali during the intestine troubles in that State, and had placed his services at the Amir's disposal; but, becoming discontented with the treatment he received, he, with true Oriental treachery, deserted Mozuffer-Eddin and went over to the enemies of the State which had helped him in his distress. The Russians believed that Omar Bek's attack had been made in retaliation for Iskander Khan's desertion, and Kaufmann therefore decided to strike a blow which should finally break the power of Bokhara and reduce the Amir to a condition of complete vassalage. Hastily collecting a force, he marched to Jizakh, and from thence moved forward towards Samarkand, driving before him the small parties of Bokharan irregular troops which attempted to bar his progress. When he reached

Yani-Kurgan he received messengers from Jura Bek and Baba Bek of Shahr-i-Sebz, two of the rebellious leaders of Said Khan's faction, promising either to afford active assistance against the Amir, or to remain neutral, on the condition that their presence should not be required in Samarkand when the city had been captured by the Russians. Kaufmann expressed his great pleasure at the friendly spirit which had been displayed by the Shahr-i-Sebz chiefs, and assured the envoys that although he stood in no need of any assistance from the Beks, he would respect their wishes in the event of strict neutrality being observed. The Amir also made several attempts to avert hostilities, and sent several messengers to state that the treaty would be signed if further delay was granted. Matters, however, had gone too far, and as the Amir was believed to be desirous of gaining time for the purpose of completing his warlike preparations, the advance was continued.

On May 13 the Russians reached the banks of the Zarafshan River, and found the enemy drawn up on the hill of Chupan-ata. Here another ambassador arrived, with a treaty signed by Mozuffe Eddin, which purported to be the same that had been prepared by Kaufmann. On examination, however, it was found to differ in many important respects from the Russian original, and Kaufmann therefore demanded that the Bokharans should evacuate their position within two hours. But, instead of retiring, the Amir's troops kept up a desultory fire on the Russians, who were drawn up in order of battle; and, therefore, when the stipulated time had expired, Kaufmann ordered the attack. The fight was short and decisive, and the Bokharans soon fled in the wildest confusion, leaving their camp and twenty-one guns as trophies in the hands of Kaufmann's victorious troops.

As soon as the inhabitants of Samarkand heard of this Russian success, they closed the gates of the city against the Bokharan army, and on May 14 sent a deputation to Kaufmann offering their submission, and requesting that the place might be occupied by Muscovite troops. At the same time the other chief towns in the neighbourhood sent delegations to declare their allegiance to the 'White Czar,' the only exceptions to the general surrender being Omar Bek of Chilek, and Hussein Bek of Urgut, who declined to treat with the infidels. Samarkand was at once occupied by the Russians, and thus the ancient capital of the Timurids became an appanage of the Russian Crown.

But although the great Bokharan city had been thus easily captured, the war was by no means at an end. While the main body of troops under Golovatcheff was pushed forward in pursuit of the Amir's army, two detachments were sent against the recalcitrant chiefs of Urgut and Chilek, and another party under Abramoff was sent southwards to watch the movements of the Shahr-i-Sebz troops. At first all went well. Golovatcheff captured the town of Katti-Kurgan; Urgut was taken, although the Bek, Hussein, and his followers escaped; Chilek was forced to submit; and Abramoff, after a slight encounter with the troops from Shahr-i-Sebz, forced them to retire to the hills south of Samarkand. But in spite of the satisfactory commencement of the campaign the position of the Russians became daily more critical. When Kaufmann entered Samarkand he sent Kamal-Eddin, the Kazi Kalian of the city, to summon Jura Bek and Baba Bek to attend at the Russian headquarters—a demand which was in violation of the assurances which had been given to their envoy at Yani-Kurgan. The chiefs at first disbelieved the Kazi's story and cast him into prison; but when they found that Kaufmann had deliberately broken faith with them, they began to suspect treachery, and wrote to the Amir offering to make peace with him, and to help him to continue the struggle against the Russians. Thus these powerful chiefs were, through Kaufmann's ill-advised and unscrupulous action, turned into active enemies, and the Russians narrowly escaped a crushing disaster which might have caused the loss of all their recently acquired territory in Central Asia.

Mozuffer-Eddin, encouraged by the assistance of the Shahr-i-Sebz troops, regained confidence, and collected a fresh army to the west of Katti-Kurgan, while his cavalry cut Kaufmann's communications with Jizakh; some 15,000 horsemen were assembled at Chilek under a nephew of Abdul Gaffar, the late Bek of Ura-tepé; and the whole country round Samarkand was swarming with armed irregulars. But Kaufmann, though in great peril, and cut off from his base at Tashkent, was equal to the emergency. He decided to effect a junction with Golovatcheff at Katti-Kurgan, and then force the Amir to a decisive engagement, which, if successful, would break up the combination against the Russians. He therefore left his sick and wounded in Samarkand, with a small garrison of 762 men, all told, and marched with the remainder of his force towards Katti-Kurgan. But he had only gone a few miles when he received an alarming report from Golovatcheff, who stated that he was completely surrounded by the enemy, who were in great strength. Making a forced march, Kaufmann relieved the garrison of Katti-Kurgan, and then, on June 14, totally defeated the Bokharan army on the heights of Zara-bulak, some few miles to the west of Katti-Kurgan, on the Samarkand-Bokhara road.

But during Kaufmann's absence from Samarkand, the little garrison which had been left to defend the city were having a very anxious time. The main Russian force had scarcely left the place when parties of the Shahr-i-Sebz troops began to appear on the outskirts of the city, and Jura Bek and Baba Bek, with many other minor chieftains, advanced to try and recapture it. Major Stempel, who had been left in command of the garrison, found that it was impossible to defend the great length of wall surrounding the city, and he therefore concentrated his force in the citadel.

A determined attack commenced soon afterwards, and on June 15 the enemy succeeded in setting fire to the gates, their total destruction being only prevented by piles of sand-bags which were placed against them. The garrison was by this time reduced to great straits, and although Stempel sent seven messengers to inform Kaufmann of what was occurring, there were no signs of his return.

At this juncture, when it appeared impossible to save the place, Jura Bek received news of the Amir's defeat on the heights of Zara-bulak, and being misled by a false report that Kaufmann was marching against Shahr-i-Sebz, withdrew his forces, and left the other Beks to their own resources. They, however, still kept up a constant series of attacks until the evening of June 19, and it was not until the arrival of Kaufmann on the 20th with the main Russian army that the remaining irregulars were finally driven from their positions and forced to raise the siege. The relief came just in time. The brave garrison had lost 3 officers and 46 men killed, and 5 officers and 167 men wounded; and although the withdrawal of Jura Bek greatly weakened the attacking force, the defenders had been reduced to the very last extremity, and Stempel had decided to concentrate the survivors of his small force in the Amir's palace—a large building in the centre of the citadel—there to sell their lives as dearly as possible. Had Jura Bek continued to assist in the attack, or if Kaufmann's return had been longer delayed, nothing could have saved the

Russians, and Samarkand must have fallen into the hands of the Bokharans. Such a disaster to the Russian arms would have been the signal for a general combination to expel the troops of the 'White Czar' from Turkestan. Kaufmann would have found himself hopelessly cut off from all assistance, and the small garrisons in Tashkent and the other towns in Russian occupation, would have been attacked by the combined armies of Khokand and Bokhara, aided, most probably, by the Kirghiz and Khivans.

After Kaufmann's return to Samarkand all resistance ceased, and on July 5, 1868, a treaty of peace was signed, whereby the Zarafshan Valley, including Samarkand and Katti-Kurgan, was surrendered to Russia,[1] who also obtained the right of establishing cantonments at Kermineh,

---

[1] In order to allay the excitement which had been produced in England by the rapid advances of Russia to the borders of Afghanistan, Prince Gortchakoff informed the Earl of Clarendon on September 2, 1869, that the Czar did not intend to retain Samarkand, and stated that 'he could give no better proof of his Majesty's determination not to proceed southwards.' This promise was frequently repeated, and on February 20, 1870, the Russian Chancellor informed the British Ambassador at St. Petersburg that the city was not restored to Bokhara only 'because the Emir will not pay us the war indemnity which he is engaged by treaty to do.' The payment of this indemnity had been delayed on account of the continued rebellion of the Katti-Tiura; but although the final instalment of the contribution was paid in 1870, Samarkand was not restored to the Amir, and in April 1875 Prince Gortchakoff finally announced in the following words that all idea of its rendition had been abandoned:—

'The necessity of holding the Amir in check, and the wishes of the population, have been the principal reasons which have compelled us to retain Samarkand.'

Charjui, and Karshi. By this treaty it was also agreed:—

(1) That all Russian subjects, without distinction of creed, should be permitted to trade freely throughout the khanate of Bokhara, the Amir being responsible for the security of all such merchants, their property and caravans.

(2) That all Russian merchants should have the right to appoint agents in all towns throughout the Amir's dominions.

(3) That a maximum *ad valorem* duty of $2\frac{1}{2}$ per cent. should be levied on all Russian goods imported into the khanate.

(4) That Russian merchants trading with neighbouring States should be granted free passes through the khanate.

(5) That the Amir was to pay a war indemnity of 125,000 tillas, of which amount 10,000 tillas were to be deposited immediately, the balance being paid within one year.

By the occupation of the Zarafshan Valley the Russians obtained control over the water-supply of the city of Bokhara, and they were thus in a position to enforce complete compliance with any demands they might subsequently desire to make.

CHAPTER VIII

THE ANGLO-RUSSIAN AGREEMENT OF 1873

Conferences between Lord Clarendon and Baron Brunnow on Russia's advance towards Afghanistan and India—Prince Gortchakoff's map—Gortchakoff's assurances—Controversy on the limitary line—Russia takes time to consider the Indian Government's proposals—Final settlement of the northern frontier of Afghanistan, and Prince Gortchakoff's letter—Russian pledges to respect the integrity of Afghanistan—An incomplete settlement—Present condition of the boundary question.

As the Russian annexation of Samarkand and the Zarafshan Valley created considerable excitement in England, Lord Clarendon, the British Minister for Foreign Affairs, in the following spring had several conferences with Baron Brunnow, the Russian Ambassador, regarding the rapid advances of Russian troops towards Afghanistan and India; and he then said, that while her Majesty's Government felt neither suspicion nor alarm at these movements, yet something had to be done to allay the uneasiness of the British and Indian public. With this object, therefore, he recommended 'the recognition of some territory as neutral between the possessions of England and Russia, which should be the limit of those possessions, and be scrupulously respected by both

Powers.' Baron Brunnow communicated this proposal to his Government; but, before replying, Prince Gortchakoff wished to obtain some clear knowledge of the political geography of the countries between the Russian frontiers and India, and to this end he obtained from Sir Roderick Murchison—then President of the Royal Geographical Society—a map of Persia, Afghanistan, and Beluchistan, which had been prepared by Mr. Weller, a well-known cartographer. In compiling this map, Mr. Weller had been guided more by the ethnographical than by the political divisions of the country; and, therefore, instead of colouring the whole of Afghanistan with one distinctive colour, he showed Afghanistan proper as being bounded to the north by the Hindu Kush Range, while Afghan-Turkestan—i.e., the country between the Hindu Kush and Oxus, and extending from Badakshan to Maimana—was painted a different colour, as if it constituted an independent State.

Armed with this map, Prince Gortchakoff sent an answer to the proposals of the British Foreign Minister, in which, after expressing his satisfaction at the friendly sentiments of the English Government, and after referring with true diplomatic insincerity to the 'profound wisdom' of Lord Lawrence's policy of 'masterly inactivity,' he gave 'the positive assurance' that 'His Imperial Majesty looks upon Afghanistan as completely outside the sphere within which Russia may be called upon to exercise her influence.' Lord

Clarendon consulted the India Office before any further steps were taken for the establishment of a 'neutral zone' between India and the Russian frontiers in Central Asia; and in accordance with the opinions of the Secretary of State, he, on April 17, 1869, informed Baron Brunnow that her Majesty's Government 'had arrived at the decided opinion that Afghanistan would not fulfil those conditions of a neutral territory that it was the object of the two Governments to establish, as the frontiers were ill-defined;' and he then suggested 'that the Upper Oxus, which was south of Bokhara, should be the boundary line which neither Power should permit their forces to cross.'

From this time the idea of a 'neutral zone' was definitely abandoned by the British Government, although Russia for obvious reasons endeavoured on more than one occasion to revive the idea. It would, of course, have been to her advantage that Afghanistan—as shown in Mr. Weller's map—should have been placed outside British influence, while she was to be permitted to absorb the whole of the States lying between her frontiers and the Hindu Kush; but fortunately the Indian authorities clearly recognised the extravagance and one-sidedness of the Russian proposals, and the idea of a neutral zone was absolutely dropped so far as England was concerned in April 1869; the subsequent negotiations being based on the assumption that it was desirable to fix some limitary line beyond which neither Power should advance.

The idea of Lord Mayo's Government was that a girdle of semi-independent States should be formed on the frontier of each country—Afghanistan, Beluchistan, and Kashgar being subject to British influence; while Khiva, Bokhara, and Khokand remained under Russian control. But Russia did not relish this idea. Although the English thereby clearly displayed their desire for peace, Russia had no intention of putting a limit to her advance until she had arrived in close proximity to the frontiers of British India; and, therefore, after some further interchange of communications, this idea also was abandoned, and all that resulted was a repetition of the Russian promise that Afghanistan should be completely outside the sphere within which Russia should be called upon to exercise her authority. This guarantee, however, was of great value, and steps were then taken to arrive at a clear definition of the actual boundaries of the Amir's territories. The Indian Government insisted that the true northern boundary of Afghanistan was marked by the course of the River Oxus 'from the district of Balkh on the west to the extreme east of Badakshan;' and they based their arguments on the fact that the various khanates between the Oxus and Hindu Kush had acknowledged the sovereignty of Dost Mahommed, and had since recognised the government of Shere Ali. After reviewing the conquests and rule of Dost Mahommed, the Indian Government said: 'The north-western boundary of what, in our opinion, ought to be considered Shere

Ali's dominions, runs in a south-westerly direction from a point on the Oxus between Khoja-Sale and Karki, skirting and including the provinces of Balkh, Maimana (with its dependencies of Andkhui, &c.), and Herat (with its dependencies between the Murghab and Heri Rud). The northern boundary is the Oxus, from the same point between Karki and Khoja-Sale eastwards to Punjab[1] and Wakhan, and thereafter the stream which passes Wakhan up to the point where the range of the Hindu Kush meets the southern angle of the Pamir Steppe.' When a copy of the letter containing these remarks was forwarded to the Russian Government, M. Stremooukoff, the Director of the Asiatic Department of the Russian Foreign Office, stated that Khoja-Sale itself should be the point on the Oxus from which the western boundary should commence; and after a brief discussion this was practically agreed to, on the understanding that the district of Khoja-Sale should be considered as constituting a portion of the territories of the Amir of Kabul. From Khoja-Sale the frontier line was to be drawn towards Persia so as to include Andkhui and Maimana in Afghan territory; but M. Stremooukoff added the significant remark that 'great care would be required in tracing a line from thence (i.e., Khoja-Sale) to the south, as Merv and the country of the Turkomans were

---

[1] The meaning here is somewhat obscure. The word 'Punjab' is evidently a misprint for Panjah, and the Indian Government evidently referred either to the River Ab-i-Panjah or to one of the towns on its banks—viz., Bar Panjah or Kila Panjah.

becoming commercially important;' a remark of which the full meaning was only realised some fourteen or fifteen years later when Merv was seized by Russia, and Russian troops had established themselves within easy striking distance of Herat.

Before the Russian Government gave any decision regarding the remainder of the proposed frontier line, they referred the matter to General Kaufmann, as being a person on the spot who could form the best opinion as to the correctness of the arguments put forward by Lord Mayo's Government. But months passed, and even years, without any definite reply having been vouchsafed, and therefore on October 17, 1872, Lord Granville addressed a communication to Lord Augustus Loftus, the British Ambassador at St. Petersburg, in which the northern boundaries of Afghanistan were defined in the following words :—

'For your Excellency's more complete information I state the territories and boundaries which Her Majesty's Government consider as fully belonging to the Ameer of Cabul, viz :

'(1) Badakshan, with its dependent district of Wakhan, from the Sir-i-kul (Woods Lake) on the east to the junction of the Kokcha River, with the Oxus (or Panjah) forming the northern boundary of this Afghan province throughout its entire extent.

'(2) Afghan Turkestan, comprising the districts of Kunduz, Khulm and Balkh, the northern boundary of which would be the line of the Oxus, from the junction of the Kokcha River to the post of the Khoja-Sale inclusive, on the high road from Bokhara to Balkh—nothing to be claimed by the Afghan Ameer on the left bank of the Oxus below Khoja-Sale.

'(3) The internal districts of Akcha, Siripul, Maimana, Shiberghan, and Andkui, the latter of which would be the extreme Afghan frontier possession to the north-west, the desert beyond belonging to independent tribes of Turcomans.

'(4) The western Afghan frontier between the dependencies of Herat and those of the Persian province of Khorassan is well known, and need not here be defined.'

In reply, Prince Gortchakoff, on December 7, 1872, forwarded a copy of a report which he had received from General Kaufmann, wherein the Governor-General of Turkestan disputed the Amir's authority over Badakshan and its dependent district of Wakhan, and also threw doubts on Shere Ali's claims to the districts of Akcha, Siripul, Maimana, Shiberghan, and Andkhui. But in the meantime Russia had completed her preparations for the invasion of Khiva, and it was necessary that she should do something to conciliate the English, in order that her military operations against that khanate might not be interfered with. Therefore, on January 31, 1873, Prince Gortchakoff definitely announced the Czar's acceptance of the northern frontier of Afghanistan, as defined by the British Cabinet, and thereby formally agreed to a limitary line which neither England nor Russia should cross. As this final settlement—so arrived at—constitutes one of the most important agreements between the two Powers concerning Central Asian affairs, and as it is the key-stone of the present political situation, the Russian Chancellor's letter is given *in extenso*. It was addressed to Baron Brunnow, by whom it was communicated to Earl Granville on February 5, 1873, and was as follows:—

'St. Petersburgh, January $\frac{1}{2}\frac{9}{1}$, 1873.'

'M. le Comte,—Lord Augustus Loftus has communicated to me the reply of Her Britannic Majesty's Principal Secretary of State to our despatch on Central Asia of the 19th of December.

'I inclose a copy of this document.

'We see with satisfaction that the English Cabinet continues to pursue in those parts the same object as ourselves, that of ensuring to them peace, and, as far as possible, tranquillity.

'The divergence which existed in our views was with regard to the frontiers assigned to the dominions of Shere Ali.

'The English Cabinet includes within them Badakshan and Wakhan, which, according to our views, enjoyed a certain independence. Considering the difficulty experienced in establishing the facts in all their details in those distant parts, considering the greater facilities which the British Government possesses for collecting precise data, and, above all, considering our wish not to give to this question of detail greater importance than is due to it, we do not refuse to accept the line of boundary laid down by England.

'We are the more inclined to this act of courtesy as the English Government engages to use all her influence with Shere Ali, in order to induce him to maintain a peaceful attitude, as well as to insist on his giving up all measures of aggression or further conquest. This influence is indisputable. It is based not only on the material and moral ascendency of England, but also on the subsidies for which Shere Ali is indebted to her. Such being the case, we see in this assurance a real guarantee for the maintenance of peace.

'Your Excellency will have the goodness to make this declaration to Her Britannic Majesty's Principal Secretary of State, and to give him a copy of this despatch.

'We are convinced that Lord Granville will perceive in it a fresh proof of the value which our august master attaches to the maintenance and consolidation of the most friendly relations with the Government of Her Majesty Queen Victoria.

'Receive, &c.
'(Signed) GORTCHAKOW.'

Such was the famous Agreement of 1873—sometimes erroneously referred to as the Agreement of 1872—and although Russian writers have frequently endeavoured to revive the question of a neutral zone, and have tried to explain that this agreement merely defined the northern limits of the Amir's dominions, and in no way interfered with Russia's freedom of action with regard to Afghanistan, the Czar's Government have repeatedly pledged themselves to respect the integrity of Afghanistan, and have frequently recognised that by this agreement they had bound themselves to abstain from all interference in the affairs of that State. They have stated that while they saw no objection whatever to English officers visiting Kabul, they agreed that Russian agents should not do so; and they have even gone so far as to declare that 'Happen what might, in the internal state of that country, the Imperial Government would not interfere'; and further, that 'If England found it to her interests to annex Afghanistan to the Indian Government, the Russian Government would not regard it as a menace to them, nor would they endeavour to prevent it.'

But although this agreement was satisfactory, so far as it went, the frontiers of the kingdom of Kabul were defined in such an ambiguous manner as to render it very probable that disputes would arise in the future; for while the central portion of the frontier—from the mouth of the Kokcha River to Khoja-Sale—was clearly marked by the course of the River Oxus, the eastern and western portions of the boundary were merely defined in a general way, without any attempt being made to fix the precise boundary in those parts. Thus, the north-western 'territories and boundaries' of Afghanistan—i.e., between Khoja-Sale and Persia—were said to include the internal districts of Akcha, Siripul, Maimana, Shiberghan, and Andkhui: but the limits of those provinces were not specified, and thus the frontier of Afghanistan in this direction remained undefined except in so far that it was recognised that those districts formed a portion of the Amir's dominions. Then, again, in the first clause of the Schedule, certain words were omitted by a careless copyist, and thus the clause was rendered obscure and almost without meaning.

The late Sir Henry Rawlinson, who first pointed out this error, stated that this first clause should read as follows (the omitted words being shown in italics):—

'(1) Badakshan, with its dependent district of Wakhan from Sir-i-kul on the east to the junction of the Kokcha River with the Oxus (or Penjah) *on the west; the stream of the Oxus* thus forming the northern boundary of this Afghan province throughout its entire extent.'

He then claimed that, such being the case, the frontier line between Afghanistan and the Central Asian States under Russian influence should follow the course of the main stream of the Oxus, which rises in the Chak-Mak Kul, or Little Pamir Lake, and, after running for some distance in an easterly direction, then turns to the north-west, and under the name Ak-su, circles round the elevated plateau of the Great Pamir, where it is joined by the Ak-Baital stream, from whence—under the name of the Murghab—it flows down the great Shignan Valley, and unites with the southern branch of the Oxus at Kila-Wamar, on the confines of Roshan; and, in support of this contention, he stated that this Murghab branch of the Oxus was well known to form the northern boundary of the district of Wakhan.

The ambiguity with which the north-eastern and north-western portions of the Afghan frontier were defined in the Agreement of 1873 have, as might have been expected, given rise to serious misunderstandings between the British and Russian Governments. In 1884, after the Russians occupied Merv, they took advantage of the incompleteness of the settlement, seized several important positions which had long been recognised as forming part of Afghanistan, and eventually gained possession of a large slice of territory which undoubtedly belonged by right to the Amir of Kabul; while at the present time, also, negotiations are being carried on between London and St. Petersburg regarding the north-eastern portion of the frontier.

The Pamir region is divided among the petty States of Wakhan, Shignan, Roshan, Darwaz, and Sir-i-kul Of these, Wakhan, Shignan, and Roshan, with a portion of Darwaz, have long formed a part of Afghanistan; the district of Sir-i-kul belongs to the Chinese; and that portion of Darwaz which lies to the north of the Oxus is dependent on Bokhara. During the great Mahommedan rebellion in the western provinces of China, and while Yakoob Beg was an independent sovereign in Kashgaria, the Chinese naturally lost their hold over the Sir-i-kul district; and similarly, after Shere Ali's death, and during the British occupation of Afghanistan,

Shignan, Roshan, and Wakhan were left to look after themselves. But after the Chinese had reconquered the western provinces, their troops were once again sent into the Pamirs, and in 1883 Chinese posts were re-established throughout the Sir-i-kul district; and in the same year also the Amir Abdur Rahman re-occupied the districts of Shignan, Roshan, and Wakhan. The Russians at once protested against this movement on the part of the Afghans; they denied that Shignan and Roshan had ever belonged to Afghanistan, and after pointing out that those districts were not mentioned in the Agreement of 1873, they called upon the British Government to use their influence with the Amir to induce him to cause the withdrawal of the Afghan force. After some delay the British Foreign Office replied that 'the Amir considers Shignan and Roshan are part of Badakshan, which was formally declared in 1872-73 to belong to Afghanistan'—and the Afghan garrisons have since remained in possession.

It will be thus seen that the boundary question which the British and Russian Governments are now endeavouring to settle is a very complicated one; and its settlement has been rendered all the more difficult on account of the careless omission of the line in the first clause of the Schedule of the Agreement of 1873, and also because the English Foreign Office and India Office, by an extraordinary oversight, neglected to include Shignan and Roshan in the list of districts under Afghan control, although they must have known that such was the case. The complication, moreover, has been still further increased by the Bokharan occupation of a portion of Darwaz, which lies on the left bank of the Oxus, and which the Russian Government evidently intend to adhere to as a set-off against the Afghan occupation of Shignan and Roshan.

But although the question is undoubtedly beset with difficulties, four facts remain perfectly clear, and these are: (1) Russia cannot, by any possible interpretation of the clause in question, lay claim to any influence over the territories to the south of the Sir-i-kul branch of the Oxus, and Russian incursions into the countries to the south of that branch of the river can, therefore, only be made in direct violation of the Anglo-Russian Agreement; (2) the Bokharan occupation of territory to the south of the main stream of the Oxus is totally inadmissible and unjustifiable; (3) the Sir-i-kul district to the east of Burzila-Jai, and to the north of Lake Victoria, belongs to China; (4) it would not be difficult to prove historically that Shignan and Darwaz have long formed a portion of the Badakshan province of Afghanistan, and the Amir's claim to those districts cannot therefore be lightly set aside.

CHAPTER IX

1868—1883

KULJA AND KASHGAR

'Bokharan independence'—Petty native disturbances in Bokhara—The Iskander Kul Expedition—Kulja and its history—Affairs of Kashgar, and the rule of Yakoob Beg—Russian occupation and annexation of Kulja 'in perpetuity'—Yakoob Beg defies Russia—British relations with Kashgar—Russian proposals to Yakoob Beg—Kashgar and the Porte—Treaty of commerce between the Indian Government and Kashgar—Projected Russian invasion of Kashgar—Subjugation of Kashgar by the Chinese—Rendition of Kulja to China.

AFTER the capture of Samarkand there was a brief pause in Russia's career of conquest and annexation in Central Asia. By Kaufmann's rapid and successful campaign, Bokhara had been reduced to a condition of complete subjection; for although the Amir nominally retained his position as the ruler of an independent State, he, in reality, became nothing more nor less than a feudatory chief of the Russian Empire. Had it been necessary for the improvement of Russia's strategical position in regard to her designs against India, the Czar could have annexed the whole of Mozuffer-Eddin's dominions without striking another blow, for the victories of Chupan-ata and Zara-Bulak, together with the brilliant defence of Samarkand, had completely cowed the Bokharans, and made them feel the utter uselessness of continuing the struggle against the great Muscovite nation. But it was well known in Russia that no such annexation was necessary, nor would such a step have been politically sound. By permitting the Amir to retain some semblance of independent authority, the Czar's Government avoided the expenses of a military occupation of the country, with its attendant dangers; while they at the same time were able somewhat to allay the irritation in England which had been caused by their recent advances, by pointing to their moderation with respect to Bokhara as a proof of their desire to abstain from fresh conquests. The Russians well knew that so far as the military situation was concerned, annexation would offer no advantages; for from their position in the Zarafshan Valley, commanding the water-supply of the city of Bokhara, they could enforce compliance with all their demands, and could move their troops through any portion of the country without difficulty or opposition; and their strategical position was therefore just the same as though they had advanced their frontiers to the banks of the Oxus.

They therefore decided—and decided wisely—that Bokhara should not be annexed; and they thereby, without losing any strategical advantages, avoided the dangers and expense of an occupation of the country; while the English people—who would have been reduced to a frantic state of alarm if the Russian frontiers had been actually advanced to the borders of Afghanistan—in their ignorance still cherished the belief that 'independent' Bokhara lay between Russia and the kingdom of Kabul, little dreaming that for all practical purposes 'Bokharan independence' is but an idle phrase.

But although the Russians made no further advances towards the middle course of the Oxus, they did not remain idle, but found ample employment in the consolidation of their position in their newly acquired territories, and in making preparations for fresh campaigns. Mozuffer-Eddin had rendered himself obnoxious to his subjects because he had concluded the disastrous peace whereby Samarkand and the Zarafshan Valley had been lost to Bokhara; and Russian troops had to be employed for the suppression of rebellion against the Amir's authority, and for the subjugation of certain malcontent chiefs who, having established themselves in the mountainous district to the south-east of Samarkand, kept the country in a constant state of disorder. Then, again, the rapid extension of Yakoob Beg's power throughout Eastern Turkestan was viewed by Kaufmann with the greatest anxiety; the relations between Russia and the Atalyk Ghazi thus became daily more strained; and eventually the Kulja Valley was annexed, in order that it might not fall into the hands of the remarkable ruler who had formed a new and powerful State on the western borders of the Chinese Empire. Nor were these the only important matters which occupied the attention of the Russian Government after Samarkand had been captured and Bokhara subdued. They clearly saw that the whole military position in Central Asia was a very weak one, and that until Turkestan was placed in communication with European Russia by means of some shorter and more direct line than the old Orenburg-Kazala route, the new districts would never, by their trade, repay the great military expenditure which had been—and was still being—incurred, nor would Turkestan make a satisfactory base of operations against India. Several alternative schemes for the establishment of direct communication between Turkestan and the Caucasus were therefore carefully considered, and it was not long before a Russian force landed at Krasnovodsk, on the east coast of the Caspian, to prepare the way for the conquest of Khiva, and for the final absorption of the whole of the Turkoman country from the Gulf of Astrabad to Merv and the Oxus.

It has already been mentioned that the greatest discontent and restlessness prevailed among the people of Bokhara for some time before Kaufmann invaded the State and seized Samarkand. Two parties had been in a state of open rebellion against the Amir's authority, and disturbances had broken out in Samarkand and in the city of Bokhara itself, Mozuffer-Eddin having been publicly insulted and ill-treated in his capital. The loss of Samarkand, and the disastrous peace which had been concluded with the Russians, did not tend to improve the situation, and it was not long before the general dissatisfaction manifested itself in a fresh outbreak of popular feeling against the Amir, who was considered to have betrayed his country. The Katti-Tiura—who was then at Shahr-i-Sebz, and to whom the Beks of that place had transferred their allegiance—seized the opportunity, and issued a proclamation declaring his father to be an infidel, and therefore quite unfit to rule the State.

The rebel prince then entered into negotiations with the Turkomans, Khivans, and Kirghiz; and as the revolt soon began to assume serious proportions, Kaufmann determined to take steps to show the malcontents that the Russians intended to uphold the Amir's authority. General Abramoff was therefore ordered to take the field; Jam, Kara-tepé, Urgut, and Karshi were speedily occupied by Russian troops; and when the Beks of Shahr-i-Sebz found that the Russian forces were closing round them, they sent in their submission and the rebellion collapsed.

As soon as this insurrection had been suppressed, Kaufmann was able to turn his attention to the restoration of order in the mountainous district to the east of Samarkand. During the disturbances which followed the conclusion of peace between Mozuffer-Eddin and the Russians, the Amir had marched a force into Hissar and Kulab—the two most eastern districts of the khanate of Bokhara—for the purpose of subduing the local Beks, who had endeavoured to assert their independence. While so employed, a portion of the Bokharan army had been detached towards the north to operate against Karategin, which was then a dependency of Khokand. Shere Ali, the Bek of the district, was driven out of the place, and forced to take refuge in Khokand; and Khudayar Khan thereupon complained to Kaufmann of the unprovoked invasion of his dominions by the Bokharan troops. Mozuffer-Eddin, on being expostulated with, tried to prove that Shere Ali had been secretly assisting the rebellious Bek of Hissar; but this charge could not be substantiated, and Kaufmann therefore ordered the Bokharan forces to be withdrawn, and suggested to Khudayar that he should restore Karategin to its former ruler, Mozuffar Shah, who had been some time previously deposed and kept as a prisoner in Khokand. This was done, and Karategin was thus formed into a semi-independent State between Khokand and Bokhara, while the Russians acquired some considerable influence over the affairs of the district.

But Mozuffar Shah had not long been reinstated when he in his turn invaded Bokharan territory. But, while marching to attack Hissar, his troops mutinied, and proclaimed a man named Patcha Hodja as Bek of Karategin; and thus in the course of a few months the Russian nominee was driven from his throne, and the whole of the Kohistan east of Samarkand was thrown into a state of disorder.

Under these circumstances Kaufmann determined to send an expeditionary force into the country to put an end to the constant petty warfare which was there being carried on, while at the same time the opportunity was taken of exploring the head waters of the Zarafshan, and the passes to the south of Lake Iskander Kul.

General Abramoff, to whom the charge of the expedition was entrusted, occupied Urmitan and Varsaminor, and destroyed the forts at Paldorak. He explored the Glacier of the Zarafshan, and, after two severe encounters with the enemy, returned to Samarkand.

During Abramoff's absence on this expedition, difficulties again arose between the Russians and the Beks of Shahr-i-Sebz. Prince Urusof, with a detachment of Cossacks, had been sent out into the country round Samarkand to collect taxes, and while so employed he was attacked by a band of robbers, who succeeded in killing some of his escort. In consequence of Jura Bek, of Shahr-i-Sebz, refusing the Russian demand for the surrender of the leader of the band, an expedition was promptly sent against him. Kitab [1] was carried by assault on August 26, 1870. Shahr immediately surrendered without offering any resistance; and Jura Bek and Baba Bek—the two leading chieftains of the district—fled for safety to Khokand.

The twin cities were then handed over to the Amir, in order to emphasise the great desire on the part of the Russians to abstain from further

---

[1] The name Shahr-i-Sebz, or Green City, is applied to the twin cities of Shahr and Kitab, which are about four miles apart. These two towns, with a few of the adjacent villages and cultivated fields, were formerly surrounded by a massive mud wall, some fifty-three miles in length, and were then known by the name of Kesh.

advances; and Abramoff's force returned to Samarkand, a small detachment being, however, sent once more into the Kohistan to punish the Beks of Farab and Maghian, who were believed to have been implicated in the attack on the Russians on the heights of Kuli Kalan during the Iskander Kul expedition. The two places were soon occupied, and were at once annexed to the Russian district of Urgut; and in the following year—1871 —the remaining mountainous districts were incorporated into the Russian Empire as a portion of the province of Zarafshan.

Having thus briefly reviewed the Russian operations in Bokhara subsequent to the conclusion of peace between the Amir and his Muscovite neighbours, it is now necessary to return once more to the consideration of Russia's movements on the extreme eastern frontier of Kaufmann's great province.

Far away in the very heart of Central Asia there lies a broad fertile valley, watered by a swiftly-running river and its numerous affluents, and encompassed on the north, east, and south by an apparently endless succession of gigantic mountain peaks which are clothed in a mantle of everlasting snow. This is the district of Kulja, which once formed a portion of the ancient kingdom of Dzungaria; and the name of the river is the Ili. For many centuries this well-favoured district had been the theatre of bitter intertribal warfare; and it had been occupied in succession by many of the wild races which inhabited the countries of Central Asia. In the second century before the Christian Era, the Usun—who are supposed by some to be the ancestors of the Suiones—were driven out of Mongolia by the Huns, and forced to migrate to the Ili Valley, where they settled down and became a powerful people. There, however, they found that they were much harassed by the neighbouring nomads, and in the fourth century of the Christian Era they again migrated, and left Kulja to be occupied by the Uighurs—a Turkish tribe that descended from the north and occupied the slopes of the Eastern Thian-Shan range. After the Uighurs came the Kara-Khitai, and these again were conquered at the commencement of the thirteenth century by the Mongols. When the great Genghiz Khan died, Dzungaria, with other regions, fell to the share of his son Jagatai, and his successors held the country until Timur made it a portion of his vast empire.

During the supremacy of the Mongols, Dzungaria was occupied by the three powerful Mongol tribes of Tchoros, Hoshot, and Torgot, who, towards the close of the fourteenth century, formed an alliance for the purpose of obtaining supreme power; and after having overthrown the opposing factions, they became predominant throughout Dzungaria. In the following century the Tchoros tribe became separated into two branches—the Tchoros and Durbot—and then the confederates became known by the name of 'Durben Oirat,' or 'four allies,' and extended their influence throughout Mongolia.

Thus matters remained till the commencement of the seventeenth century, when dissensions arose which led to the secession of certain petty chiefs, who, with their supporters, migrated to Siberia, where they received from the Tartars and Kirghiz the name of 'Kalmuks'—i.e., the remnant. For the next hundred years Dzungaria, under the sovereignty of successive Oirat princes,[1] was the scene of almost incessant warfare; and early in the eighteenth century the Torgot tribe was defeated by Tsevan-Rabdan, and forced to migrate to European Russia, where it settled along the banks of the Volga. In 1745 Galdan Tchirin, the son of Tsevan-Rabdan, died, and was succeeded by one of his sons; but this prince was soon afterwards murdered by his brother; the murderer in his turn was then killed by another brother, who was finally overthrown by two tribal leaders named Amursana and Davatsi. These two conspirators, however, quarrelled, when the former invoked the aid of the Emperor of China, and with the assistance of a Chinese army overthrew his opponent.

China having thus acquired an influence in the country, had no intention of abandoning it, and Amursana thus found himself to be merely in the position of a Chinese governor instead of being an independent sovereign as he had expected to be. He therefore instigated his followers to rise and expel the Chinese forces; but was defeated, and fled to Siberia, where he died in 1757.

[1] These were Kho-no-kho-tsin (or Batur Kun-taitsi), Zenga, Galdan, Tsevan-Rabdan, and Galdan Tchirin.

The Chinese, after having gained this victory, determined to prevent a repetition of the rebellion, and they therefore at once proceeded to indiscriminately massacre the remaining Dzungarian population. This was done so completely that about 600,000 persons were either killed or forced to save their lives by fleeing from the country.

By these drastic measures the Emperor of China found himself to be the happy possessor of a fertile province, but one which was entirely without inhabitants, with the exception of the few soldiers who had effected its subjugation. This difficulty was, however, speedily surmounted by enforced colonisation. Agriculturists were sent from Eastern Turkestan, who became known as Tarantchis (from taran—i.e., millet); criminals, called Tchampans, were deported from the prisons of Southern China; while military colonies were drafted wholesale from Manchuria; and thus in a short time Dzungaria was re-inhabited by a new population entirely under Chinese subjection.

Some years after this (in 1771) the Kalmuks—i.e., the Torgot tribe—who had settled on the banks of the Volga, having heard of the depopulation of Dzungaria by the Chinese, returned there, expecting to find themselves masters of the province on their arrival. Finding, however, that the Chinese were in full possession of the country, they had no alternative but to tender their submission, when they were granted lands on the banks of the Tekes and Kunges Rivers.

The population of the district thus consisted

of a number of different tribes; and, in addition to these, another new race gradually became settled in the Ili Valley during the Chinese *régime*. These were the Dungans, a hardy, temperate tribe of Mahommedans from the Chinese provinces of Shensi and Hansu, who, on account of their being more robust than the Chinese, were chiefly employed as carriers. These people monopolised the carrying trade between China and Kulja, and gradually settled in considerable numbers in the latter province.

The Chinese appear to have relied to a great extent on the race-hatred between these various nationalities for the safe government of the province, as only a small number of regular troops appear to have been kept there. They, however, succeeded in carrying on the government for more than a century, and it was not until the end of that period that general discontent began to manifest itself on account of the oppression of the Chinese officials. In 1836 troubles began. In that year there was an attempt at rebellion, which, however, was easily put down, when the leaders were executed or banished from the country; and again, in 1860 and 1863, other rebellions occurred, but these also were similarly suppressed.

But the general insurrection of the Mahommedan populations against Chinese authority was rapidly gaining ground throughout the empire.

The Chinese garrison of Urumchi was attacked and the city captured by the rebels, who are stated to have massacred 130,000 of the loyal inhabitants and garrison. The Dungans, by the possession of Urumchi, isolated Kulja from China proper, as the direct roads ran through that city. But they were not satisfied with this success, and advanced to Kucha (Kut-che), and also towards Kashgar, while at the same time a force moved to Manas, thus threatening the Ili province.

On receiving intelligence of their compatriots' successes, the Dungans of Kulja again broke out into rebellion in March 1864, but were again suppressed, and the Chinese Governor-General then despatched a strong force to attack the insurgents who had advanced from Urumchi towards Manas. The Chinese troops were defeated and driven back to Kulja, and this was the signal for a renewed rising on the part of the local Dungans, who were shortly after joined by the Tarantchis. Ili (Mantchu-Kulja) and Bayandai were besieged by the Dungans, and disturbances broke out in Old Kulja.

The Kirghiz now joined in the revolt, and commenced plundering the Chinese settlements; and eventually the Dungans, finding that the Chinese were incapable of decided action, grew bolder, and stormed the fort of Bayandai in the spring of 1865, and, having captured it, massacred the garrison and inhabitants. Suidun, Losigun, and Khorgos were in turn besieged, and the insurrection spread to Tarbagatai, while the siege of Ili dragged on.

Matters now appeared to be in as hopeless a condition for the Chinese as can well be imagined; but they seemed determined, by mismanagement, to throw away every possible chance of success. The Kalmuks, who had hitherto held aloof, becoming incensed at a Dungan attack on their great temple, took up arms, and inflicted a severe defeat on the rebels near Ili; and if the Chinese had then, by diplomatic measures, taken advantage of this movement in their favour, it might have still been possible for them to regain their ascendency. They, however, by their ill-advised actions, succeeded in completely alienating the Kalmuks, who interfered no more in the conflict, and on their departure from Ili, the rebels resumed the siege with redoubled energy, and completely surrounded the place, which was reduced to a state of starvation. Finally, in January, 1866, when the provisions had become entirely exhausted, and hundreds of the garrison and inhabitants had died from disease, the city was assaulted. The rebels forced their way into the town, where a horrible butchery took place, in which no consideration was paid to sex or age, and the entire city was converted into a disgusting slaughter-house.

The capture of Ili was a deathblow to Chinese domination in the province, for it was shortly followed by the fall of their remaining strongholds in the north of the district, where the Dungans and Tarantchis became masters of the situation. They, however, could not long agree, and early in 1867 commenced fighting among themselves, to the ultimate advantage of the Tarantchis.

At the time when these disturbances were taking place in Kulja, the Russian district of Semiretchinsk formed a portion of the Siberian province of Semipalatinsk. Russia at that time was fully engaged in her advance towards the frontiers of Khokand, and was therefore not in a position to undertake a forward policy in Kulja, with the risk of being drawn into a quarrel with China, and the Russian frontier officials thus maintained an attitude of strict neutrality, and abstained from all interference in the Ili Valley. In July, 1867, however, Semiretchinsk was removed from Siberian control, and incorporated in the newly-formed province of Turkestan. This change resulted in the adoption of a new line of policy towards Kulja—a policy which was dependent in a large measure on Kaufmann's dealings with the States on his south-eastern frontier.

In the early ages, the territory known by the names of Kashgaria, Alty Shahr, Little Bokhara, or Eastern Turkestan (that is, the country extending from the Alai Range on the west to Lob-Nor on the east, and between the Kuen-Luen and Thian-Shan Mountains), appears to have been subject either to the Chinese or to some of the wandering tribes which inhabited Mongolia. During the eighth century the doctrines of Mahomet began to take root in the country; but owing to the predominance of Buddhism the religion of the Prophet at first made but little headway, and it was not till five centuries later that Mohammedanism began to obtain the ascendency.

During the fourteenth and fifteenth centuries several teachers, or Seids, who were said to be the descendants of the Prophet, and who had the reputation of saints and workers of miracles, appeared in Eastern Turkestan, where they were received with great respect and even enthusiasm; and one of these men, named Hodja-Makhturmi-Aziam, gained considerable renown as a theologian. After this man's death, his two sons, Imam-Kalian and Hodja-Isaac-Vali, were treated with a similar amount of veneration, and from this time the Hodjas (or Khojas) began to obtain a position of great authority through Kashgaria, which has been maintained to the present day. The followers of Imam-Kalian were called Ishkias, and the disciples of Isaac-Vali called themselves Isakias; and subsequently these branches became known as 'White Mountaineers' and 'Black Mountaineers' respectively. These two parties soon became hostile to one another; and although at first their rivalry was confined to religious matters, as each became stronger and gained adherents, their dissensions soon developed a secular turn, and ended in a struggle for political supremacy.

During the following centuries Kashgaria was the scene of almost continual strife, until, in 1865, it fell into the hands of Yakoob Beg, the Khokandian, who had been one of the most prominent opponents of the Russian advance on the Syr Daria, and Chinese supremacy was entirely broken for several years.

Yakoob Beg first entered the country as the 'Batyr Bashi,' or commander-in-chief, of a Hodja claimant to the throne, named Buzurg Khan. But when the Chinese troops had been defeated, he struck out a line for himself, and after defeating his former master in a pitched battle outside Kashgar, was proclaimed ruler of the State. He then entered upon a course of conquest, which, in a few years, extended his rule as far eastwards as Turfan, and to Khotan in the south, thus becoming in a short space of time one of the most powerful sovereigns in Central Asia. He, however, never lost his inveterate hatred towards the Russians, and declined to permit their traders to enter his dominions.

There is no doubt that the rapid successes of Yakoob Beg caused the greatest alarm to the Russian authorities, who could not watch the growth of a strong, independent State so close to their frontier without serious misgivings, especially as the ruler of this State took no pains to conceal his strong anti-Russian proclivities. At first, however, they were far too much occupied with their own operations against Khokand and Bokhara to attempt any interference in Kashgarian affairs, and when Yakoob Beg was proclaimed supreme ruler of Eastern Turkestan, they contented themselves with merely refusing to recognise his position as an independent sovereign.

But in 1867 matters began to assume a different aspect; for the Russians began to display unwonted activity in the Naryn Valley to the north of the Thian-Shan Mountains, and, although they still refused to recognise his status as an independent prince, they nevertheless applied for permission to construct a bridge across the Naryn, and make a military road across the Thian-Shan range. Yakoob Beg, however, emphatically refused to grant this request; he clearly saw that the construction of such a road would place Kashgar at the mercy of the Russians whenever they might wish to seize it; and the Russians, being much irritated at the rebuff which they had received, hastily commenced the construction of a fort in the Naryn Valley, and began to make preparations for an invasion of Kashgar.

This fort was completed in 1868, and in the spring of that year an enterprising Russian trader, named Khludoff, set out from Vernoye with the intention of proceeding to the city of Kashgar by way of Uch-Turfan. He, however, had scarcely crossed the frontier when he was attacked and driven back; but the Russian authorities speedily assisted him to collect another caravan, and, having obtained a certificate from General Kolpakoffsky (the Governor of the district of Semiretchinsk) to the effect that his enterprise was a purely commercial one, he once more crossed the frontier, and on this occasion succeeded in reaching Yakoob Beg's capital. There he combined diplomacy with trade, and by his shrewd conduct managed to persuade the Atalyk Ghazi to enter into negotiations with the Russians.

Khludoff returned to Vernoye in August 1868, accompanied by Yakoob Beg's nephew, Shadi Mirza, who brought with him a letter addressed to General Kaufmann. Kaufmann, however, had just gone to St. Petersburg, after the conclusion of peace with Bokhara, and Kolpakoffsky, therefore, did not permit the Kashgarian envoy to continue his journey to Tashkent. He replied to Yakoob Beg's letter, and sent the answer by Captain Reinthal, who was also instructed to try to conclude a commercial treaty with the Atalyk Ghazi, and at the same time to demand the surrender of certain Kirghiz marauders, and the return of some prisoners whom these men had captured.

Reinthal was received in Kashgar with due consideration, and he was treated during his stay in a hospitable manner. But his movements were closely watched, and he was not allowed to visit other parts of the country; and, on his return, he was forced to confess that he had been able to do little or nothing to remove the misunderstandings between the Atalyk Ghazi and the Russian authorities. Shortly afterwards Kaufmann, while in St. Petersburg, received a report of Shadi Mirza's mission, and gave orders for the envoy to be sent to the Russian capital. On his arrival there, however, Yakoob Beg's ambassador failed to obtain an audience of the Czar, and he therefore returned to Kashgar in January 1869 without having been able to arrive at any satisfactory settlement. Thus the relations between Russia and Kashgar continued on their former unsatisfactory footing.

During this period Yakoob Beg had been consolidating his power over Western Kashgaria, and had steadily extended his authority over the country towards the east. He at first endeavoured to enter into friendly relations with the Dungans and Tarantchis, but failing in this, he soon changed his tactics and picked a quarrel with them. At first they succeeded in holding their own, but after occupying Karashar, Kucha, and Sairam, he, in the spring of 1870, besieged Turfan, which place also surrendered to him, after a defence of four months, in July 1870.

As these movements appeared to be directed against Kulja, the Russians at last determined to occupy that province, so that it might not fall into Yakoob Beg's possession. They therefore occupied the Muzart Pass as a preliminary step to hold the Kashgarians in check while they carried out the annexation of the district. The Russian authorities, however, considered it necessary to bring forward some grievance against the Tarantchis to justify their action, and this was easily obtained. During the revolt of the Dungans and Tarantchis against the Chinese, the Kirghiz had (as has already been mentioned) joined in the insurrection, and from that time they carried on a system of raids both in Russian and Kulja territory. This gave rise to mutual complaints between the Russians and Tarantchis, which were never satisfactorily settled. The Tarantchis repeatedly sent envoys to Vernoye to assure the Russians of their friendship and desire to retain friendly relations; but a ready cause for Russian interference existed, although it is probable that the chief delinquents were Russian Kirghiz, who took advantage of the unsettled state of the border to commit their depredations, and who then took refuge in the mountains outside the Russian territory. Yakoob Beg's advance to Kucha and Turfan having brought matters to a climax, the Kirghiz raids were put forward as the immediate reason for the Russian advance.

At the end of 1870 Baron Kaulbars was sent to Kulja, ostensibly for the purpose of coming to terms with Sultan Abil Ogla (the ruler of the Tarantchis); but there is reason to believe that it was not intended that a satisfactory solution should be arrived at, and the negotiations fell through.

On his return preparations for an advance were begun. On June 24, 1871, General Kolpakoffsky left the town of Borokhudzir with about 1,800 men, and commenced a rapid advance on Kulja. On June 28 he defeated about 4,000 Tarantchis at Alim-tu; and two days afterwards gained another victory in front of Chin-cha-ko-tsi, which town fell into his hands on the same day. On July 1 he occupied Suidun, and two days later, while near Bayandai, received an embassy from Sultan Abil Ogla, who formally tendered his submission. In the evening of the same day the Sultan arrived in the Russian camp and delivered himself up, and on the next day (July 4) Kolpakoffsky occupied Kulja just too late to prevent the massacre of over 2,000 Dungans and Chinese, who had been mercilessly slaughtered by the Tarantchis as soon as they heard of the surrender of their chief.

Kulja—or 'Dzungaria,' as it was called in the proclamation—was shortly afterwards annexed to Russia 'in perpetuity,' and received the name of the 'Priilinskaya Gubernaya,' or the Government of Priilinsk. The Russian Foreign Office, however, immediately informed the Chinese Government that the province would be restored to China as soon as the Emperor could send a sufficient force for the permanent occupation of the country, so as to preserve it from external attacks and to maintain order among its turbulent inhabitants.

It is now necessary to return for a moment to Kashgar to follow the fortunes of its remarkable ruler. As direct relations between Russia and the Atalyk Ghazi had been suspended, General Kaufmann turned to Khudayar Khan of Khokand, in hopes that that chief might be persuaded to attack Kashgar, and thus save Russia the trouble and expense of military operations beyond the Thian-Shan range. He tried to work on the Khan's vanity, and explained how Yakoob Beg and his best lieutenants had been his former subjects, and that, therefore, Kashgar should form, not an independent and rival administration, but a province subject to Khokand. Khudayar was therefore urged to invade Eastern Turkestan, and to add the country to his dominions.

The Khan, however, had no desire to be drawn into a quarrel with his powerful neighbour. He declared that Yakoob Beg had given him no offence; and then with bitter irony he pointed to the map and showed how Khokand should extend further towards the west, and ended the matter by saying that the conquest of the plains of Kashgaria would be but a poor equivalent for the loss of Tashkent and Khojent. He, however, promised to use his influence to persuade Yakoob Beg to come to terms with the Russians, and he therefore sent Sarymsak Udaitchi with a letter to the Atalyk Ghazi, counselling him to make peace with Russia. Yakoob, however, while receiving the envoy with respect, declined to enter into negotiations with the Russians, as they had refused to acknowledge his position as the ruler of an independent State; and in reply to the suggestion that he should enter into commercial relations with Russia, he said, 'The Russians that have come here, into my State of Kashgar, look at these localities and become acquainted with the state of the country; and therefore it is better to forbid their coming, for they are a treacherous and crooked-minded people.' This defiant reply clearly demonstrated to Kaufmann that the Atalyk Ghazi was determined to insist on being treated as an equal, and that he had no intention of being frightened into granting any political or commercial concessions.

But just before the receipt of this bold letter, Kaufmann had himself written a letter to Yakoob Beg threatening war if he did not mend his ways and enter into friendly intercourse with the Russians, in the same manner as had been done by the Khokandians and Bokharans; in other words, Kashgar was to become subservient to Russia, or otherwise the country would be attacked and probably annexed. Nor was this an idle threat. Russia had fully determined to go to war if nothing else would bring Yakoob Beg to reason. But, before taking this final step, Kaufmann tried still once again to bring about the re-establishment of diplomatic relations with Kashgar through the good offices of the Khokandians. He therefore induced Mirza Hakim to write a letter to a certain Khokandian named Akhrar Khan, who had formerly held high office under Khudayar Khan, but had since migrated to Kashgar, informing him of the Russian preparations for the invasion of Eastern Turkestan, and advising him to induce the Atalyk Ghazi to adopt a more conciliatory line of conduct. To this letter Akhrar Khan replied that his master Yakoob Beg considered it was useless for the Governor-General to attempt to establish diplomatic relations through the agency of the Khan of Khokand; and that if the Russians really desired to form an alliance with him, they could send an embassy, when the envoys would be well received and the matter favourably considered. 'The Badaulet'—it was said—'does not deny either the power or resources of Russia, but as a brave man he places his trust in God, and will never refuse to fight, for he does not fear death, and all he aspires to is to die for the faith.'

Thus, for the first time in the history of Russia's dealings with the States of Central Asia, an Asiatic ruler, by his dignified independence, completely nonplussed the Czar's officials; and in this way Yakoob Beg forced Kaufmann to make the first move to effect a reconciliation. The Governor-General of Turkestan began to realise that he was confronted by a determined chieftain whose power was daily increasing, and who might, unless propitiated, set himself up as the champion of Islam, and incite the Mahommedan States of Central Asia to undertake a holy war against the Russians. He therefore decided to send a mission to Kashgar, and in May 1872 Baron Kaulbars set out from Kulja for Yakoob Beg's capital, accompanied by an engineer, a topographer, and a merchant. Meanwhile, however, the warlike preparations were continued, troops were massed along the Russian frontier to the south of Lake Issik Kul, a military road was made across the mountains, and stores were collected at the Naryn Fort.

The objects of Kaulbars' mission were threefold. He, firstly, was to acquire information regarding the country, and to ascertain if Yakoob Beg really was the powerful ruler he was generally supposed to be. Then he was to endeavour to obtain a monopoly of the trade in order that the British might be shut out from commercial relations with the country. And, finally, he was to find out what the Atalyk Ghazi's intentions were regarding Kulja and Khokand.

Russia at this time was very jealous of English interference in Kashgarian concerns. Some few years previously—in 1868—after Yakoob Beg had established his position in the country, he had sent a man named Mahommed Nazar to the Punjaub to take notes of the strength and resources of the Indian Empire. Mr. Shaw, who was then in Ladakh, then told this envoy that he greatly desired to visit Kashgar, and after some little delay the Atalyk Ghazi's consent was obtained, and Shaw entered Eastern Turkestan in December 1868, being the first Englishman who had ever set foot in that country. He remained there for three months as the guest of the Atalyk Ghazi, who treated him most hospitably and had several friendly interviews with him. While there, Mr. Hayward—who afterwards was murdered in the wild country north of Gilgit—also reached Kashgar, and although this fresh arrival for a short time rendered Yakoob Beg suspicious and caused him to detain the two Englishmen in a kind of honourable captivity, the matter ended happily, and the first two English explorers of Eastern Turkestan returned to India in safety.

While in Kashgar, Mr. Shaw had strongly urged Yakoob Beg to maintain a representative in the Punjaub, and some months after the Englishmen's return to Ladakh, the Atalyk Ghazi de spatched Akhrar Khan on an embassy to India, to urge the British Government to enter into commercial relations with Kashgaria, and to send a British officer to his dominions as an official representative of the Indian Government. In response to this invitation, Mr.—afterwards Sir Douglas—Forsyth was sent as the first British envoy to Eastern Turkestan. Accompanied by Mr. Shaw and Dr. Henderson, he reached Yarkand in 1870, but there heard that Yakoob Beg was away on the far eastern frontiers of his dominions, engaged in suppressing the Dungans of Turfan and Urumchi; and, as nothing could be effected, the mission was obliged to retrace its steps in September 1870. In the following year, however, Yakoob Beg once more sent Akhrar Khan to India to renew his protestations of friendship, entrusting him with letters to the Queen and Viceroy of India.

Thus while the Atalyk Ghazi was persistently refusing to negotiate with the Russians through the mediation of the Khokandians, he was openly displaying his friendship towards the English, and this fact, no doubt, greatly influenced Kaufmann in his decision to send Baron Kaulbars to Kashgar.

When the Russian ambassador first reached Yakoob Beg's capital, he was received in the most cordial manner. At the first audience the Atalyk Ghazi said: 'Ye are guests sent to me from heaven; sit upon my knees, on my bosom, or where ye like;' and then a short time later, after the Russians had been shown all the objects of interest in the neighbourhood, and had attended reviews of the Kashgarian troops, he again said: 'I look upon the Russians as my best friends; if I did not, should I have shown you my military power? Surely it is not usual, even with you Russians, to make known one's actual condition to a possible enemy.' But when he found that the Russians were still continuing to mass troops on his northern frontiers, his manner soon changed, and he declined to sign the proposed commercial treaty until the warlike preparations had been stopped.

Eventually, however, the treaty was signed on June 22, 1872; but Baron Kaulbars, in order to prove the complete success of his negotiations, had it dated June 2 (old style, May 21) or St. Constantine's day, and then wrote to Kaufmann saying that, as a mark of especial goodwill, Yakoob Beg had insisted on signing the treaty on that day in honour of Kaufmann's patron saint. This, however, was a little too much even for Kaufmann's vanity, and he therefore, in forwarding the despatch to St. Petersburg, substituted the name of the Grand Duke Constantine (the Emperor's brother) for his own. This treaty, however, remained a dead letter, and no good feeling sprang up between the two countries; the mutual distrust continued, and trade languished.

Soon after Baron Kaulbars had left Kashgar, Yakoob Beg sent his nephew Seid Yakoob Khan—commonly called the Hadji Torah—on a return mission to St. Petersburg, where the envoy was treated in the most princely fashion. After concluding his business in the Russian capital, Hadji Torah turned southwards, and after visiting Moscow and Odessa, he arrived in Constantinople, from whence he returned to Kashgar viâ the Suez Canal and India. While at Constantinople this ambassador concluded certain secret negotiations with the Sultan, and it shortly afterwards became generally known that the Sultan had conferred the title of 'Amir-ul-Muminin' on Yakoob Beg, who in his turn acknowledged the suzerainty of the Porte, and even began to issue a new coinage bearing on one side the head of Sultan Abdul Aziz. When this became known in Russia, the military party at once declared that such an alliance between the two Mahommedan States constituted a great danger to the Russian position in Central Asia, and they clamoured for an expedition to be sent to finally subdue the haughty ruler of Kashgar. But at that time the Czar's Government had decided to invade Khiva, and peremptory orders were issued that operations beyond the Thian-Shan range were on no account to be undertaken; and thus the projected invasion of Kashgar was once more postponed.

The troubles about trade meanwhile continued, and in 1873 a Russian caravan was sent to Kashgar under a man named Somof, the clerk of a Mr. Pupysheff, who had large business connections with most parts of Central Asia. On arriving at Kashgar, however, Yakoob Beg himself bought up the greater part of the goods, and prohibited Somof from making any commercial expeditions to Yarkand and Khotan. This wholesale purchase of stores was a very astute move on the Atalyk Ghazi's part, as thereby he gave the Russians no excuse for lingering at Kashgar; but when payment was made the merchant found that he received his pay in Chinese coins at a value fixed by the Atalyk Ghazi himself, which was considerably above their real commercial value, and in this way the trader lost some 15,000 roubles. The Russian authorities took up the matter, and, after considerable delay, Yakoob agreed to pay

12,000 roubles, which was the final amount claimed after the matter had been investigated by a commission at Tashkent.

In the meantime the English Government decided to send another mission to Kashgar in response to Yakoob Beg's second invitation; and in the autumn of 1873 Mr. Forsyth once more set out for Eastern Turkestan, accompanied by Colonel T. E. Gordon, Dr. Bellew, and Captains Chapman, Trotter, and Biddulph. The learned Dr. Stoliczka[1] also joined the party, and there was an escort of ten sowars, and one naick and ten sepoys of the Corps of Guides. On reaching the frontier district of Sanju, the embassy was joined by the Hadji Torah, who had pushed on by forced marches as soon as he reached India, and from this time he, by his tact and good-will, did much to assist Forsyth in the execution of his delicate task. On December 4 the mission reached Yakoob Beg's capital, and seven days later Forsyth had his first formal interview with the strange chieftain who had become so famous throughout the wild countries of Central Asia, and who, by his bold and clever policy, had made both England and Russia anxious to cultivate his friendship. Forsyth and his companions were received with the utmost distinction and cordiality; they were permitted to move freely about the country, and the Kashgarian officials, and even the common people, vied with each other in their efforts to display their friendly feelings

---

[1] This gentleman unfortunately died in the Passes from the effects of the rarefied atmosphere.

towards the British Elchi and his staff. Throughout their stay they travelled free of all expense, and Yakoob Beg insisted on paying his subjects for whatever service they rendered to the members of the Embassy.

On February 2, 1874, Yakoob Beg signed a treaty of commerce with the Indian Government, whereby the subjects of either State were to be permitted to trade freely and without restriction in the dominions of the other contracting party; and on March 16 Forsyth took leave of the Atalyk Ghazi, and commenced his return march to India; Colonel Gordon, with a portion of the escort, turning westward to explore the little known regions of the Pamir Plateau, which had previously been visited by only one Englishman—the intrepid Captain John Wood of the Indian Navy.

The Russians were by no means pleased at the conclusion of this commercial treaty between England and Kashgar, as they had no wish to see British traders competing with theirs in the markets of Eastern Turkestan. They therefore considered it necessary that immediate steps should be taken to increase their influence in Yakoob Beg's dominions, and for this purpose Colonel Reinthal (the same officer who visited Kashgar in 1868) was sent to demand that Russian consular agents should be permitted to reside in the chief cities in Kashgaria. But Yakoob Beg too clearly realised the dangers which would follow the establishment of such Russian agents in his dominions, and he resolutely set his face against any such concessions. In

Article III. of the Commercial Treaty of 1872 it had been stipulated that 'Russian merchants shall, if they desire it, have the right to have commercial agents (caravan-bashis) in all the towns of Djety-Shahr (i.e. Kashgaria), whose business it is to watch over the regular courts of trade, and over the legal imposition of customs dues,' and Reinthal contended that this clause was intended to mean that Russia could appoint consular agents in the chief towns of Yakoob Beg's kingdom. The Atalyk Ghazi would, however, permit no such construction to be placed on the article in question. A caravan-bashi—as both he and the Russians knew full well—means the leader of a caravan, who is generally an uneducated and unimportant personage, who merely looks after the personal affairs of the traders. He had no intention of permitting this personage to be supplanted by a prying Aksakal or Mirza, who would foster intrigues and foment rebellion against his authority for the advancement of Russia's aggressive designs; and he therefore rejected Reinthal's proposals, and the Russian ambassador was forced to return without a vestige of success.

On his return the Turkestan authorities decided that force should be used to remove the objectionable ruler who had so often thwarted their designs, and had even rendered them ridiculous in the eyes of the other chiefs in Central Asia. Preparations were, therefore, once more made for commencing a campaign against Kashgar: stores were pushed forward to Kulja and the Naryn Valley, and a

Russian mission was sent to Khokand to obtain Khudayar Khan's consent to the passage of a subsidiary column through his dominions, in order that Kashgaria might be simultaneously invaded from the north and from the west. But, as will be subsequently described, a serious rebellion broke out in Khokand, when Khudayar was driven out of his dominions, and bands of Khokandians crossed the Russian frontiers and even threatened Tashkent and Khojent. Thus the projected invasion of Eastern Turkestan was turned into an attack on Khokand, which resulted in the annexation of that province to Russia. But even after the conquest of Khokand the relations between Yakoob Beg and the Russians still continued to be most unsatisfactory; and Kaufmann was seriously meditating an invasion of Eastern Turkestan, when events occurred which rendered such a step unnecessary. The days of the remarkable Atalyk Ghazi, or Amir of Kashgaria, were fast drawing to a close, and China, by once more establishing her authority throughout the countries to the south of the Thian-Shan range, deprived Russia of any further excuse for interference in Kashgarian affairs.

In the autumn of 1876 messengers arrived in Kashgar, bringing to Yakoob Beg strange and terrible news from the north-eastern frontier of his dominions—strange on account of its very unexpectedness, and terrible to the Atalyk Ghazi, because the message thus brought clearly proved that the Emperor of China had, after many years of apparent forgetfulness, once more turned his attention towards the West, and determined to employ the whole strength of his Empire to overthrow the usurper, and to re-establish Chinese supremacy throughout Eastern Turkestan. The intelligence thus suddenly brought to Kashgar was to the effect that a large Chinese army, under Tso Tsung Tang, had appeared in the country to the north of the Thian-Shan range, and, after capturing Urumchi, was closely besieging the town of Manas, while a subsidiary force, under another Chinese general, Chang Yao, was in possession of Hamil, to the south of the mountains.

The Atalyk Ghazi at once nerved himself for the conflict, and hastily collected an army of some 17,000 men, he marched eastwards to do battle in defence of his kingdom.

He occupied the towns of Turfan and Toksoun, on the extreme eastern frontier of Kashgaria, and there halted, after detaching a small force of 900 men and two guns to the village of Devanchi, at the southern entrance to the Devan Pass. But here he was fairly caught in a trap. Chang Yao, in the middle of April 1874, seized the towns of Chightam and Pidjam, to the east of Turfan; and then a simultaneous advance was made by the Chinese armies from the north and east, which soon resulted in the complete overthrow of the Atalyk Ghazi's army and his headlong flight towards Kurla, where—on May 1, 1877—he was assassinated by Hakim Khan Torah, the chief of Kucha and son of his old master and subsequent enemy, Buzurg Khan Hodja. Thus ended the career of this remarkable soldier of fortune, ' who, without birth, power, or even any great amount of genius, constructed an independent rule in Central Asia, and maintained it against many adversaries during the space of twelve years.'

After some months' halt in the neighbourhood of Turfan, the Chinese armies again began to move forward in August 1877 for the complete subjugation of Kashgar.

All hope of resisting the invaders vanished, and after an absence of fourteen years, the Chinese regained complete ascendency over the whole of Eastern Turkestan. By this remarkable campaign China thoroughly vindicated her right to take her place as one of the three Great Powers of Asia, and clearly demonstrated to the startled politicians of Europe that she is a potent factor in the Central Asian Question.

As soon as the Chinese had thus firmly reestablished themselves in Eastern Turkestan, the Emperor determined to remind Russia of her promise to restore Kulja to China as soon as the Pekin authorities could send a force sufficiently strong to maintain order in that province. Such a force had undoubtedly established itself in Kashgaria, and China now was perfectly capable of fulfilling the Russians conditions with respect to Kulja; and Tso Tsung Tang therefore preferred a formal demand that the Ili Valley should be handed over to him. This request, though by no means unexpected, was nevertheless most annoying to the Russians, and they plainly showed that they had no intention of quietly abandoning one of their richest provinces in Central Asia. Eventually, after some months' delay, a high Chinese official named Chung Hao was sent to St. Petersburg for the purpose of arriving at an amicable settlement of the difficulty; and in September 1879 this ambassador concluded a treaty at Livadia, wherein it was stipulated that a portion of the Kulja province was to be restored to China, Russia however retaining the Tekes Valley and the passes of the Thian-Shan leading into Eastern Turkestan. China was further to pay five million roubles to defray the expenses incurred in the temporary occupation of the country, and as indemnity to the Russian traders for losses incurred through Mahommedan revolts and the oppression of the Chinese officials. The treaty also contained clauses granting to Russia some important trade privileges, and some important references were also made to the boundary line between Khokand and Kashgaria.

Chung Hao returned to Pekin early in January 1880, but on his arrival there he was greeted with a perfect storm of popular indignation. He was declared to have betrayed his country, was deprived of his State offices, and was handed over to a competent tribunal for trial and punishment. On January 28 the commission recommended that he should be dismissed from the public service; and he was then cast into prison, an order being shortly afterwards issued for his decapitation. Marquis Tseng, the Chinese ambassador to England, was then appointed special ambassador to the Russian Court for the negotiation of a fresh treaty, as the Chinese Emperor absolutely refused to ratify the Livadia Convention. Russia, however, declined to resume negotiations unless Chung Hao was first pardoned and set at liberty; and for many months the relations between the two countries were very strained. Both parties made energetic preparations for war; Chinese armies were massed along the Amour and on the frontiers of Kulja, while the Russians in turn pushed forward reinforcements to the Ili Valley; and for a time it seemed as if nothing could prevent the outbreak of a tremendous struggle between the Chinese and 'the Barbarians of the West.' All the foreign ambassadors at Pekin, however, supported the Russian demand for Chung Hao's acquittal, and finally—on August 12—an order for his release appeared in the Pekin Gazette. The negotiations between Russia and China were then resumed; and after a lapse of what, under the circumstances, may well be considered a very short period, Tseng succeeded in inducing the Czar's Government to agree to the rendition of the whole of the Kulja province, except a small and unimportant portion which was to be used as a refuge for such Dungans as might desire to remain under Russian protection. In other respects this treaty differed but little from the previous one which had been negotiated by Chung Hao; but the Chinese had made up their minds that Kulja should be recovered, and, once that point had been gained, the national sentiment was satisfied, and they paid but little heed to the other points.

Tseng's treaty was concluded at St. Petersburg on February 12, 1881, and was ratified within six months, but it was not until the spring of 1883 that the Russians finally evacuated the Ili province. Early in March of that year the garrisons were marched across the newly-defined frontier into Russian territory, leaving a small detachment of Cossacks in the town of Kulja for the protection of the Russian Consul and traders in that place. They, however, had scarcely left when troubles broke out among the tribes, who were by no means friendly to the Chinese, and serious disputes also occurred between the Chinese and Russian frontier officials, owing to the Russians having advanced some five miles beyond the boundary line as fixed by the treaty. The matter was, however, soon arranged, the delimitation of the new frontier was speedily concluded, and a protocol was signed at Chuguchak on October 19, 1883, by the plenipotentiaries of the two Empires.

CHAPTER X

1869—1873

CONQUEST OF KHIVA

Occupation of Krasnovodsk and its object—Gortchakoff's explanations to Great Britain—Protestations from the Khan of Khiva and the Persian Government—Kirghiz insurrection—Skobeleff and Markozoff's reconnaissances—Council at St. Petersburg—Advance to Khiva and march of the Russian columns—Disasters of Markozoff's column—Bombardment of Khiva—Surrender of Khiva and Kaufmann's triumphal entry—Treaty of peace—Reaction in England against Russia.

SHORTLY after the capture of Samarkand, and while the Russians were engaged in restoring order in the Khanate of Bokhara, and in subduing the petty Bekships in the mountainous districts round the head-waters of the Zarafshan, another important movement was being made far away to the west. In November 1869 a small Russian detachment quietly left the port of Petrovsk, and shortly afterwards landed at Krasnovodsk, on the eastern shores of the Caspian Sea. The force which thus established itself at the mouth of the ancient bed of the Oxus was under the command of General Radetsky, the officer who afterwards distinguished himself by his successful operations in the Shipka Pass during the last Russo-Turkish war. A site was at once selected for the construction of a fort, and as soon as the garrison had been properly established, Radetsky returned to the Caucasus, when the command devolved on Colonel Stolietoff, who afterwards led the Russian mission to Kabul in 1878.

This occupation of Krasnovodsk, though apparently insignificant in itself, was nevertheless an act of the very greatest importance, for thereby Russia initiated the most important movement in the whole of her great scheme for empire in Central Asia—a movement which has not only resulted in the connection of Turkestan with the Caucasus and the consolidation of Russian power in Central Asia, but which has brought the Czar's troops within close striking distance of the most vulnerable portion of Afghanistan. It is well, therefore, to clearly understand why this move was made, and to consider the reasons which induced the Russians to deliberately occupy a position on the eastern shores of the Caspian, where they would assuredly come into collision with the warlike Turkoman tribes who inhabit the countries between Persia and the River Oxus.

While the Russians were advancing along the Syr Daria from Fort Aralsk towards Tashkent and Samarkand, their position in Central Asia was one of considerable strategical weakness. Reinforcements could only reach Turkestan from Orenburg after great delay and toilsome marches across the Steppes, and had any serious disaster occurred to the Russian arms, it would have inevitably been followed by a complete collapse of Muscovite supremacy in the countries to the south of the Kirghiz Steppes. Thus it was clear that, for military reasons alone, it was most necessary that Turkestan should be linked to European Russia by means of some shorter route than the old Orenburg-Kazala line. Then, again, there were financial and administrative reasons for such a step. Hitherto the Czar's Asiatic provinces had been a constant drain on the resources of the Empire. Vast sums had been expended in fitting out the expeditionary forces which were necessary for the conquest of the country, and constant military expenditure was needed for the maintenance of garrisons at the main strategical points in the newly-acquired territories. All this time but little or no revenue was received, and it was clear that until a short and safe trade route could be established between Europe and Central Asia, the Czar's Government could expect to gain no profit from the occupation of their new provinces. And, finally, there was the question of offence to be considered as well as defence. The Turkestan army could never be of any use for an attack on India until it could readily receive reinforcements and supplies from European Russia; and as the possibility of an attack on India has never been lost sight of in Russia, this point was no doubt carefully considered when the question of better communication with Turkestan came to be discussed.

A glance at the map will show that the shortest line of communication between European Russia and the Russian provinces in Central Asia would start from some point on the east coast of the Caspian Sea, and must pass either through the Khanate of Khiva or through some portion of the adjoining territory which is inhabited by the Turkomans, some of whom were subjects of the Khan of Khiva. But the greater portion of this tract of country is nothing better than a barren sandy desert which appeared to offer an almost insurmountable obstacle to any advance in that direction, and it can well be understood why the Russians for some time hesitated before they seriously set to work to open up communication with Turkestan by a direct line from the east coast of the Caspian. In 1868, however, General Romanoffsky brought out a pamphlet on Central Asian affairs, which attracted a considerable amount of attention in Russia at the time, in which he pointed out the urgent necessity of at once establishing direct communication between the Caucasus and Turkestan, in order that the military resources of the southern province might be utilised in Central Asia. In this *brochure* Romanoffsky suggested three alternative routes which might be adopted, viz. :—

1. From Krasnovodsk along the ancient bed of the Oxus to Khiva.

2. From the mouth of the River Emba round the north of the Sea of Aral, to Kazala on the Syr Daria. And

3. Across the Ust-Yurt plateau, through Khiva to the Oxus.[1]

[1] This third alternative line had been previously recommended

He himself recommended the adoption of the third line; and there is no doubt that the first and last were the only two routes which were ever seriously considered by the Russian authorities; for the line from the Emba round the northern shores of the Aral Sea was a long and circuitous one, and considerable outlay would have been required to provide water in the portions on the skirts of the Kara-Kum sands near the mouth of the Emba. After some consideration the Russian Government decided to make Krasnovodsk the starting-point for the new route to Central Asia, and thus, as has been mentioned, a force sailed across the Caspian in November 1869, and occupied that place.

Now it will be well to pause and inquire why the Czar's advisers selected Krasnovodsk as the western terminus of the proposed route to Turkestan, instead of adopting the more northerly line across the Ust-Yurt plateau, which would have been shorter and would also have been safe from flank attacks from the direction of Persia. It must be borne in mind that in the year of grace 1869 but little was known concerning the regions to the north of Persia, and the general geography of Central Asia was but little understood. The English, however, knew of the existence of Khiva, and they believed that Russia's object in landing

by Prince Bariatinsky, who suggested that a railway should be constructed across the Ust-Yurt plateau between the Mertvii-Kultuk Bay on the Caspian and Chernishef Bay on the Aral Sea. The execution of this project had for some years been seriously contemplated by the Russian Government.

on the eastern coast of the Caspian was in order that she might obtain a more convenient base of operations from which Khiva could be successfully attacked. Such, no doubt, was partly the object of the occupation of Krasnovodsk; but, although the English people did not know it, Russia had another and more important object in view which could not have been attained if the Ust-Yurt line had been adopted, and if a point on the Mertvii-Kultuk Bay had been occupied, instead of Krasnovodsk. Russia knew full well that between the Caspian and Turkestan there were only two possible lines of communication, viz.: one through Khiva, and the other along the northern frontiers of Persia, and thence through Merv to Bokhara. By occupying Krasnovodsk she gained a position from which she could push forward on either or both of these lines as the opportunity might occur, while, from the Mertvii-Kultuk Bay, she could have only dealt with the route through Khiva. Thus it will be seen that the occupation of Krasnovodsk marks the commencement of a most important design, not merely for the conquest of Khiva, but it was also part and parcel of a more elaborate scheme for the connection of Turkestan with Europe by means of a direct route from the eastern shores of the Caspian, and for the subjugation of the Turkoman tribes between the northern frontiers of Persia and the River Oxus.

For some years it was not realised in England that the chief danger from this new development of Muscovite activity lay in the possibility of a

Russian advance along the northern borders of Persia towards Merv and Herat. Sir Henry Rawlinson and a few other experts did indeed clearly explain how Russia would assuredly obtain a formidable and threatening position on the borders of the Herat province as the natural result of this preliminary occupation of Krasnovodsk; but their warnings were unheeded, they themselves were believed to be alarmists and Russophobes, and the English people, after some slight show of interest, once more relapsed into their usual condition of calm indifference to Central Asian affairs, happy in their belief that the Turkomans would, by their resistance, offer a barrier to the Russian advance which would at least last for many years, and that, even if that obstacle were overcome, Herat would still be safe behind the mythical range of snow-clad mountains with which cartographers delighted to embellish their maps.

But, although the danger of a Russian advance towards Merv and Herat was at this time imperfectly understood, such was not the case with the Khiva question. The British Ambassador at St. Petersburg at once demanded explanations regarding the occupation of Krasnovodsk, and Prince Gortchakoff then stated that the proposed establishment at that place 'would be merely a factory, which would, however, of course, require to be protected by a small armed force.' He further observed that 'its object would be entirely commercial, as it would open a shorter caravan route to Central Asia, and also give increased security to trade by restraining the predatory practices of the Turkomans, and by warning the Khan of Khiva that hostility on his part would not be tolerated hereafter.' But, as persistent rumours began to obtain circulation to the effect that an expedition on a large scale was being prepared for the conquest of Khiva, Sir A. Buchanan again, on December 1, 1869, asked Prince Gortchakoff whether there was any truth in the reports; and the Russian Chancellor then repeated what he had previously said as to the commercial objects of the occupation of Krasnovodsk, and went on to deny in the most positive manner that the Czar had any intention of attacking Khiva. His Excellency said that, unless the Khan gave provocation by the renewal of intrigues among the Kirghiz,[1] there

---

[1] As the Khivans were accused of instigating the Kirghiz to revolt in 1869 and 1870, and as the final conquest of the Khanate was undertaken on the pretext that the Khan was always interfering with the Kirghiz and inciting them to rebellion, it will be interesting to see what General Tchernaieff says on the subject. This distinguished officer, who thoroughly understood what he was writing about, made the following statements in the *Russki Mir* of February 14, 1875:—

'The Khivans did not incite the Kirghiz to rebellion, but, on the contrary, they were made to rebel by the introduction of the new regulations prepared by the Ministry of War, the liberal and humane aims of which, for some reason, always meet a strange fate. So it was in the present instance. Instead of the expected gratitude of the population for the introduction of the humane and liberal regulations, the only reply was rebellion.

'When Cossack detachments were sent out to put down these disturbances, the Kirghiz threw the blame on the distant Khivans, and the officials accepted these excuses to cover their own mistakes. In this way the idea grew up at St. Petersburg of the instigation of the Kirghiz by the Khivans, who had no thought for foreign undertakings when they could scarcely maintain themselves at home

was 'no idea of going to war with him, much less of occupying his country, the possession of which would only be an embarrassment to the Government.'

In spite of these declarations of the Russian Chancellor, there is, however, no doubt that at this time the subjugation of Khiva was seriously contemplated by the Russian Government; for immediately after Krasnovodsk had been occupied General Kaufmann reported to the Ministry of War the necessity of adopting harsh measures with Khiva, and proposed that the Khanate should be attacked by two forces, one acting from the Krasnovodsk base, while the other advanced from Tashkent; and it is now well known that this suggestion was approved of in a letter dated March 25, 1870, wherein the Minister of War informed General Kaufmann that his views had met with the Emperor's approval. The projected attack was, however, postponed, not out of respect for the pacific assurances which had been given to the British Government, but because the Russian troops in Central Asia were occupied in the Iskander Kul and Kulja campaigns, and it was also necessary that the country through which the columns would have to move should be thoroughly reconnoitred.

The seizure of Krasnovodsk created a profound

against the Turkomans. We must remember, too, this fact, that when we are quiet, our neighbours are quiet, but as soon as we excite the discontent of our own Kirghiz, some of our neighbours are immediately found to be to blame.'

impression in Khiva, where it was generally believed that the Russian landing was but a preliminary step to an immediate invasion of the Khanate. The Khan indignantly protested against the occupation as being an unwarranted seizure of a portion of his dominions, and a direct menace to the safety of his kingdom, and he quickly despatched an envoy to the Caspian, to complain of the encroachment. Stolietoff, however, was instructed to abstain from entering into negotiations with this ambassador, and the man was thus obliged to return without having even obtained an audience. The Persian Government also displayed considerable concern at the establishment of the Russians at the mouth of the Balkan Bay, and they at once asked for explanations as to the Russian intentions in that direction. They clearly recognised that the chief danger to be expected from this new movement lay in the probability that other points further to the south would be similarly seized, and that Russia, after establishing herself on the shores of the Gulf of Astrabad and along the banks of the Atrek and Gurgen rivers, would gradually push forward either through Khorassan itself or along the skirts of the hills to the north of Bujnurd and Kushan, in the direction of Merv and Herat. After somewhat prolonged negotiations on the subject, however, the Russians gave a clear promise that the Persian frontier line of the Atrek would be carefully respected by Russia, and the Shah's Government were obliged to be content with this assurance.

In the meanwhile the Kirghiz subjects of Russia had been engaged in one of their periodical rebellions, on account of the mismanagement of the Russian officials. Amongst these nomads there is a tribe known as the Adaieffs, who for years had been subject to the Khans of Khiva, and had been in the habit of paying tribute to the rulers of that State. But when the Russians built the Fort of Novo-Alexandrovsk, on the north-eastern shores of the Caspian, they also began to tax this tribe, and thus much discontent was caused. The wretched nomads, however, were forced to submit to the arbitrary exactions of their two stronger neighbours, and no serious trouble occurred until 1869, when the Russians increased the taxes by as much as 150 per cent. This naturally created the very greatest dissatisfaction, and in the spring of 1870 the Adaieffs displayed their resentment by making a determined attack on the Russian position in the Mangishlak Peninsula. A party of Russians, under Colonel Rukin, was surprised by the nomads near the Kochak Bay, on which occasion fourteen Cossacks were killed and the remainder carried into slavery, Rukin himself committing suicide to avoid capture. The Kirghiz then closely besieged Fort Alexandrovsk, and in spite of the fact that the fort was armed with fourteen guns, the garrison were reduced to the greatest straits, and were on the point of surrendering, when reinforcements arrived from the Caucasus, and the Adaieffs were completely overcome. The

Russians at once accused the Khivans of having instigated this serious attack, and this supposed act of hostility on the part of the Khivan Khan was added to the list of offences which was to be put forward as the reason for invading the Khanate, as soon as the preparations for a combined attack had been completed. It is impossible to say whether the Khivans did support the Adaieffs or not; and it is not impossible that they did incite the nomads to make this attack; but it is far more likely that they were driven to rebellion by the long series of errors which General Tchernaieff has so forcibly referred to, and which culminated in the arbitrary and extortionate increase of taxation in 1869.

As soon as Stolietoff had established his position at Krasnovodsk he began to send out reconnoitring parties into the neighbouring country; and proceeding eastwards along the northern shores of the Balkan Bay, he built a small fort at a place called Tash-Arvat, at the foot of the western slopes of the Great Balkan range, where there was a fair supply of water. By the occupation of this point, the Russian commander expected to be able to get a firm hold over the Yomud tribe of Turkomans, who were in the habit of migrating every year from the south to the Ust-Yurt plateau; but in this he was disappointed, for the nomads in their annual migrations used a route far to the east of the fort, and thus kept well out of striking distance. Shortly afterwards the Russians built a second post at Michaelovsk; but as at this place there was little or no drinking water, and all the water for the garrison of 100 men had to be brought from Krasnovodsk, at a cost of about three roubles per bucket, another fortification was built, some fourteen miles to the east of Michaelovsk, at a place called Mulla Kari, where good springs were found.

In the spring of 1870 the Russian Government determined to develop their position on the eastern shores of the Caspian; and, in accordance with the orders issued from St. Petersburg, Prince Mirsky, who was then entrusted with the direction of affairs in the Caucasus, sent instructions to Stolietoff to form Krasnovodsk into an extensive fortified base of operations, from which he was to commence energetic offensive movements against the Yomud and Tekké tribes of Turkomans. A good excuse for such an attack on the Turkoman settlements was soon afforded by the Turkomans themselves, who in the spring of 1870 assaulted the Michaelovsk post. This attack was easily repulsed; and in the following November Stolietoff, acting on the instructions received from Tiflis, marched round the head of the Balkan Bay, and, crossing the barren Steppe to the east of Mulla Kari, reached the Turkoman fort of Kizil-Arvat on the skirts of the Kuren Dagh Range. The Tekkés had however abandoned the place and disappeared with their families and possessions into the Akhal Oasis, further towards the east; and as Stolietoff was not prepared for a prolonged campaign, he destroyed the Tekké fort, and returned to

Krasnovodsk, his first considerable venture into the Turkoman country having thus been of very doubtful utility.

But while Stolietoff was marching against the Tekkés a far more important reconnaissance was being made in the direction of Khiva. Captain Skobeleff, the future hero of Plevna and idol of the Russian army, set out from Krasnovodsk with a small party of Cossacks, and after a trying and adventurous march in a north-easterly direction, reached the Sari-Kamish Lake in safety. But this brilliant officer was by no means satisfied with this achievement, and he therefore pushed on, accompanied by only three Cossacks, all disguised as Usbeg merchants, as far as Dekche, on the borders of the Khivan Oasis. Having thus reconnoitred the route from Krasnovodsk to Khiva, Skobeleff returned with an excellent sketch of the country traversed, and by the following summer was in Tiflis, when he was able to add very considerably to the meagre stock of knowledge respecting these regions which was then possessed by the Caucasus authorities.

In the spring of 1871 Stolietoff was recalled, and Colonel Markozoff was then appointed to the chief command at Krasnovodsk. This officer received orders to carefully examine the country to the north-east of the Balkan Bay, as far as Tuar, a spring some few miles from the eastern shores of the Kara-Bugaz Gulf; and, in accordance with these instructions, he assembled a column at Mulla Kari, and set out on the proposed reconnaissance.

Proceeding northwards, he reached the Gezli-Ata Wells without difficulty, and after he had there constructed a small fort for a garrison of forty or fifty men, he continued his march towards the north-east. At the Chagil Wells another small fort was built, and on October 3 the force reached Tuar, which is situated in a trough-like depression at the foot of a precipitous range of hills. Here a third fortification was constructed, and with it the actual instructions of the Tiflis authorities had been successfully carried out. But Markozoff, taking advantage of the excellent condition of his troops, determined to extend the reconnaissance on his own responsibility; and he therefore, on October 5, set out from the Tuar post, and reached the Kum-Sabshan Wells on October 9. There a halt was made for some days to permit of the construction of a fort for a garrison of fifty infantry, twenty Cossacks, and one gun; and while this was being built, the commander of the force started off to examine the wells at Dapmi and Dirin, which are situated at a distance of some twenty miles to the north-west of Kum-Sabshan. On his return he resumed his march towards Kazakhli, and on reaching that point he let the column continue its march towards Uzun-Kuyu, while he, accompanied by a few Cossacks, rode to the spring of Dakhli, some miles to the south of Kazakhli. He then hastened back and overtook the main body while still on the march to Uzun-Kuyu, which point was reached after terrible sufferings from want of water; and another fort was there built for the reception of all the Cossacks and their horses and fifty infantrymen. From thence the remainder of the force pushed on towards the Sari-Kamish Lake, reached Haji-Kuyusi on October 29, and two days later struck Skobeleff's route at the Sari-Kamish Wells. There he left the bulk of his force, and with fifty men and all his camels he pushed on to Dekche, which he reached on the same day, and found the banks of the ancient channel of the Oxus clothed with verdure, saxaul bushes, and even trees twenty feet in height and some eight inches in diameter. Here the Russian advance was checked by the Turkomans, who attacked the party, and although they were easily driven off, Markozoff felt that it would be a highly injudicious proceeding to venture any closer to Khiva. He therefore commenced his return march towards the Caspian, and although the Turkomans followed the column as far as Chagil, they kept at a respectful distance and never ventured to make any serious attack. From this point Markozoff sent a portion back to Krasnovodsk by a new route through Portokup and Yangi-Su, while he himself with the rest of the column marched to Kuhnughir, on the eastern shores of the Kara-Bugaz Gulf. On his return from thence to Gezli-Ata, another detachment was sent back to Krasnovodsk, and the Colonel with the remainder of the troops marched eastwards, viâ Kimal and Alti-Kuyurukh to the Topatan Wells and Lakes in the Uzboi, or ancient channel of the Oxus. There some more Turkomans were encountered and several slight skirmishes ensued, but the nomads were easily repulsed, and on November 25 Markozoff returned to Mulla Kari.

This expedition, though but little known, had very important results, for during the two months it lasted all the routes to the north-east of Krasnovodsk, and between that place and the borders of Khiva, had been thoroughly examined, and the Russians thus acquired valuable information as to the difficulties which might be expected in an advance against Khiva from this direction. But the indefatigable Russian commander had no intention of resting content with his achievements; the winter was yet young, and he had many other important matters still to attend to. It had been found that camels could not be procured at Krasnovodsk in sufficient numbers for the projected invasion of Khiva, while it was known that they could be more easily obtained from the Goklan tribe of Turkomans which inhabit the country near the Atrek and Gurgen Rivers, and for this purpose, and also to emphasise the Russian claims to the country north of the Atrek, it was decided that a fort should be erected at the mouth of that river. Therefore, after a brief halt of four days, he once more set out from Mulla Kari, but on this occasion he moved in a southerly direction towards the Atrek River and the settlements of the Goklans. He reached Chikishliar, about twenty miles to the north of the mouth of the Atrek River, on December 13. Here he was attacked by the Turkomans, but they were easily driven off, and the construction of the fort was commenced. On the following night a more serious attack was made, when Markozoff narrowly escaped assassination. A small band of nomads suddenly burst into the Russian camp, cut down the guards, and made their way into the Colonel's tent with the evident intention of killing the commander, who had proved to be such a relentless and energetic foe to the Turkoman tribes. He, however, was at the time fortunately absent on a visit to the picquets, and thus escaped, and the marauders were soon forced to retire with some slight loss. After the fort had been built, Markozoff proceeded a short distance up the river, with the intention of crossing it; but the stream was much swollen by the recent heavy rains, and it was found that even horses could not live in the current. The idea was therefore abandoned, and after leaving two companies and two guns as a garrison for the new fort, Markozoff returned to Krasnovodsk, and from thence proceeded to Teheran, where he concluded a definite treaty with Persia respecting the Atrek frontier line. After this he went to Tiflis to report the result of his recent operations, and to receive orders as to what was to be done during the following winter.

In the meanwhile the Russians in the Mangishlak Peninsula had not been idle. After the death of Rukin that officer had been succeeded first by Major-General Komaroff, and then by Colonel Lomakin, and both of these officers made several reconnaissances between the years 1870 and 1872, in order to introduce the new system of administration among the Kirghiz which it was hoped would insure the speedy settlement of the country. For this purpose small Russian detachments constantly visited the 'Auls' of the nomads, who were thus soon convinced that they were completely under the power of the Russians, and that the best thing they could do was to submit quietly to the new order of government.

In Turkestan also Kaufmann had been energetically exploring the country between his frontier posts and the Oxus, and was quietly preparing for the projected invasion of Khiva. As soon as he arrived in Tashkent he wrote a letter to the Khivan Khan, Mahommed Rahim, in which he informed him of his appointment and arrival. He at the same time sent small columns from Kazala and Fort Perovski as far as Irkibai, for the purpose of examining the northern portion of the Kizil Kum Desert, and for the protection of Russian caravans; and in his letter to Mahommed Rahim he mentioned the despatch of these columns, and stated that they had been sent out to punish the marauders who had pillaged certain caravans. In the following February a reply was received from the Khivan Kush-Begi, claiming for Khiva all territory to the south of the Syr Daria, protesting against the violation of the Khan's dominions, and promising to punish all persons who molested traders crossing the Steppes to the south of the Jaxartes.

For some time following this Kaufmann was

engaged in the war with Bokhara, and in the subsequent pacification of that Khanate, and Khivan affairs therefore for a time became of secondary importance; but in 1869 the outbreak of the Kirghiz rebellion gave the Governor-General of Turkestan an opportunity for renewing his interference with Khiva, and on August 24 of that year he wrote a letter in which the Khan was told that inflammatory proclamations had been sent to the Kirghiz and Turkomans, that his officials accompanied by troops had crossed the Russian frontiers for the purpose of fomenting rebellion amongst the subjects of the Czar, that Russians had been carried off to Khiva with the full knowledge of the Khan, and that rebels and marauders had evaded punishment by taking refuge in Khiva, where they had been hospitably received.[1] At about this time also a detachment was sent from Kazala to the Yani-Daria, while another force was sent from Jizakh to the Bukan-Tau Mountains.

These movements, and the occupation of Krasnovodsk, caused the greatest alarm in the Khivan capital, and the Khan began to take measures for the defence of his kingdom. A small fort was constructed at Cape Urga; the chief branch of the Oxus was diverted, and canals were cut to render it shallow and impassable for any of the ships of the Aral Sea flotilla; a new citadel was built for the protection of the capital, and it was

---

[1] This is Kaufmann's version of the causes of the Kirghiz rebellion. Tchernaieff, however, as has already been seen, attributed the rising to Russian maladministration. (See footnote to page 280.)

armed with twenty guns; and a force of cavalry was sent out to poison the wells on the road to Krasnovodsk by throwing dead dogs into them. The Khan also insisted on the recognition of his undoubted right to the country in the vicinity of the Bukan-Tau Mountains; asserted with a considerable show of reason that the disturbances in that region had been caused by the dissatisfied Kirghiz subjects of the Czar, and had in no way been encouraged by the Khivan officials; and, finally, after once more bitterly complaining of the violation of his territories, he concluded one of his letters by saying: 'If, relying on the strength of his armies, the White Czar wishes to make war against us, then before the Creator of heaven and earth, before the Great Judge of all earthly judges, all are equal, both the strong and the weak. He gives the victory to whomsoever He wishes, and nothing can be accomplished against the desires and predestination of the Most High.' This letter was written in April 1870, after much previous correspondence which clearly proved to Mahommed Rahim that the Russians were fully determined to find some excuse for invading his dominions. He plainly saw that his enemies were gradually encompassing him on all sides, and that he was marked down as the next victim to the insatiable lust after territorial aggrandisement which is the leading characteristic of the Russian rule in Central Asia. His alarm gradually increased as the Russian reconnoitring parties pushed forward closer and closer to his capital, and at the close of the year 1871, when Markozoff was advancing to Dekche on the west, and when another detachment under Colonel Golovatcheff had been sent from Jizakh through the Bukan-Tau Mountains to the Oxus, he decided once again to try to come to terms with his formidable enemies. He therefore, early in 1872, sent two embassies, one to Tiflis and the other to Orenburg, bearing letters addressed to the Czar, in which he declared that he had always been actuated by feelings of friendship towards Russia. After reviewing the numerous threatening expeditions which had advanced into his dominions, both from the direction of Turkestan and from the Caspian, he asked that a treaty might be concluded whereby each of the two Powers should agree to be content with its existing frontiers, and he then offered to return all the Russian subjects who remained captive in the Khanate. 'But,' continued the Khan, 'if these prisoners serve you only as a pretext for war against us with the aim of extending your dominions, then a decree will descend from Providence whose purposes we cannot alter.'

Of the two embassies sent to Russia, one proceeded viâ Fort Novo-Alexandrovsk and Petrovsk to Tiflis, while the other went to Orenburg. But they were not allowed to continue their journey to St. Petersburg, and were informed that negotiations with Khiva would not be entered into until every Russian captive in the Khanate had been released. The Khan then sent an envoy to the Indian Government asking for assistance, but this messenger was informed that he could expect no help from England, and the Khan was advised to restore the Russian captives and to come to a reconciliation with the Russian authorities; a reply which must have greatly pleased the Muscovites, who now clearly learnt for the first time that England had no intention of waging war in defence of Khiva.

During the autumn of the year 1872 important reconnaissances were made, both from Fort Alexandrovsk and Krasnovodsk. On September 20 Colonel Lomakin left the former place, successfully explored a considerable tract of the adjacent country, and marched 670 miles in thirty-two days without loss of either men or horses.

In the meanwhile Markozoff had returned to Krasnovodsk, and was busily engaged in preparing for more extensive operations in the Turkoman country. In June 1872 he left Krasnovodsk and made a careful examination of the Caspian coast between that point and Chikishliar. Landing at a small bay about half way between the two Russian forts, he captured some three hundred camels, and after exploring the neighbouring country returned to his headquarters. But the great summer heat of those regions and the scarcity of water rendered it necessary that no extensive military movements should be carried out until the winter had fairly set in, and thus nothing of much importance was done until September. Then, however, troops were concentrated at Krasnovodsk, Belek, and Chikishliar, and on the 10th of the month the Krasnovodsk and Belek troops left the latter place and marched through Tash-Arvat and Burudji to Topatan, where they were to join hands with the Chikishliar detachment, which started on September 23 under the command of Markozoff himself. The two columns united at Topatan on October 7, and the combined force then consisted of about 1,450 men and fourteen guns.

It was at first intended that this force should rapidly advance on Khiva and try to gain possession of the capital of the Khanate by a sudden attack. But this idea was eventually abandoned, for just as Markozoff was on the point of commencing his advance from Topatan, and before any encounter with the Turkomans took place, an officer arrived from Tiflis, bringing strict orders from the Grand Duke that the attack on Khiva was on no account to be attempted, and Markozoff therefore had to rest content with a less exciting campaign against the Akhal Tekkés. Leaving Topatan on October 16, the column reached Jamala on the following day, when they at once began the construction of a small fort. While thus employed they were suddenly assailed on all sides by some two thousand Turkomans, but after a sharp fight the enemy were driven off, and the Russians shortly afterwards continued their march eastwards along the Uzboi. Igdi was reached on October 28, and after a three days' halt at that place the column marched southwards towards the Tekké settlements in the Akhal Oasis. Kizil-Arvat, Bami, and Beurma were in turn visited, and after some slight skirmishes with the Tekkés Markozoff turned westward, and marched down the Sumbar and Atrek valleys to Chikishliar, where he arrived on December 30. There he heard that it had been definitely decided that Khiva should be invaded in the following spring, and he started at once for Tiflis to confer with the military authorities in the Caucasus regarding the part which was to be played by the Krasnovodsk troops in the coming campaign.

Colonel Markozoff's operations on the eastern shores of the Caspian have received little or no notice from English writers on Central Asian affairs, and have generally been dismissed in a few words as though they were absolutely insignificant and devoid of important results. As a matter of fact, this indefatigable officer, who is but little known in England, except as having been the unfortunate commander of the one Russian column which failed to reach Khiva in 1873, laid the foundation of Russia's present position at Merv, and on the frontier of the Herat province of Afghanistan. His operations in the winter of 1871 were completely successful, and by them all the routes between Krasnovodsk and Khiva were thoroughly examined and surveyed; but the subsequent expedition of 1872 was even more important in its results, for thereby he gained complete information regarding the various routes from Krasnovodsk to the Tekké country north of the Kuren Dagh Range, the alternative line of advance from Chikishliar along the Atrek and Sumbar Rivers was also explored, and, above all, by his successful advance to

Beurma, he took the first important step in that great movement towards Herat, which, after many intervening checks and disasters, has been so successfully completed, through the military skill of Skobeleff, and the subsequent intrigues and unscrupulous actions of Komaroff and Alikhanoff. In England the full significance of the Russian operations on the borders of the Akhal Tekké country was completely lost sight of, owing to the great importance which was attached to the independence of Khiva, and on account of the ever-increasing belief that Russia was steadily preparing for the annexation of that Khanate; and it was only several years later, when Skobeleff broke the power of the Turkomans at Denghil Tepé, that the people of England fully realised that the Russians had acquired a position which, as a base for offensive operations against India, was of infinitely greater value than the whole of Russia's other conquests in Central Asia put together.

But the Russians in all their movements in Central Asia have displayed remarkable patience and caution, and they have never undertaken any fresh advance until they have thoroughly secured their existing position. In this instance they knew full well that it would be useless to attempt the conquest of the Tekkés or to try to gain a footing at Merv and at the gates of Herat until Khiva had been first subdued, and therefore in December 1872 the Czar finally issued orders for the immediate preparation of a large expedition for the invasion of that Khanate. In the previous August,

General Kaufmann left Tashkent for St. Petersburg in order to strengthen his position in the eyes of the Czar against the numerous and frequent attacks which were being made against his administration of the Turkestan province, and also to gain the Czar's assent to the despatch of an army against Khiva, in order that by a successful campaign he might be able to divert public attention from the maladministration of Turkestan, and gain the sympathies of the powerful military party in the country. On his arrival at the Russian capital, the Grand Duke Michael (Governor-General of the Caucasus) and General Krijhanoffsky (Governor of the Orenburg district) were summoned to St. Petersburg to give their opinions regarding his proposed scheme for the invasion of Khiva. He suggested that, while one column advanced under his command from Turkestan, another force should operate from Krasnovodsk or Chikishliar. A small subsidiary detachment was at the same time to start from Fort No. 1 on the Syr Daria, and join the Tashkent troops at some point on the Oxus, and when the eastern and western armies had united at some point in the Khivan Oasis, they were then to carry out combined operations under the supreme command of General Kaufmann himself. On the recommendation of General Krijhanoffsky, it was afterwards decided that a strong detachment should advance from Orenburg in addition to those proposed by Kaufmann; and minor changes were also subsequently introduced into the plan of campaign on account of the difficulty experienced in procuring a sufficient number of camels. The Caspian column was divided into two distinct and independent forces, one of which under Markozoff was to start from Chikishliar, while the other under Lomakin was to operate from Fort Alexandrovsk; and thus, by the final orders for the expedition, it was arranged that five different detachments should converge on the oasis, viz. two from the Caspian, one from Orenburg, and two from the Russian provinces east of the Sea of Aral. These orders were sanctioned by the Emperor in December 1872 at a council at which, it is said, that thirty-five of the members voted for the annexation of the Khanate, while the small minority of nine (among whom was Prince Gortchakoff) voted against such a step, believing that it would be better rather to punish the Khan and retire than to retain possession of the country.

Having thus definitely decided that Khiva should be invaded in the following spring, the Russian Government at once determined to break the news as gently as possible to the British Government; for it was well known that public opinion in England was strongly averse to any Russian interference with Khiva, and as the Czar's Government had so frequently disavowed any intention of attacking the Khanate, it was clearly incumbent on them to at least explain the reasons which had caused such a change in their declared policy. For this purpose, therefore, Count Schouvaloff, a statesman enjoying the full confidence of the Czar, left St. Petersburg for London, by the express command of the Russian Emperor, and on January 8, 1873, had an interview with Lord Granville, when he made an important statement regarding Russia's intentions concerning Khiva, and of the Czar's general policy in Central Asia. After expressing surprise at the amount of excitement and susceptibility displayed by the English regarding Central Asian affairs, and after he had then asserted that an agreement regarding the Afghan frontier might be expected at an early date,[1] this trusted adviser of the Russian Czar then went on to say that: 'With regard to the expedition to Khiva, it was true that it was decided upon for next spring. *To give an idea of its character, it was sufficient to say that it would consist of four and a half battalions.* Its object was to punish acts of brigandage, to recover fifty Russian prisoners, and to teach the Khan that such conduct on his part could not be continued with the impunity which the moderation of Russia had led him to believe. *Not only was it far from the intention of the Emperor to take possession of Khiva, but positive orders had been prepared to prevent it, and directions given that the conditions imposed should be such as could not in any way lead to a prolonged occupancy of Khiva.*' Schouvaloff then went on to say that this positive assurance might be given to the British Parliament as a proof of the friendly and pacific intentions of his master the Czar.

---

[1] As has already been seen, this matter was settled on January 31, 1873, by the formal recognition by Russia of the northern frontier of Afghanistan as defined by the British Government.

When this emphatic denial of any intention on the part of the Russian Government to retain possession of Khiva became known, the English public readily accepted the Czar's promises, and it was generally believed that, as soon as the Khan had been punished for the barbarous acts which he was said to have committed, the Russian troops would once more be withdrawn to their former positions, and that Khiva would still remain an independent State between Afghanistan and the Russian frontiers in Central Asia.

It is but natural that Schouvaloff's voluntary declarations should have had a tranquillising effect, for his position as the confidential ambassador from the Russian Emperor was well known, and it was implicitly believed that, although Russian diplomatists might be found who would tear up treaties and repudiate their engagements, still the pledged word of the Russian Czar could never be broken. It was indeed a natural belief, but one which was destined to be rudely shaken; and it will be seen how Russia did retain possession of a large slice of Khivan territory, and how, to use the words of the late Sir Henry Rawlinson, 'an Emperor's word had been weighed in the balance and found wanting.'

In spite of Count Schouvaloff's declaration that the force would be limited to four and a half battalions, the total strength actually amounted to sixty-one companies of infantry, twenty-six sotnias of Cossacks, and several sappers, with fifty-four guns, four mortars, and five rocket detachments.

The four and a half battalions had in a few weeks expanded into a formidable army.

The Turkestan column, under the supreme command of General Kaufmann, comprised two detachments, which started from Kazala and Jizakh, and were commanded respectively by Colonel Goloff and Colonel Golovatcheff. The Orenburg column was commanded by Lieutenant-General Verefkin; the Kinderly column by Colonel Lomakin; and the Krasnovodsk column by Colonel Markozoff.

In the orders which were issued for the conduct of the operations, it was stated that the Jizakh column was to proceed by the road running along the Bokharan frontier to Min Bulak, in the Bukan-Tau Mountains, where it would be joined by the Kazala detachment, and the united forces were then to march in a south-westerly direction towards the village of Shura-Khana, on the right bank of the Oxus In pursuance of this design, the Kazala force began its advance on March 11, 1873, and on the 25th of the same month the head of the main Turkestan army marched out of Jizakh. But when Kaufmann, on April 13, reached the Wells of Aristan-bel-Kuduk, about 100 miles from the appointed rendezvous, he suddenly issued fresh orders, changing the routes by which the two detachments were to advance to the Amu-Daria. By these fresh instructions the Jizakh force was to turn off towards the west, and proceed, viâ Khala-ata and Adam-Krilgan, to Uch-Uchak, on the river

Oxus; while the Kazala detachment was directed to continue its march in a southerly direction and effect a junction with the main column at Khala-ata.

This change of route was most ill advised, and very nearly resulted in the complete loss of the whole Turkestan army of invasion. It is not clear what possible advantage Kaufmann expected to gain by it, for the route originally selected had been previously reconnoitred and was well known, whereas the new line was quite unexplored.

The two columns successfully joined hands at Khala-ata on May 6, and a halt was then made for some days, in order that the troops might be rested before they began their march to the Oxus, and for the purpose of building a fort to guard the line of communications. It was also necessary that the country between Khala-ata and the Oxus should be examined, and for this purpose a small detachment was sent forward, under Colonel Ivanoff. This party arrived near the Adam-Krilgan Wells, where they encountered a band of Turkomans. A smart fight followed, and the Turkomans retired, after wounding the Colonel in two places and killing two of his escort.

The Russians then proceeded to improve the wells by digging, so that in a short time a sufficient supply of water was obtained for the whole column; and on May 12 Kaufmann moved forward, leaving a small garrison in the fort at Khala-ata.

Up to this time the Russian troops from Jizakh

and Kazala had experienced but little hardship, but the weather now became excessively hot, and the most trying portion of the march began. No one knew how far the Oxus really was, but, although it was believed that no wells existed in the intervening desert, it was confidently expected that the column could reach the river in three days. On the morning of May 17 the advance was resumed, a supply of water for three days being carried with the troops. It was intended that the force should start every day at dawn and march until about 10 A.M., rest till the afternoon, and then continue the march in the evening, when the great heat had somewhat abated, by which means it was expected that the columns could cover thirty miles a day. But this calculation was completely upset by the great heat which was experienced, by the heavy shifting sand through which the advance was made, and chiefly on account of the extreme weakness and miserable condition of the camels.

During the very first day's march from Adam-Krilgan the troops consumed the greater portion of the precious supply of water which was to have lasted till they reached the Oxus; and the position of the force at last became so critical, that Kaufmann gave himself up for lost, and even nominated the officer who should take command in the event of his death. Advance through an unknown desert without water was, of course, quite impossible, while a retreat would have had a most demoralising effect, not only on the troops composing the force, but on all the tribes and nationalities of Central Asia. Russia's position in Central Asia depended largely on the prestige which the troops of the White Czar had gained by their wonderful successes in the wars against Khokand and Bokhara, and any reverse at this time would have destroyed that belief in Russian invincibility on which the foundations of the Czar's empire in Asia rested. The Amir of Bokhara was known to be watching for a favourable opportunity for attacking his old enemies, and the Khan of Khokand was no less hostile. A retreat would, therefore, have been the signal for a general attack on the Russian garrisons in Central Asia; and, instead of conquering Khiva, it is probable that the Russians would have had to fight for the retention of their existing possessions on the Syr Daria.

But at this juncture, when defeat and disgrace were staring him in the face, Kaufmann was saved by an insignificant and hitherto despised member of his force. While the Kazala detachment was advancing from Irkibai, a ragged Kirghiz offered his services to Colonel Dreschern, and begged that he might be employed as a guide without any pay, in order that he might witness the punishment of the Turkomans who had killed or enslaved most of his relations. This man now came forward, and said he could find water in the immediate vicinity of the camp. Kaufmann took out his flask, and promised to give the guide a hundred roubles if he would bring it back full of water; and, after the Kirghiz had been absent for a short time, he returned with the flask full of water—filthy and nauseous, it is true, but, nevertheless, water which would save life. On being questioned, he stated that this foul liquid had been obtained from three wells which existed some four miles to the north of the Russian camp, and that a sufficient supply could be obtained for the whole army. Orders were immediately given for the force to move to the spot referred to, and on arrival there it was found that the guide's story was correct. Kaufmann had three more wells dug,[1] but even then the supply was very unsatisfactory, and the troops were limited to a daily allowance of one pint per man, which merely supported life, but did not relieve them from intense suffering.

As there was not sufficient water for the camels at this place, they were sent back, under an escort of 600 men, to Adam-Krilgan, in order that they might have a good drink and get a fresh supply for the force before the final attempt was made to reach the Oxus. While this convoy was at Adam-Krilgan it was attacked by some 500 Turkomans, under their renowned leader Sadyk, who had taken service under the Khivan Khan, and who now tried to cripple the Russians by capturing their transport animals. The attack was made in the early dawn, and the Turkomans, led by their brave chief, advanced to the attack with considerable determination; but they were unable to

[1] The place thus became known as 'Alty Kuduk,' or 'six wells.'

stand for long before the fire of the Russian breech-loaders, and were soon obliged to retreat.

A week elapsed before the camels returned to Alty-Kuduk with a fresh supply of water for the force, and during this time the troops had been reduced to a deplorable and apparently hopeless condition. To add to Kaufmann's difficulties it was found, when the convoy did return, that the camels were so reduced in numbers through sickness and death that it would be impossible to convey all the baggage to the Oxus. The greater part of the stores had therefore to be left behind at Alty-Kuduk under a guard of two companies, and out of six iron boats which had been specially constructed for the passage of the Amu Daria, only two could be carried forward with the advancing army. Taking with them only absolute necessaries, the troops continued their advance; and after hard marching, and exposed throughout the whole of the last day to incessant attacks from the enemy, the force arrived on the banks of the Oxus at the foot of the Uch-Uchak hills on May 23.

As soon as the safety of the column was assured by its arrival on the banks of the river, Kaufmann, who had hitherto remained strictly on the defensive, proceeded to attack the enemy, who were collected in masses at the foot of the neighbouring mountains. The Turkomans were quickly dispersed, and pursued for several miles along the banks of the river, and eleven 'Kayuks,' or Khivan boats, were captured, which proved most invaluable when the Russians crossed the Oxus a few days later.

Continuing its march down the right bank of the river, the column reached Shura-Khana on May 28; but the boats, without which the passage of the river could not be effected, had not then arrived, and Kaufmann, in his anxiety for their safety, rode some three or four miles up the bank to see if there were any signs of their coming. While thus riding along, a Khivan battery on the opposite side of the stream suddenly opened fire on the group of officers, and, by their excellent practice, made it exceedingly unpleasant for the Russian staff for a short time. As this battery would have endangered the safe passage of the boats, the Russian commander determined to silence it, and therefore, on the next morning, a portion of his force, under General Golovatcheff, moved up from Shura Khana and commenced to bombard the Khivan position. The Russians opened fire from two six-pounder guns, and after a short engagement, in which the enemy were completely overmatched, the battery was silenced, and the Khivans were seen to be withdrawing their guns out of range. This engagement has received the name of the 'Battle of Sheikh Arik,' from the fact that the Khivan fort (which was a miserable structure some thirty feet in diameter) stood on one of the embankments of the Sheikh Arik canal, which conducts water during flood-time to the interior of the Khivan oasis.

In the meanwhile the boats had arrived from Uch-Uchak, and preparations were then made for crossing the Amu Daria. It had originally been intended that the river should be crossed at Shura Khana, but after the affair at Sheikh-Arik, Kaufmann decided that it would be better to cross over at the latter place; and at daybreak on May 30 the Russian troops were put in motion and concentrated at the spot where Golovatcheff's detachment had stood the day before. The river at this point was about 1,200 yards wide, and it took each boat an hour to make the trip to the left bank and back again, for the current being strong, the boats were carried some distance down stream, and had then to be hauled back to their original starting place; and it was not until June 3 that the whole of the troops had been transferred to the left bank. The safety of the operation was, however, quickly ensured, for early on the first day two companies of infantry and four light guns were landed on the left bank, and taking possession of the deserted fort and adjacent canal embankments, they completely covered the crossing of the remainder of the army.

On June 4 the town of Hazarasp was occupied without resistance, and Kaufmann, who was thus within forty-five miles of the capital, there received a letter from the Khan stating that all Russian prisoners had been liberated, and declaring his willingness to comply with the Russian demands, but requesting that the further advance of the column might be stopped.

One of the other columns was fated to experience even greater difficulties and hardships than Kaufmann's force had gone through; and in spite of desperate endeavours to push forward and thus to share in the ultimate triumph, it was compelled to abandon the attempt and retreat in disorder to the Caspian. This unfortunate column was the one which advanced from Chikishliar under Colonel Markozoff. It started from that place on March 31, and reached Igdi on the 29th of the following month. There the advanced guard had a sharp fight with some Turkomans, who were easily defeated with considerable loss, and the force soon afterwards set out for the Ortakuya wells, which were believed to be about fifty miles distant. But the column had not proceeded far before the terrible heat began to tell on the troops. The water-supply soon became exhausted, and although the guides suggested that the store should be replenished from the wells of Bala Ishem, which were at no considerable distance from the line of march, Markozoff decided to continue the advance in the hope of being able to capture Khiva before the other columns could reach the khanate. But the attempt failed. The whole force rapidly fell into a state of disorder, and was at last forced to retreat to the Caspian.

On May 26—while Kaufmann was marching down the right bank of the Oxus, and two days after Verefkin and Lomakin had joined hands near Kungrad—the last stragglers of this ill-fated detachment reached Krasnovodsk, utterly broken down in health, half-starved on account of the scarcity and bad quality of the provisions which had been supplied, and displaying unmistakable traces of the utter defeat and demoralisation which had been caused through the rascality of the army contractors and the reckless indiscretion of the commander, who, in his ambitious desire to capture Khiva before the other columns could assist in the undertaking, pushed blindly on into the waterless desert, when a halt and rest at the Bala Ishem wells would have refreshed his jaded troops and enabled them to make a fresh start with some hope of ultimate success.

Early in January 1873, when the troops for the Orenburg column were being assembled at Orenburg, Orsk, and Uralsk, news was received that a Mangishlak chieftain, named Kaphar-Karajigetoff, was urging the Adaieff Kirghiz to migrate into the desolate regions in the centre of the Ust-Yurt plateau, in order that they might not be compelled to give up their camels to the Russians for use in the Khivan campaign. This man was so successful in his agitation that the Adaieffs actually began to move eastwards with the whole of their camels and household goods; and Colonel Lomakin was therefore ordered to march into the Buzachi peninsula to restore order. On arriving near the Kara-Kitshu-Tuz lake, he came across a considerable number of nomads, who were making their way towards the Ust-Yurt with some 10,000 camels. The Kirghiz at once attacked the Cossacks, and a hard fight ensued, which ended in the defeat of the nomads, who, however, managed to drive off their camels. This defiant attitude of the Adaieffs was one of the reasons why the Russian Government decided that the Caspian column should be split up into two detachments, one being sent from the Mangishlak peninsula to keep the Kirghiz in check during the campaign; and at the same time Cossack detachments were sent to Sam, Djebisk, and to the Mogadjarsk Mountains to prevent inroads of the nomads into Russian territory, and to keep up communication between the Orenburg and Kinderly columns.

Colonel Lomakin, who commanded the Kinderly column, experienced much difficulty in getting a sufficient number of camels, and the detachment was obliged to start with an insufficient number; but at length 380 camels and 110 horses were captured from the Adaieffs, in addition to some 3,000 sheep and goats.

On April 26 the column set out from the Kinderlinsk Gulf and commenced their march to Kungrad by way of Kaundi, Senek, Bishekti, Iltegi, and Kizil-Aghir. It was not long before the troops began to experience all the trials and sufferings of a desert march. The heat was excessive, and the wells were far apart, while such water as was obtainable was brackish, muddy, and full of insects. The camels soon began to die off, and within the first few days the force found that it was opposed by an enemy far worse and more powerful than any possible combination of nomad tribes. During the march from Kaundi to Senek— a distance of about sixty miles—sickness broke out among the soldiers, and it was found necessary to utilise the cavalry horses for the conveyance of the men who were stricken with fever, dysentery, or sunstroke. But Lomakin steadily pushed forward, and passing Senek, reached Bishekti on May 2, when a small fort was built enclosing the six wells.

The sufferings which had been experienced during the march from the Kinderlinsk Gulf to Bishekti were but a foretaste of what was in store for the Russians during the whole of their march to the borders of the Khivan Oasis. Intense heat, aggravated by the blinding glare from the sand, accompanied by a most serious scarcity of water and with a steady and rapid increase in the death-rate among the camels, marked the progress of the column.

During the march from Bishekti to Kilzil-Aghir there were many anxious moments, when it almost appeared as if the force was doomed to destruction. On May 9, when the headquarter staff and its escort reached Kol-Kinir, the well was found to be so deep that no means could be devised for bringing the water to the surface, and although the next known well was thirty-four miles further on, there was no alternative but to make an attempt to reach it. The party, therefore, pushed on; but by mid-day on the 10th they had still some thirteen miles to march before they could get a drop of water; the men could go no further; 'and everybody, even the officers, with their horses, sank down helplessly into the burning sand. Not a drop of water was left in the column; round about as far as the eye could reach there was nothing but the white sand.'

But while the troops were in this hopeless condition, Lomakin, in his search for water, came across a dried-up channel, and sent two Kirghiz to explore it, when they found a small well about one and a half mile to the north of the place where the troops had halted. By this fortunate discovery the headquarter staff and its escort were saved, and, after a rest, they once more pushed on and reached the wells of Iltegi on the following day.

While there, a messenger arrived with the news that the main body of troops under Colonel Grodekoff had come to a complete standstill at a point some three miles short of the wells, and were unable to proceed any further as their water-supply had been completely exhausted, and the men were dying from thirst. Lomakin at once sent back every available animal with vessels containing water, and after the troops had been thus refreshed, they continued their march to Iltegi. There a square redoubt was built to enclose the two wells, and on the afternoon of May 14 the force once more resumed its journey eastwards.

Kizil-Aghir was reached at 1 A.M. on the 15th, and as it was known that Khiva was not far distant, a council of war was held to decide what steps should be taken to ensure complete co-operation with the Orenburg column. It had been originally intended that the Orenburg and Kinderly columns should meet at some point on the dried-up inlet of the Aral Sea called Lake Aibugir, and orders were therefore issued that the main body of troops should move to Bai-chagir, and thence turn northwards through Itibai, while a force was detached under Colonel Skobeleff to reconnoitre the country in the direction of Kone Urgenj. But on the 16th, when the column was a short distance beyond Bai-chagir, Lomakin received a message from General Verefkin, in which he said that he hoped to reach Urga on the Sea of Aral by May 18, and directed the Kinderly column to march northwards and join him at that place, so that the two columns could make a combined attack on the town of Kungrad. Messengers were therefore sent to recall Skobeleff; but this was no easy matter, for Skobeleff never let the grass grow under his feet, and before the order reached him he had on the 17th had an encounter with a large body of Turkomans who were escorting a caravan to Khiva. In this fight the gallant colonel was wounded, but he quickly defeated the enemy, and captured 15 prisoners, 150 camels, and a large store of provisions.

On receiving a second message from Verefkin, Lomakin determined to push forward by forced marches with his staff and cavalry, leaving Lieutenant-Colonel Paduroff to follow on with the infantry. Throughout the three days' march which followed, only one well was found, and this had been poisoned by the Khivans, who had cast dead animals into it. But, although Lomakin's party suffered considerably from want of water, they, on May 23, crossed the dried-up bed of the Aibugir Lake, which was thickly covered with reeds from 15 to 20 feet high, and on the following day the flying column arrived in the Khivan oasis, where, after two months of incessant privations and suffering, they again saw green fields and flowing water, and knew that their troubles were over, and that they were within reach of the goal towards which they had struggled so bravely. Lomakin reached Kungrad at about one o'clock in the afternoon of May 24; but found that the Orenburg column had left the place a few hours previously in its rapid advance on the capital—a strong detachment having been left in possession of the town. He, therefore, pushed on after an hour's halt, and succeeded in joining Verefkin at nine o'clock in the evening. He was, however, ordered to wait for his infantry, and on Paduroff's arrival to push on as rapidly as possible with the whole force.

In the meanwhile the infantry under Paduroff had been advancing along the regular route through Irbasan and Kara-Kuduk. The force was divided into two detachments—the main party being under the command of Paduroff himself, while the other was under Major Avarsky. The march from Uk-Alan commenced at 2 A.M. on May 20, and during the first day some water was obtained *en route*, but it was brackish and almost undrinkable; on the second day's march the troops had to rely on the scanty supply of water which was carried with them, for the wells which were passed were found to have been poisoned; while on the third day they were absolutely without any water at all. In fact, throughout the whole march to the outskirts of the Khivan oasis the force was almost entirely without water, and the infantry of the Kinderly column cannot be too highly praised for their splendid endurance under most trying circumstances. However, at three o'clock in the afternoon of May 23, they reached Irali-Kotchkan, on the borders of the oasis, and a couple of days later were met by Lomakin, who, after a short rest, advanced with the whole column towards Khojaili.

Before describing the advance of the combined Orenburg and Kinderly columns towards the capital, it is necessary now to give a brief account of the march of Verefkin's force from Orenburg to Kungrad. Although General Krijhanoffsky only received definite orders regarding the despatch of a column from Orenburg at the beginning of January, yet by the end of the following month all the preparations had been completed, and the troops began their march towards the Emba River from Orenburg, Orsk, and Uralsk on February 25, 26, and 27. In spite of tremendous snowstorms and severe frost, and the terrible condition of the roads, the Emba post was reached on March 15, 16, and 17, and after a three weeks' halt the force resumed its advance towards Khiva on April 7. By this time the weather had become much milder, and the Russians experienced but little difficulty in their march to the western shores of the Aral Sea, and then along the coast to Yani Kala on the borders of the Khivan Oasis, where the column arrived on May 14.

Up to this time no resistance had been encountered, the Khivans having merely contented themselves with sending messages demanding the withdrawal of the Russian forces. On the 19th, when Verefkin was a short distance from Kungrad, he received an amusing letter from the Khivan governor of that town, requesting that the march of the force might be delayed for three days until the garrison had been reinforced by some artillery which was daily expected, on receipt of which he would be ready to oppose the Muscovite advance; but it was stated that, if the Russians blindly persisted in moving forward before the guns arrived, the Khivans would absolutely decline to fight. Verefkin, however, did 'blindly persist' in continuing his advance, and when he reached Kungrad on the following day he found that the Khivan commander had kept his promise. The place was deserted, and the Russians took possession of it without firing a shot.

On May 23 the advanced guard of the Orenburg column marched out of Kungrad under Colonel Leontscheff, and at about four o'clock in the afternoon it was violently attacked by a large number of Khivans, who succeeded in forcing their way to the very centre of the Russian camp, but were eventually driven off with the loss of several killed. Verefkin, as has been already mentioned, left Kungrad with the main body of the Orenburg troops on the morning of the 24th, and steadily pushed forward to the capital without seeing any further signs of the enemy, either on that day or on the 25th. But at 5 A.M. on the 26th the advance was continued toward Kara-Baili, and at noon, while the column was resting on the banks of a stream, the sound of firing was heard towards the front, and a Cossack arrived with a report that while an officer of the Topographical Department was making a reconnaissance of the country ahead of the column, he had been attacked by a numerous body of Khivans, who had succeeded in killing one of the escort and wounding two others, besides capturing several horses.

Colonel Leontscheff at once galloped forward with two sotnias of cavalry, but on reaching the scene of attack, he found that the enemy had disappeared, and although he advanced some miles further he failed to see any signs of them, and he was obliged to abandon the pursuit. He had, however, scarcely returned to the main body, when shots were again heard on the flank of the column, and on this occasion he overtook the Khivans and inflicted considerable loss on them. From one of the prisoners taken during this fight it was learnt that these two attacks had been made by some 400 or 500 Turkomans who had been detached from a large Khivan army which had been sent under the command of the Khan's brother to defend the town of Khojaili.

On the same evening Lomakin rejoined with the whole of the Kinderly column, and from this time the combined columns came under the command of General Verefkin, who at once issued orders regarding the formation of the column during its advance on the capital.

The force left Kara-Baili at daybreak on May 27, and, after a slight skirmish, reached the gardens and enclosures on the outskirts of Khojaili at about four o'clock in the afternoon. Skirmishers were then sent forward, and the force steadily pushed on till it arrived within about 500 yards from the walls of the town. Here a deputation of the leading inhabitants presented themselves before Verefkin, informing him that the Khivan troops had evacuated the place, and begging that they might not be punished. At 5 P.M. the Russians marched through the town and took up a position three-quarters of a mile to the south, where the force remained for two days.

On May 30 the advance was continued, and early the following morning the outposts were attacked by large bodies of Turkomans, who, however, as usual, fell back as soon as a few shells had been fired. Leontscheff pursued them for several miles, and on his return he reported that the Laudan Canal on the way to Manghit was impassable for infantry, as there was no bridge over it. A detachment of sappers and two sotnias of cavalry were therefore sent forward with the cask-bridge equipment, but on reaching the canal they were received by a heavy fire from the Khivans, who were hidden in the undergrowth on the opposite bank. The Cossacks, however, swam across and drove the enemy away, and the bridge was then so rapidly constructed that by 8.30 A.M. the whole force had crossed, and after a short march camped on the banks of the Oxus at a place called Djelan-

Cheganak, where the river was about three-quarters of a mile wide.

The remainder of the day passed quietly, and although a night-attack was expected, no further signs of the enemy were seen until the following morning (June 1), when, just as the Russians were striking their camp, a couple of shots were fired from some Khivan guns on the opposite bank of the Amu Daria. These, however, fell short, and the column shortly afterwards set out towards Manghit, where the enemy was known to have taken up a strong position barring the Russian line of advance.

At 7 A.M. Verefkin came into touch with the Khivan army, which was drawn up on a plain covered with reeds and high grass—the village of Manghit and several neighbouring sandhills being also strongly occupied. As soon as the Russians arrived within about three-quarters of a mile from the position, the Khivan horsemen, uttering fiendish yells, galloped forward with the apparent intention of charging the Russian centre; but they soon changed their course, and in a few minutes spread themselves out into a long line some seven or eight miles in extent, which encircled the column on the south, east, and north-east. The four guns in the Russian centre then opened a heavy fire, and Verefkin sent three other pieces to reinforce the left flank which was seriously threatened. The Khivans, however, made a series of determined charges, and at one time they succeeded in pushing forward to within a couple of hundred yards of the general and his staff, while Leontscheff's cavalry on the right flank was so hardly pressed that they were obliged to dismount and fight like infantrymen before they could beat off the assailants. As soon as this front attack was repulsed, the Khivans made a furious onslaught on the rearguard, which they apparently expected to find weak and unprovided with artillery. But they were soon undeceived, for they were received with a heavy infantry and artillery fire, which caused them to recoil in confusion, when they joined their companions in flight towards Manghit.

A short time afterwards the attack was renewed, but on this occasion the Khivans did not attempt to come to close quarters, and soon retired once again towards the south. Verefkin then ordered a general advance, and Manghit was occupied at three o'clock in the afternoon. Here the Russians were fired upon by some of the enemy who were lurking in the village, and in retaliation the troops set fire to the place and commenced an indiscriminate massacre of the inhabitants, in which no respect was paid to either sex or age. The force then continued its march and took up a position on the banks of the Arna Canal, about a mile to the south of the smouldering ruins of Manghit, from whence Skobeleff was sent with two sotnias of Cossacks to destroy the village of Kubetan, the inhabitants of which had taken a leading part in the hostile operations. This affair was the most serious engagement of the whole campaign. The Russians lost one officer and eight men killed, and ten men severely wounded, whilst many others received slight wounds. The Khivan loss is unknown, but it must have been very heavy.

On June 2 the force continued its advance, and after repeated encounters with parties of Turkomans, reached the Attnalick Canal. On the following day the enemy still continued to harass the column, but they were unable to delay its progress, and it was not till June 4 that any further serious fighting took place. At 6.45 A.M. on that day, however, just as the Russians had struck their camp, they were assailed on all sides by dense masses of the enemy. Their position for a time was most critical, for they were in a closely built Usbeg village which was surrounded by a network of gardens and irrigation channels, and they were unable to get a clear field for their fire. The Khivans were most determined in their attacks, and returned again and again to the charge; and it was not until 11 A.M., when the Russians had broken down some of the surrounding walls and brought their guns into action, that the assailants were finally forced to retire. The staff then halted at the village of Udott, and in the afternoon went into a camp some miles to the south.

In this fight, in spite of its serious character, the Russians only lost five men wounded, which is due to the fact that the Khivans were only armed with swords and spears, and had but few guns of a very primitive make. Thus, while they invariably lost heavily from the fire of the Russian breech-loaders, they themselves, like all savage races, were unable to inflict any serious loss on their opponents, because they were always defeated before they could come to close quarters. This defeat near Udott, together with the previous lesson they had received at Manghit, appears to have completely disheartened them, and they made no more serious attempts to resist the advance of Verefkin's troops towards the capital, and the Russians from this time encountered no greater difficulties than were caused by the destruction of bridges over the numerous canals which crossed their line of march.[1]

The Khan, however, made one further attempt to persuade Verefkin to grant a truce. On June 4 a messenger arrived in the Russian camp bearing a letter from Mahommed Rahim, in which he declared his friendship towards Russia, and stated that nothing would please him better than to be able to entertain such distinguished visitors in a befitting manner. He therefore begged that an armistice might be granted for three or four days to enable him to make the necessary arrangements for their reception; but he urged the general not to abstain from attacking the Turkomans, who, he declared, had opposed the Russian advance in opposition to his wishes. Verefkin, however, was not to be deceived by such a palpable attempt to gain time, and he therefore pushed on; and passing through Kyat-Kungrad on June 5, and Kush-Kupir on the following evening, the combined

---

[1] At Klytch Niaz Bai a bridge 189 feet long had to be built over the canal before the Russians could continue their march.

Orenburg and Kinderly columns on June 7 encamped in the Chanakchik, or pleasure-gardens of the Khan, which are situated some three miles from the northern gate of the Khivan capital. Here the troops remained for two days, during which time the advanced guard under Skobeleff was incessantly attacked by the enemy, who invariably delivered their assaults in the mornings, and daily lost 400 or 500 men besides many guns and horses.

Verefkin at this time was in complete ignorance of Kaufmann's movements; for, although on June 5 he had received a letter from the Commander-in-Chief which had been written three days previously, and which contained news of the engagement with the Khivan forces at Sheikh Arik and successful passage of the river, no further intelligence had been received regarding the position or movements of the Turkestan column. It was, moreover, rumoured that Kaufmann, after advancing to Hazarasp, had been compelled to return to the Oxus, and that he was then about sixty miles away from Khiva.

Verefkin, therefore, decided to attack the city without waiting for the arrival of the Turkestan troops, and at about eleven o'clock on the morning of June 9 the troops advanced from Chanakchik for the purpose of making a reconnaissance in force so that the breaching batteries could be placed and the bombardment commenced. At noon the column reached Skobeleff's advanced posts, which had just had their usual morning's fight with the Khivans, and shortly afterwards the reconnoitring party found the enemy strongly posted in the gardens and suburbs in front of the north gate. A few rounds from the guns, however, soon caused them to disappear, and a quarter of a mile further on the column got into a narrow road, scarcely four yards wide, with an almost impassable network of canals, gardens, and buildings on each side.

While in this confined position, and buried in clouds of dust which rendered it impossible to see even a few yards ahead, the Russians suddenly found themselves exposed to a heavy fire. Without knowing it they had arrived in close formation within a couple of hundred yards of the city walls, which were lined with Khivans, who opened a tremendous fusillade on the astonished Russians. Fortunately, however, for Verefkin's men the fire was badly directed, and most of the bullets passed high over the heads of the troops. For ten minutes the Russians were in this unpleasant position before they could get out of the defile; but they at length got under cover, the guns were brought to the front and opened a well-directed fire against the north gate of the city, and the infantry moved forward on the right and left of the road, preceded by a line of skirmishers, who kept up a heavy fire on the walls. In a short time several of the Khivan guns were put out of action, and the Russians pushed on to a brick building just in front of the canal bridge outside the north gate.

Here their further advance was delayed by a

well-built barricade which had been erected across the road about 100 yards in front of the gate, and which contained four pieces of artillery. In front of this there was a deep, wide canal, over which there was a narrow bridge, which the Khivans had stupidly neglected to destroy. The fire from this barricade proved most galling to the Russians, and Major Bourovzoff charged across the bridge at the head of four companies of infantry, and in a few moments forced his way into the work, where the Khivan gunners were bayoneted beside their guns.

This storming party, which was exposed to a heavy fire from the city walls, then took shelter behind the canal embankment, and as an assault on the town would have probably been less dangerous than retirement, Lieutenant-Colonel Paduroff, who commanded the attack at this point, sent back and asked Verefkin for scaling-ladders. The general, however, did not intend to risk an assault, and decided to confine himself to a bombardment till Kaufmann arrived, and he therefore ordered the troops to retire. Bourovzoff's party then fell back, and in spite of the heavy fire to which they were exposed, they succeeded in dragging off three of the Khivan guns. This advanced party suffered a loss of four men killed and twenty-two wounded, including their gallant leader, who was wounded in three places.

During the engagement Verefkin was also severely wounded in the right eye, and after giving directions regarding the breaching batteries which were to be employed against the defences, he was obliged to hand over the command to Colonel Sarantschoff. The cavalry and staff then retired, and were shortly afterwards followed by the main body of infantry, Skobeleff remaining in his usual post at the front to continue the bombardment and watch the movements of the enemy.

The guns kept up a steady fire on the city until about 4 P.M., when an envoy arrived from the Khan asking for a suspension of hostilities, and saying that within an hour an ambassador would be sent to arrange the terms of capitulation. Colonels Sarantschoff and Lomakin informed this messenger that the Russians would cease fire and grant an armistice only on the understanding that not another shot was fired from the walls, but that the conditions of peace could only be arranged by General Kaufmann. The Russian batteries, in accordance with this arrangement, ceased firing at 4.30 P.M.; but soon afterwards the fire from the ramparts recommenced, and although a second messenger then appeared declaring that the Khan was not responsible for this hostile demonstration, as the culprits were Yomud Turkomans, over whom the Khan had no control, the Russians very naturally ignored the excuse and resumed the bombardment, which was maintained till 10 P.M., when the city was on fire in several places.

An hour later a letter was received from General Kaufmann, stating that the Turkestan column, which had left Hazarasp on June 8, was about seven miles from Khiva, and directing Verefkin to stop the bombardment and to meet him at eight o'clock on the following morning at a bridge some three miles from the eastern gate of the city, when the Khan's uncle, Seid Emir-ul-Umar, would be present to arrange the terms of surrender. Verefkin was unable to go to the rendezvous on account of his wound, and he therefore sent Sarantschoff and Lomakin. At the appointed place they met Kaufmann at the head of the Turkestan column, and there Seid-ul-Umar, Ata Jan (the Khan's younger brother), and other influential persons offered their complete submission and formally surrendered the city to the Russians.

While Kaufmann was thus peacefully obtaining the capitulation of Khiva, certain fiery spirits on the opposite side of the city appeared determined to keep up the contest as long as possible; for while the Russian and Khivan leaders were proceeding to the rendezvous to settle the terms of surrender, the Turkomans at the north gate reopened fire on the advanced party under Skobeleff, who at once recommenced the bombardment. By a few well-directed shots the gate was destroyed, and then a storming column of about 1,000 men, led by Skobeleff and Count Schouvaloff, rushed to the assault and speedily gained possession of the gate and adjoining ramparts. But the Turkomans still maintained a running fire from the houses and alleys of the city, and Skobeleff, pushing on, cleared the streets with rockets, and finally, with a loss of only fifteen men, penetrated as far as the

Khan's palace, where he heard that Kaufmann, at the head of the Turkestan column, was entering the town by the Hazarasp gate with all 'the honours of war.' Skobeleff therefore discreetly fell back, and marching his force out of the city by the gate at which he had entered, left the Commander-in-Chief to continue his triumphal progress undisturbed.

After remaining at the Khan's palace for a few hours to make arrangements for the protection of property and disarmament of the inhabitants, Kaufmann visited Verefkin's camp and inspected the wounded in the hospitals; on the following day a 'Te Deum' was sung and Mass said for the repose of the souls of Peter the Great (whose birthday it was) and of those soldiers who had perished in the previous wars against Khiva; and on June 13 the troops evacuated the city and marched into camps in the adjacent gardens, small detachments being, however, left to guard the gates of the town.

In the meanwhile, as Mahommed Rahim, being alarmed at the bombardment by Verefkin's force, had fled to Imukchir, near Iliali, and there taken refuge among the Yomuds, his younger brother, Ata Jan, was temporarily appointed to the khanship; but, on the 13th, Kaufmann wrote to Mahommed Rahim advising him to return, and on the evening of the next day he presented himself at the general's camp, where he was reinstated, a special council or 'divan,' partly composed of Russian officers and partly of Khivans, being appointed to assist in the government of the khanate.

On June 24, the Khan, by Kaufmann's direction, issued a decree abolishing slavery, and commanding all his subjects to set their slaves at liberty. The captives were permitted, if they so desired, to remain in Khiva, or to return to Persia if they preferred to do so. Those wishing to return to their homes were directed to assemble at certain bazaars, where they were to be registered, and thence sent to Persia, viâ Krasnovodsk. In spite of this order, however, it appears that not more than one-sixth of the whole number of slaves were released by the time the Russian forces left the oasis.

Shortly afterwards the Russian troops were employed in a campaign against the Yomud Turkomans, which lasted till late in the month of August; and, on his return from this expedition, Kaufmann, on August 24, 1873, concluded a treaty of peace with the Khan, the draft of which had been previously sent by a courier to St. Petersburg for the Emperor's sanction, and which had been returned duly approved by the Czar. By this treaty the Khan renounced his right to maintain direct relations with any of the neighbouring rulers or Khans, or to undertake any military operations without the knowledge and permission of the Russian authorities in Central Asia; the whole of the right bank of the Amu Daria and the lands adjoining thereunto[1] which

[1] On the 10th of the following October Kaufmann concluded a

had formerly been considered as belonging to Khiva were annexed to Russia, and the ancient bed of the Oxus was fixed as the boundary between the Russian and Khivan dominions to the west of the oasis; the navigation of the Oxus was exclusively reserved for Russian vessels, Khivan or Bokharan boats being only permitted to sail on the river by special permission from the Russian authorities; the Russians were to have the right to construct wharves and factories at such points on the left bank of the Amu Daria as might be considered necessary or convenient; Russian merchants were to have the free right to travel throughout the khanate without payment of any taxes, and to be permitted to establish agents in Khiva or in any of the other towns of the khanate; and, in addition to many other clauses, it was finally agreed that the Khan should pay a war

treaty with the Amir of Bokhara, whereby the strip of territory on the right bank of the Oxus, from Kukertli to Meshekli, and thence to the Russian frontier, was handed over to Bokhara as a reward for the Amir's neutrality during the war. By this treaty it was also agreed that the Russians might establish wharves and factories at any places on the Bokharan bank of the Amu Daria; that all towns and villages in the khanate should be open to Russian trade; that all goods belonging to Russian traders—whether imported or exported—should be subject to a tax of 2½ per cent. *ad valorem*; that Russian merchants should have a right to transport their goods through the khanate free of all duties; that Russian traders might establish caravanserais and appoint commercial agents wherever they pleased; that Russian subjects should be permitted to purchase real property and to engage in any trade or craft permitted by the Shariat; that no persons should be permitted to enter the khanate from Russian territory without passes from the Russian authorities; and that a Bokharan envoy should reside in Tashkent, a Russian resident agent being also appointed to remain in Bokhara.

indemnity of 2,200,000 roubles, payable in certain instalments, the last of which was to be paid on or before November 13, 1893.

Such were the conditions imposed on the Khivans as the result of their disastrous overthrow. The Khan was turned into a mere puppet who was to be entirely under Russian guidance; the great River Oxus was to be thenceforward completely under Russian control, from its mouths to the borders of Afghanistan; and in spite of the Russian Emperor's solemn declaration that he had no intention of occupying the khanate, and had even given positive orders to prevent it, and that the final conditions to be imposed should be such as could not in any way lead to a prolonged occupation of Khiva—in spite of this voluntary and emphatic promise, a large slice of Khivan territory was annexed to Russia, Khivan independence was completely destroyed, and instead of abstaining from a prolonged occupation of the khanate, a considerable Russian force was permanently established in a fort on the Oxus within two marches of the Khan's capital.

It is not to be wondered at that when this treaty was published the British public felt that they had been completely duped. It is true that three years previously they had been taught how little value Russia attaches to her treaty obligations;[1] but in spite of the cancelment of the Black

---

[1] On October 31, 1870, during the Franco-German War, Prince Gortchakoff wrote a circular note to the Russian Ambassadors at Foreign Courts, wherein he declared the intention of Russia to be

Sea clauses of the Treaty of Paris, they could not bring themselves to believe that the assurances voluntarily given at the instance of the Russian Czar himself would not be scrupulously observed; and, therefore, when they found that their confidence had been misplaced the reaction was complete.

no longer bound by the Black Sea clauses of the Treaty of Paris. The time was well chosen: France was then vainly endeavouring to stem the tide of invasion, and was powerless to take action against Russia. England was thus left alone, and as she did not feel inclined to go to war in support of the treaty, a conference was assembled, at which, after much delay, it was agreed that the Black Sea clauses were to be cancelled; and although it was declared that no Power had a right to liberate itself from treaty engagements, this was very little to set against the tangible advantages which had been gained by Russia. In this way, by a stroke of the pen, the fruits of the Crimean War were practically destroyed, and yet some Englishmen were still to be found who believed in the good faith of Russia.

END OF THE FIRST VOLUME.

www.ingramcontent.com/pod-product-compliance
Lightning Source LLC
Chambersburg PA
CBHW030309240426
43673CB00040B/1105